Born in Orange, NSW, Scott McGregor has
tools, having spent much of his spare ti
antiques and restoring vintage railway carriages. He is a graduate of
NIDA who has appeared in countless TV dramas, films and plays and
presented numerous documentaries on Australian history and railway
journeys. He was the DIY presenter on Channel Seven's *Better Homes
and Gardens* and the host of the highly successful series *Room for
Improvement*. For many years Scott also owned the railway-buff mecca
called 'Off the Rails', specialising in industrial antiques.

Scott writes a weekly DIY column for the *Sun-Herald* called
'Weekend Workshop' and as if that's not enough you can find him regularly appearing at Ladies Nights at Bunnings hardware stores where he
shares his passion for shellac (amongst other things). Scott's biggest
'fix it' project is his railway retreat, Ruwenzori, near Mudgee, which is an
ongoing labour of love.

FIX IT

How to do all those little repair jobs around your home

SCOTT McGREGOR

First published in 2007

Allen & Unwin
83 Alexander Street
Crows Nest NSW 2065
Australia
Phone: (61 2) 8425 0100
Fax: (61 2) 9906 2218
Email: info@allenandunwin.com
Web: www.allenandunwin.com

National Library of Australia
Cataloguing-in-Publication entry:

McGregor, Scott, 1957- .
Fix it : how to do all those little repair jobs around your home.

Includes index.
ISBN 9781741753264 (pbk.).

1. Do-it-yourself work - Amateurs' manuals. 2. Dwellings - Maintenance and repair - Amateurs' manual. 3. Repairing - Amateurs' manuals. I. Title.

643.7

Edited by Michael Wall
Internal photographs by Wendy Gray
Indexed by Russell Brooks
Text designed by Seymour Designs
Set in 10 pt Grotesque MT Lt by Midland Typesetters, Australia
Printed and bound in Australia by Griffin Press

10 9 8 7 6 5 4 3 2 1

To my wife, Wendy Gray, for all your hard yakka, keyboard work and laughs. Your support, dedication, and direction has been the force keeping this little two person team firmly ON the rails.

To Poss and Doug (Mum and Dad) for your inspiration. Thanks for putting this sign up in the sunroom:

The person who says it can't be done is likely to be interrupted by somebody doing it.

Special thanks to Darryl Chapman my right-hand man in all matters handy, for being a fine hunter of the 'how-to' and a gatherer of great stuff.

And thanks to my agents Lisa Hanrahan and Mark Byrne for your ideas, encouragement and advice.

CONTENTS

1.   **HOW I GOT HOOKED**   **1**

2.   **TOOLS**   **9**
The basic toolkit   9
A DIY shadow board   17
The more advanced toolkit   19
And then there are the power tools …   24
Hiring tools   31
Looking after your tools   32
Sharpening tools   32

3.   **PRODUCTS AND MATERIALS**   **37**
Key ingredients   37
Fasteners   41
Glues, sealants and fillers   46
Cleaners   52
Tapes, strings, ropes, straps and wires   53
Timber and boards   54
Timber finishes   56

4.   **SAFETY WHILE YOU WORK**   **59**
Number one important thing, grasshopper!   60
Invisible dangers   62
Electrical safety   63
Fire hazards   64
Ladder safety   64
What to do about lead paint   65

5. MAKING YOUR HOME MORE ENERGY EFFICIENT   68

Installing or updating your insulation   69
Draught-proofing your house   70
Refrigerators   75
Air conditioning   76
On standby   76
Reducing energy used for hot water   77
Saving water   78

6. WALLS AND CEILINGS   81

Repairing plasterboard   81
Fixing corner chips on masonry walls   85
Repairing holes in masonry walls   86
Fixing cracks in rendered walls   87
Fixing timber-lined homes   89
Removing wallpaper   89
Soundproofing your house   91
Dealing with damp   93
Hanging pictures on your walls   97
Installing shelves on your walls   101
Hanging mirrors   103
Repairing or installing a new cornice   105
Attaching a new ceiling rose   107

7. FLOORS . . . AND WHAT'S UNDERNEATH   109

Fixing creaky floorboards   109
Fixing creaky timber stairs   113
Fixing gaps in floorboards   116
Fixing a damaged tongue and groove floorboard   117
Protecting your polished floors   119
Pests in flooring and under the floor   122
Under-floor ventilation problems   126

Other types of flooring 127

Carpet 130

8. DOORS AND WINDOWS **133**

Fixing a rattling door 133

Fixing doors that won't close properly 134

Restoring door furniture 137

Fixing dents on door and window frames 142

Repairing a mullion or a muntin 143

Repairing a broken door or doorframe 144

Fixing sliding doors 145

Maintaining sash windows 149

Replacing putty around glass in your windows 153

Fitting locks on your windows 154

Fixing hinges on your windows 157

Making and fixing flyscreens 158

Maintaining powder-coated aluminium windows 162

Removing old masking tape from windows 164

Removing bubbling tint from windows 164

9. BUILT-IN CUPBOARDS **166**

Kitchen cupboard doors that no longer line up 167

Fixing sagging corner cupboard doors 168

Fixing swinging wardrobe doors 168

Fixing drawers 169

Shelf supports 170

Looking after and updating your laminate kitchen 171

Timber benchtops 174

Other benchtops 175

Replacing cupboard door handles 176

10. FURNITURE **178**

Fixing dents and scratches in timber furniture 178

Removing white heat rings from timber 181
Restoring timber furniture 182
Fixing chairs 186
Fixing creaky wardrobe doors 188
Fixing timber veneer that's lifting 189
Cane and bamboo furniture 190

11. WET AREAS **191**
Tiling 191
Getting rid of mildew on walls 198
Replacing grubby silicone 199
Fixing a sliding glass screen door 200
Rejuvenating an enamel bath 201
Rejuvenating an acrylic bath 202

12. ELECTRICAL AND PLUMBING **203**
Electrical 203
About circuits, watts, amps, fuses and your fusebox 204
Fixing a blown fuse 204
Illumination 206
Plumbing 210
Dripping taps 211
Repairing leaky PVC pipes 212
Water hammer 213
Changing taps in your bathroom or laundry 214
Leaky shower recess 214
Clearing a blocked trap 215
Fixing a leaky loo 215
Looking after your hot water system 216

13. PAINTING AND OTHER FINISHES   218

Paintbrushes and rollers   218
Types of paint   222
Painting—the basics   226
Painting with enamel paint   239
Getting a good, straight edge   241
Storing and disposing of paint   242
Staining timber surfaces   243
Waxing   245
French polishing   246
Applying tung oil   248
Applying oil-based urethane   250
Painting the outside of your house   251

14. THE OUTSIDE BITS—YOUR HOME'S EXTERIOR   253

Cleaning and fixing gutters   253
Looking after your deck   256
Fixing outdoor timber stairs   264
Removing rot from outdoor timber areas   267
Repairing cracks in brickwork   269
Waterproofing   272
Patching damaged render   274
Bagging a wall   275
Repairing a cracked concrete path   278
Cleaning canvas blinds and awnings   280
Removing stains from concrete and masonry   281
Fixing chalky concrete   283
Fixing efflorescence on concrete   284
Rejuvenating tessellated tiles   284
Cleaning sandstone doorsteps   285
Refinishing a balcony railing   285

15. YOUR GARDEN AND YARD   **287**

Fixing your fence   287
Lifting a sagging gate   291
Fixing outdoor timber furniture   293
Fixing your rotary clothesline   294
Waterproofing retaining walls and planter boxes   295
Removing rust from outdoor metal   296
Looking after your BBQ   298

16. USEFUL INFORMATION   **302**

Safety while you work   303
Energy saving   303
Timber and furniture restoration   304
Timber finishes   305
General timber info   307
Building protection   308
Doors and windows   309
Kitchens and wet areas   310
Paint and other finishes   311
Gutters   315
General/miscellaneous   315

INDEX   **317**

Chapter 1
HOW I GOT HOOKED

The weekend is upon us and in the ideal world the sun is shining, the birds are singing and the kids are happily mucking round in the yard. The missus is indulging in some quality 'me' time, and so am I. 'If anyone wants me I'm in the shed,' I holler as I gallop off to the inner sanctum of my big boys' toy shop. They know I may be some time.

My day of doodling is a journey that may involve making, restoring or fixing something, doing projects that could be straightforward or more of a challenge. But often it's simply play time, R&D in the laboratory of home improvement if you like. A trip to the hardware can end up being hours of hard-core study; having the blokes around to join in on a debate at the 'Institute of Backyard Studies' (thanks to Mark Thompson) can lead to some surprising results. But it's all in the name of being able to Do It Yourself.

It seems all my life I've been in homes or jobs that have encouraged me to be handy, but in the beginning I was thrust into a DIY mindset by a family philosophy founded on the pioneering and Depression era mentality of fixing everything and making use of anything. Dad's mantra was that there's nothing you can't fix with a bit of tie wire and some Araldite. Exactly what this combination did was always a mystery to me, but he was never without these ingredients in his messy little fixing kit.

Together he and Mum would scour the country auctions and clearing sales for bargains, hauling these dilapidated 'treasures' back home to be transformed. In the process they turned our backyard and our various sheds into smelly furniture-restoration sweatshops, but over the years they successfully furnished the old farmhouse with an impressive collection of bargain basement antiques.

The last thing I wanted to do as a kid was get my hands dirty with paint stripper and metho—the clay walls of the local creek and the creativity of my mate Flarkie were far more appealing DIY options, as was the distraction of the nearby railway and its passing parade of monstrous steam trains, which I just loved to watch. But I was always amazed at the results of Mum and Dad's hard work as another piece of cedar would eventually be added to the Victorian clutter of 'Rahiri' (near Orange), making the place look like a cross between the set of *On Our Selection* and *The Madness of King George*.

Something must've rubbed off, because at the age of 13 I found myself compelled to put up my hand at a local auction sale, and ended up spending seven dollars of my hard-earned paperboy pocket money on a twee little blue-painted cedar meat safe. Over the next few months, in between projects for woodwork at school and learning lines for the school plays that I'd also become addicted to, it got the full treatment as my first serious fix-it project. I've still got the piece and it's a survivor, unlike the things I built in woodwork, reminding me that even then it was evident that my skills were more attuned to fixing and restoring than to building stuff. It's no wonder that the family tradition of trying to fix things myself was to be my main direction.

In my twenties, when I actually had a bit more than a paperboy's wage from a couple of lead roles in TV miniseries, I hit upon the potential for a really big antique restoration job that would act as a weekender-with-a-difference on our family acres at Mudgee: a vintage railway carriage. Now, even though the purchase and moving costs were less than knocking up a simple shed, the real attraction was the idea of living a bohemian existence in a train, a quirky place to play and stay for friends and family, and a restoration challenge for the novice McGregor with his grand vision for an off-the-rails Orient Express.

At Ruwenzori, my own DIY life-size train set!

This exercise was to set in train, pardon the pun, a journey that opened up a range of opportunities and cultivated my interest in the arena of hard-core DIY. The search for spare parts for my new train took me to the far corners of the railway network at a time when the dismantling of this vast empire was well underway. Each new acting job meant a new carriage—an instant extension if you like. Regular assistance, additions and advice from mates, some of whom were carriage builders themselves, was adding simultaneously to my knowledge bank in a big way, as well as breathing new life into these old trains.

I soon had more spare parts than I needed, and selling a few of my bits and pieces seemed like a good move. I soon had a great little business called *Off the Rails*, trading and restoring all kinds of ex-railway and industrial age antiques. The *Off the Rails* shops kept me busy, but I was most at home in the workshop. Crowded with the remnants of a dozen railway factories and reeking of the nutty smells of beeswax, shellac and gum turps, the creative gang in the workshop—Pete, John and Tony especially—perfected the process of restoration. The team was invariably all like me, self-taught and passionate tinkerers, and together we delighted in solving the many problems that arose, fixing and restoring the variety of weird, wonderful and mostly derelict stuff that came our way.

After a decade of trading I was looking for new directions and, like some kind of fairy godmother, a casting agent came to my call. It was a gift; I was asked to screen test as the new handyman on *Better Homes and Gardens*. To get the job I had to construct an artist's easel in ten minutes. The end product was a joke, but the drawing I did of St Paul's Cathedral as an artist's impression of my next DIY project took the focus away from my folly. It was most likely the presence, up on the workbench with me, of my little spotted cattle-collie cross, Patsy, with her eye-catching features and great camera presence, that clinched the deal for me. Incidentally, she went on to become a regular as well (but is now, sadly, in DIY doggie heaven).

Even my doodles are over the top!

There was a point in my career not so long ago when the DIY thing got completely out of hand. In the middle of my regular work as the handyman on *Better Homes and Gardens* and the ongoing renovation of my old carriages at Mudgee, I began hosting a crazy makeover show called *Room for Improvement*. It was about the maddest thing I've ever done with a tool belt on. Each week while frantically unpacking the truck—my energy levels already off the Richter scale—I would gush down the barrel of the camera, 'We've got just two days and seven and a half thousand dollars to completely make over this house, and what we don't spend we're going to give back to the person we're surprising.'

With a huge crew behind the scenes, and the on-screen talent (four of us) pretending to do all the work, we built, fixed and laughed our way through a kind of DIY cook-off, a fixing frenzy that teetered on anarchy. We did the renos in two days and made the half-hour TV show as we went along, and I was always amazed, and extremely relieved, when it all came together (often with only minutes to spare) before the arrival of the unsuspecting homeowner (not always, I might add, to their delight). The show rated its socks off and I couldn't walk down the street without some wally shouting out, 'Hey, mate! Come and do up my place', but it was a brilliant experience fixing these places up and learning a lot about what could be done to revamp a place without too much hassle.

It's the constant discovery of new info and finding new ways to do things that's the really stimulating aspect of being a serial DIYer. Over the years I've been a sponge absorbing all sorts of info and, like most DIYers without swags of spare time to devote to courses and study, the best education has come from knowledgeable tradies, teachers and mates. These generous and passionate individuals who've shared their expertise, knowledge and enthusiasm have also, often unknowingly, been a source of great inspiration.

I want to name them all but this book is mostly about fixing things so we'll leave the exhaustive list of great fixers for another volume. However, I have to mention Kiwi (Ian Christieson), the carriage builder from Eveleigh Railway Workshops who taught me that perhaps my hand was not the best kind of hammer, and then there's Warwick Mead, fellow carriage owner and DIY legend who took away the fear of tackling the bigger jobs. More recently there's Brett Ley, who held the other end of the timber (and my hand) during much of my on-screen days, and Darryl Chapman, who took over from Brett and has done a lot of the research for this book.

Unlike my golf swing, my learning curve has been accelerating lately, especially during the process of writing this book. Another, recent, big project was probably the most challenging and rewarding of my career as I went back to Mudgee and tackled the big reno. Together with my great buddy and caretaker of the trains, George Lecke, and a team of tradesmen, fellow wood butchers and human bobcats, we transformed my sleepy collection of now historic railway carriages, buildings and paraphernalia into a unique, palatial, themed retreat which has subsequently opened to the public as a self-contained guesthouse. Yes, it's time for the shameless plug: if you want to have a look at the end results of my biggest DIY project, check out www.ruwenzori.com.au.

Not for a minute do I pretend that I'm a professional tradesman—I'm a 'fixer', not a builder. I'm also not pretending that this book covers every little thing you'll ever want to fix around your house—you'd need an encyclopaedia to cover every job in the average home. (I'll have to talk to my wonderful publisher, Jude McGee, at Allen & Unwin about that for next time.) No, this book just covers some of the most common problems, and you'll notice there's a strong focus on timber and natural timber finishes—two of my great passions.

Talking of which, the girls at home—two smallish ones (Sophie and Hayley), one biggish one (Wendy)—are, no argument, my greatest passion, and the fact they're an appreciative audience for my DIY performances is truly heartwarming. If the kids keep me happily distracted with frequent workshop visits to shellac their school projects or make holes in wood with the cordless, then Wendy keeps me happily on track with her extraordinary powers of suggestion (often referred to as 'whip-cracking'). When Wendy submits her 'to-do list' to stop the house falling down, it's all I can do to stay focused on a new bridge for the train set or some other masterpiece in the shed. Seriously, Wendy has a brilliant ability to motivate (just ask the film crews she works with in her role as a TV producer), and during the course of our long relationship she's been the 'architect' behind many of our projects, including this book. As a team comprising brains and brawn (you guess which one is which), we've achieved some classic DIY triumphs together.

Today I find that my DIY chickens have come home to roost, and putting this book together has just confirmed the old family philosophy I offer to those who look at this book—that, if possible and when appropriate, to be able to fix it yourself is a masterful and rewarding thing.

Chapter 2
TOOLS

Every home needs a good toolkit. It doesn't have to be large; you can cre-ate one without a lot of expense, and with a bit of looking after you can start to 'fix it' with confidence. Try to always buy the best quality you can afford. Good-quality tools will not only last longer, they're safer to use and make your job easier. Chances are the whole set will cost you less than a couple of days' labour by an experienced tradesperson.

The basic toolkit

This is what I think you need in your basic home-fix-it toolkit. There's no doubt that the list I've settled on is open to interpretation, especially from those of you who are seasoned DIYers, but here goes. In Chapter 3 you'll find a list of all the products and materials these tools are used with.

Safety equipment. The first and most important items to have. At the very minimum you need disposable dust masks, protective goggles, ear muffs and gloves. See Chapter 4, 'Safety while you work', for a full rundown on gear and tips.

Claw hammer. This is the standard hammer that most people would recognise—one side of the head has a flat face with either a smooth or textured surface and is used for, well, hammering. The other side of the head curves down and splits in the middle, forming a 'V' shape—this is most commonly used for extracting nails from wood. Choose a medium-weight one with a comfortable grip and good balance, preferably with a one-piece head and handle construction.

Tack hammer. A much smaller lightweight hammer useful for hobby, craft and light work like picture framing, it's got a small rectangular head that has no claw but tapers down to a small, thinner face. Use for narrow spots or small 'brad' nails and pins. The thin end of the head is split for extracting tacks. These hammers usually have a wooden handle and a magnetised head.

Tape measure. 8 metre/24 ft metric/imperial combination measures are handy if you're still stuck in the old system. If you really want to get serious about measuring and marking angles, add a **steel rule**, a **combination 'square'** and a **sliding bevel**.

Hand wood saw. There are various types of hand wood saws. Crosscut saws have saw teeth that are shaped like a series of tiny knives, and are used to cut across the grain of timber. Rip saws feature a series of tiny chisel-like edges which are used to cut along the timber grain. A good inexpensive all-round saw to have in your kit would be one of the new hard-point multipurpose saws; it will allow you to cut wood with or across the grain, and the handle will double as a combination square for marking 90 and 45 degree angles. These saws have hardened teeth that will stay sharp 6–8 times longer than a standard saw, but cannot be resharpened and will need to be replaced once they become dull.

Keyhole saw (or compass saw). A small, tapered, thin-bladed saw with a grip at one end, a bit like a serrated knife. It's ideal for cutting holes or short curves, or for using in tight spots where a larger saw won't fit.

A keyhole saw in action

Hacksaw. For cutting metals and plastics. It's a fine-toothed saw with an interchangeable blade under tension in a frame.

Screwdriver set (or combination screwdriver with a range of tips). The combination driver will take up less space and the spare tips are usually stored inside the handle. Make sure you have at least one Phillips head (or cross-head) screwdriver, as well as flat-tipped screwdrivers and an insulated screwdriver for electrical work such as replacing fuses.

WHAT'S A POZIDRIV SCREWDRIVER?

A Pozidriv screwdriver is different from a Phillips head in that the driver bit has four extra smaller ridges between each of the four main driving ridges. These aren't quite compatible with your standard Phillips head screws. Don't go out and buy a Pozidriv screwdriver, though, as there are some great new universal screwdrivers available—they'll not only fit your Pozidriv screws but a whole range of different-sized Phillips head screws around the house as well. So with just one screwdriver in your kit you'll be set for every little job around the house, from assembling new furniture to changing the batteries in the kids' toys.

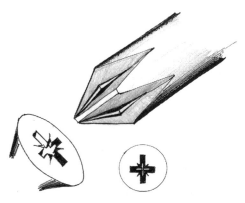

Pozidriv screwdriver

Utility knife with retractable blade (often called a Stanley knife, which is a brand name). It has replaceable blades and will cut through all manner of things from carpet and lino to cardboard boxes to built-up paint around windowframes.

Pliers. These are great for not only gripping and twisting metal objects, but come with built-in cutters for cutting through wire and cable. Standard snub-nosed pliers have flat gripping faces between the jaws at the front with concave gripping faces behind these and then the cutters nearest the pivot for maximum leverage. Be sure to buy some with insulated handles. There are variations on this basic style for performing other tasks:

- pliers with sharp side cutters, for cutting
- needle-nose pliers, for electrical and finer work
- locking pliers (or Vice-Grips, which is a brand name), for clamping onto objects
- fencing pliers with longer handles, for a stronger grip, and
- diagonal pliers with angled jaws, for getting into difficult spots.

Multigrips (or slip-joint pliers). A bit like pliers but these will adjust to allow the jaws to open wider for a larger grip such as holding pipes, nuts and bolts.

Shifting (or adjustable) spanner. Has a screw which changes the size of the jaw to fit different nuts and bolts. Choose a medium-sized one to suit the average nuts and bolts that hold together furniture, bicycles and other household objects. Or you can lash out and get small, medium and large shifting spanners in a set which will basically cover any spanner job that arises. By the way, those crazy Americans call spanners 'wrenches'.

300 mm spirit level. Very important for checking if surfaces are level ('plumb'), and indispensable for hanging pictures straight.

Quick-fitting clamps. You'll need a pair of medium-sized quick-fitting clamps for safely holding things down while you saw or drill them, for assembling projects and for holding together repairs and glue jobs. These are like having a second pair of hands—very strong hands.

Spring clamps. A couple of simple spring clamps (imagine a large metal spring-loaded peg) are good for small, quick clamping jobs such as gluing broken toys, doing craft work or holding up plastic sheeting.

CRAMP OR CLAMP?
Have you ever seen the term 'cramp' used in woodworking books and wondered if it's a typo? Well, traditionally the word 'cramp' referred to devices that use a screw mechanism, such as a G-cramp or sash cramp. 'Clamps' use a brace, clasp or band to fasten items together, such as strap clamps or quick grips. But these days we tend to call them all just 'clamps'.

Wood chisels. A chisel (or three) kept sharp is very handy for any woodworking project—you can use it to shape, carve and trim. Start with a 19 mm one and then perhaps a larger one; look for plastic split-proof handles as these will withstand blows from a standard hammer.

Pry bar (or cat's paw). A flat bar made from spring steel with a flat lever at one end and a hook-shaped lever at the other which also includes slots for the removal of nails. Often used in combination with a hammer, it's an essential tool for prising open timber joins, removing trim and dismantling structures.

Paint scraper and/or putty knife. Scraping, mixing and patching are just a few of the uses for these handy items. It's good to have a couple of different sized flat-bladed scrapers, but also consider the curve-bladed putty knife and a profile scraper, which gives you a number of options for scraping with its multi-shaped blade.

Caulking gun. A device for dispensing glues and sealants from bulk pack tubes. Essential for weatherproofing, waterproofing and preparing for a paint job. Modern designs are compact, with easy-squeeze handles and (much appreciated) drip-proofing mechanisms.

Magnet. A small but powerful magnet will often come in handy.

Brushes and rollers. See Chapter 13, 'Painting and other finishes'.

Sharpening stones. See 'Looking after your tools' below for details.

Awl. A screwdriver-looking tool with a sharp point. Good for marking things and starting small drill holes. A 'brad awl' may sound like a character in a soap opera, but it's actually an awl with a bevelled tip useful for starting holes for screws.

Plunger. No, not the coffee variety, but the rubber suction cup on the end of a wooden handle. Essential for cleaning drains and unblocking sinks. You can coat the rim of the plunger cup with petroleum jelly to get a better seal.

Punch set. My mum and dad had a punch set which consisted of a cut crystal bowl with funny little cups hanging off the side; often used at cocktail soirees. However, *nail* punches have a hollow tip and are usually used to drive the heads of nails below the surface of timber. Centre punches have a pointed tip and are used to basically start off the hole you'll later drill into, particularly in metal. You'll need at least one centre punch, and a few different-sized nail punches.

Ladder. A 2.4 metre double-sided A-frame ladder will serve you well for many odd jobs from painting to pruning. In a pinch you can even lay it on its side to support timbers for cutting, in lieu of a pair of saw-horses.

WHAT'S A BEVEL AND WHY SHOULD YOU CARE?

My wife, when reviewing this book, pointed out that I'm always going on about bevels, but some people may not have any idea what they are. So basically, a *bevel* is the meeting of any two surfaces at any angle other than a right angle. A *chamfer* is a type of bevel restricted to 45 degrees. You'll have bevels and chamfers everywhere around your house—often the edges of tabletops, mouldings and picture frames are bevelled or chamfered and the glass in mirrors is often bevelled around the edge for decorative effect. You may also hear about the *arris*, which is basically the sharp edge where the two surfaces meet, such as the face and edge of a piece of timber. Bevels and chamfers are created primarily for aesthetic reasons, but can also be used as a safety feature, e.g. to remove a particularly sharp arris. They're also used to protect sharp-edged timbers from splitting and denting easily.

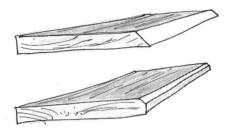

A bevel (top) and a chamfer (bottom)

A DIY shadow board

As you get your basic toolkit together (and add to it—see 'The more advanced toolkit' below) you'll really need to work out how best to store your tools. Setting up a shadow board on the wall of the garage, laundry or garden shed is the go. You could even convert an old wardrobe into a mini shed, add some shelves for bulky power tools and hang your shadow board on the inside of the doors.

Shadow boards are often made from a sheet of perforated masonite (peg board). I prefer a sheet of plywood as you have more flexibility with your tool positioning. You can use screws, nails or any of the various screw-in hooks available at the hardware store to hang your tools off. A few tips:

- Don't try to arrange the layout while it's on a wall. Lay the board on a horizontal surface, then spread and arrange all the tools until you're satisfied with their positions.
- Next, lay the tools down and trace outlines of each tool, then remove them. Paint in the silhouettes, hang the board on the wall and then add the various hooks as needed.

- If you are hanging tools directly onto a wall, then adopt the method in the photo below.

Setting up a new shadow board

A DIY PORTABLE WORKBENCH

An easy way to set up a workbench just about anywhere is with two sawhorses and a sheet of plywood or MDF about 1200 mm x 800 mm, and at least 19 mm thick so it won't bow.

The more advanced toolkit

Once you've got the basics sorted, and you want to do some slightly more complicated jobs, you'll need more tools! (As far as I'm concerned, you can never have enough tools!) Here are the other things in my shed that I use most often, though it's FAR from an exhaustive list.

Spiral ratchet screwdriver. A screwdriver that has a spring-return handle, which means you can drive more screws in quickly—also has a reverse setting for taking them out. It has interchangeable tips, so it's extremely versatile.

Reversible ratchet socket spanner. Basically a handle with a ratchet mechanism on one end which contains a one-way mechanism. This allows the socket (a hollow cylinder that fits over one end of a nut or bolt head) to be turned without removing it from the nut or bolt, simply by cycling the handle backwards and forwards. You can fit a variety of sockets on it, as well as other attachments, to quickly tighten or loosen nuts, bolts and screws.

Long-nosed pliers. Exactly what they sound like. Very good for doing anything with wire and also very small screws and bolts. And removing nasal hairs—only joking!

Wire cutters (or side cutters). Dedicated tools for cutting wires and cables. They'll do this job more cleanly and efficiently than the cutters in a pair of pliers.

Files. Can be used for shaping and fine-tuning both wood and metal. There are a variety of different shaped files that come in handy around the shed—a round file is useful for making small concave surfaces (e.g. to thread a lead through) or enlarging smaller holes. A triangular file is good for squaring the corners of holes. A half round file (i.e. rounded on one side, flat on the other) is used for shaping both curves and straight edges. Don't use your files to prise things open, as they can snap!

Rasps. Come in a variety of shapes, much like files, but are used for shaping wood quickly (a rasp has larger, more serrated teeth than a file).

Tin snips. Like spring-loaded heavy-duty scissors designed to make cutting sheet metal easy. Select a pair that are straight cutting and have a safety catch to keep them closed when not in use.

Mallet. Used when a softer blow is called for than that which a metal hammer would deliver—for example, forming sheet metal, forcing tight-fitting parts together or shifting plasterboard into place. It's basically a large rubber-headed hammer (sometimes it has plastic on one side and rubber on the other). Wooden mallets are less common and mainly used in woodworking.

Tenon saw and mitre box. A very sexy bit of work, this. As the name suggests, tenon saws are traditionally used for cutting away timber for the 'tenons' in a traditional mortice and tenon joint. They have fine teeth and a ridged back; as a result they're ideal for extra-smooth crosscuts in small timber and are good for controlled-depth cuts. A mitre box is a simple 3-sided box (open at the top and ends) with slots cut into the side to guide the handsaw to make precise mitre (angled) cuts in a board. Using the saw in the mitre box, you can make clean accurate straight or angled cuts. Pre-cut slots in the box allow you to adjust the saw to cut the different angles. Use this combination for cutting items that have to have tight-fitting angled joints such as architrave corners, beading and picture framing timber.

Coping saw. Has a narrow, ribbon-like blade tensioned between two lugs by a screw handle and a high-backed stiff metal frame. You'd use it to cut out shapes in wood or metal—particularly good for shaping the ends of skirting boards to fit snugly around the adjoining board.

Pull saw (particularly of the Japanese variety). These saws have very fine blades with little or no set (or angle) on the teeth. They're designed to cut at the pull stroke rather than the traditional push stroke. The result of this type of action is greater accuracy and less effort, meaning you can cut timber straighter, faster and cleaner both across the grain and with it.

Cold chisel. The tool, not the band. A rectangular or hexagonal rod of tempered steel bevelled to a cutting edge at one end. Once struck with a hammer, a cold chisel can cut metal rods, bolts, rivets or chains. More commonly used around the home for working masonry.

Bolster. A masonry chisel with a thick handle and a wide steel blade, used for accurately snapping bricks or stone.

Plugging chisel. Has a thin tapered edge and is used for cleaning out old mortar from between bricks and stone.

Lump or club hammer. A heavy one-handed hammer that relies on its extra weight for inertia to drive down on masonry chisels or for driving metal or wooden stakes into the ground.

Bricklayer's trowel. A flat diamond-shaped metal scoop with a handle, used for levelling, spreading and shaping concrete, plaster and mortar.

Float. A flat-bottomed rectangular tool made from metal or wood, used for smoothing concrete and render.

Pointing trowel and hawk. For cement or mortar work. This is a small diamond-shaped metal trowel used for masonry jobs like patching mortar between bricks (i.e. pointing). The 'hawk' is the flat tray device you carry the mortar around on.

Staple gun. A great toy and very useful if you're applying fabric to anything. Basically like a really big stapler which hammers in large staples with a single blow from a spring-driven plunger. You can also use it to attach thin plywood, plastic and metal. Mine often gets used for doing interesting things with cardboard for school projects. Cheap and efficient electric staple guns are also worth considering.

Plane. This is a woodworking tool basically used to smooth off sections of wood—it has a metal blade which shaves off the top layer of timber. Can also create bevels. It's adjustable so you can dictate how much wood is shaved off. The most common type is a jack plane—usually around 350 mm long and requiring two hands to operate. Block planes are also common—they're designed to cut end grain and are small enough to be used with one hand.

Woodworking vice. A clamp device, usually bolted down to a sturdy bench or table, which has adjustable 'jaws' that hold items firm for sawing or drilling whether in a vertical or horizontal position.

G-clamp (or 'G-cramp'). A clamp that looks like a capital G and has an adjustable screw part which enables you to hold pieces of work together for gluing, sawing or drilling. Two 150 mm clamps should be enough for most jobs.

Pipe wrench. Used for gripping circular objects like pipe; it has an adjustable 'jaw'. You can also use a pipe wrench to move nuts that have damaged corners.

Allen key set. If you've even bought build-it-yourself furniture then you'll know about Allen keys—those thin metal keys with a bend at one end and a hexagonal profile. Usually used to secure handles, plumbing fittings (like taps) and knobs, as well as for assembling pre-packaged whitewood and melamine furniture.

Jeweller's screwdriver. A tiny screwdriver which usually comes in a set. Very useful for fixing spectacles, clocks and other fiddly things.

Window scraper. A specialist tool designed for scraping paint off glass. Usually comes with a replaceable blade.

Pinch bar (also called a wrecking bar). Long metal bar, made from hardened steel with an angled wedge. More heavy duty than a pry bar and good for demolition work. Ideal for situations where you have to prise hardwood frames apart or lift timber floorboards. The split wedge at one end helps in removing large nails.

Stud finder. I have some female friends who are very interested in this tool. OK, bad joke. This is an electronic device used to locate hidden structures inside your plasterboard walls (the 'studs' are the upright timbers inside your wall cavity). This tool can also locate things like wiring and metal water pipes inside your walls, and some types also have extra cool functions like emitting an infrared beam to use as a level.

And then there are the power tools . . .

Cordless drill

For your first power tool purchase I'd definitely suggest you buy a **cordless drill**. With a vast array of drill bits, drivers and other attachments available, it's virtually a toolkit in itself. A 12-volt unit should give you all the grunt needed for most jobs without too much weight, but higher voltage drills are really not that much more expensive. Spend a little extra and buy one with a smart charger included, as this will extend your batteries' useful life, and will also switch off when it's hot so you won't burn the house down if you forget to unplug it. Also, more expensive drills have 'hammer drill' functions as well—very handy for all those masonry drilling jobs. See 'About cordless drills and batteries' below for information about the different sorts of batteries. For your cordless drill you'll need:

- Drill bit kit
- Screwdriver bits—slotted, Phillips, possibly Pozidriv
- Masonry drill bits—if your drill has a masonry drill function

Your cordless drill can be made even more useful with the aid of various special attachments—for almost every job you want to do, you're likely to find a specific drill attachment that will make the job easier. For example:

■ Magnetic bit holders, which hold metal screws in place and allow a quick exchange from drill bit to screwdriver bit.

■ Combination drill bits (or Step drill bits) are also useful. These are specially shaped drill bits which will cut a pilot hole, clearance hole and countersink all in one operation.

■ Angle attachments, which allow you to use your drill at a right angle to the face you're working on; ideal for tight situations.

■ Driver bits for plasterboard screws, which prevent the screw from going too deep by automatically stopping once the screw is flush with the wall.

About cordless tools and batteries

Cordless technology is everywhere in professional workshops and construction sites, and cordless drills, saws and sanders also offer amateur renovators much in the way of convenience and flexibility.

Different chemical combinations and better design have resulted in batteries that are more powerful and hold a charge for longer so they'll now drive tools that are thirsty for power, like high-speed saws. There are three main properties of a battery to think about when buying a cordless drill:

■ **Voltage (V).** The voltage indicated on the side of batteries refers to the actual power available to drive the tool—the higher the voltage the more capable of high-powered jobs the battery is. For cordless drills voltages generally range from 12 to 24 volt, but around 14.4 volt is usually a good balance between power and weight for most DIY users.

- **Amp hours (Ah).** The other number quoted is amp hours; this is often compared to the size of a fuel tank in a car, as it tells you how much charge the battery will hold. A 2.4 Ah battery will run longer than a 1.5 Ah unit, for example, but, like a car, the more powerful or inefficient the motor, the quicker this energy will be used up.
- **Chemistry.** The three main battery types are:

  1) Nickel cadmium (NiCad), which will not hold a charge for as long as the other types and will lose charge quickly when stored. They're less expensive and will take more charge cycles in their effective life, but they're more susceptible to the so-called 'memory effect' which is where the amount of power a battery is able to store is reduced by not discharging it completely before recharging;

  2) Nickel metal hydride (NiMH), which typically offer longer life per charge and are more resilient to memory effect. Each charge will last longer, but the batteries will take fewer charges before the cells start to break down. They're more expensive than Ni-Cads and are usually only found on higher-quality tools;

  3) Lithium ion (Li-Ion), which are more expensive at this stage but will soon become the next stage of evolution for cordless tools as they allow longer operating times and greater power in smaller and lighter battery packs, and won't develop memory effect. Li-Ion batteries are easy to care for as all the failsafes (such as overload protection and heat sensors) are built into the battery rather than the charger.

To take care of your drill's batteries:
- Never leave batteries sitting in a charger. I know of at least one fire caused by this, and my local tool repairer tells me that many chargers come in with the battery literally melted into them.
- Never charge a battery while it's still hot from operating.
- Never push your battery tool beyond its capacity. Sometimes it's

worth pulling out the old corded tool for heavy-duty jobs, as overloading a cordless tool may damage both the tool and the battery.

More expensive tools come with a smart charger that will solve a number of these issues. Good-quality chargers will charge a battery in as little as half an hour.

Electric drill

The next step up from the cordless is an **electric drill**, which has more grunt and can drive more attachments. Fittings available for your electric drill include:

- Plug cutter—cuts round wooden plugs used to conceal holes in timber.
- Counterbore bit—very useful at parties. No, actually this bit sinks a hole with straight sides and a flat bottom that will hold a bolt head that is required to sit flush with or below the surface.
- Countersink bit—creates a tapered, cone-shaped hole for a wood-screw, allowing it to be flush with or below the surface.

A countersink bit

- Grinding attachments—which come in different grades. You can use them to cut or shape metal, remove rust, sharpen your tools (see 'Looking after your tools' below), cut or shape tiles or to remove burrs from freshly cut or drilled metal.
- Wire brushes—which come in many shapes and sizes. The soft steel bristles are great for removing rust and paint, for cleaning files and other tools, and for cleaning away pitted surfaces, especially metal.
- Sanding attachments—see Chapter 3, 'Products and materials'.
- Polisher—a lamb's wool covering tied around a flexible rubber pad, used to buff wood and metal. Also good to use with an angle grinder.
- Nibbler attachment—will cut through sheet metals by taking a continuous row of very small bits from the metal along a line.
- Paint mixer attachment—will blitz even old lumpy paint.
- Hole saw—a cylinder of metal with cutting teeth on the bottom edge that spins around a central drill bit. Used for cutting holes through various materials larger than those made by drills.
- Auger drill bit—for deep wood drilling.
- Forstner drill bit—for low, flat holes like those required for kitchen hinges.

These are just a few examples of the various attachments available to fit drills; you can even get an attachment to sharpen dull drill bits!

SNAP IT ON
Snap-on lock drill attachments are becoming more common. These are great for fast and efficient bit exchanging. The days are numbered when attachments will be held in with 'chucks'.

More advanced electric tools

I could go on forever, but here are some that I think are pretty handy.

Angle grinder. A very popular tool—the motor drives an arbor mounted at a right angle to the machine's body. Into this arbor, stone discs are mounted that can be replaced when worn. Disks come in different weights and styles, and you can also attach wire brushes, diamond-cutting wheels and polishing pads. You can use your angle grinder for grinding, cutting and wire brushing but BE WARNED—these tools cause more injuries than any another and it's VITAL you wear protective goggles when using one.

Jigsaw. A versatile electric saw that has interchangeable straight blades fitted vertically into the machine. As the name suggests, this tool is ideal for cutting curves and awkward shapes, but it can be used for straight and even bevelled cutting. Metal cutting, wood cutting and special-purpose blades like scroll blades are available.

Circular saw. Has a spinning vertical circular blade and is used for sawing timber. Circular saws are portable and versatile—use them for making long cuts through sheet material, crosscuts, rips and bevels, depending on the blade you've fitted. Make sure the one you buy has a fixed upper blade guard and a lower blade guard that springs into position when a cut is finished—these can be very dangerous tools if not used with care.

Electric sander. Fantastic if you have to do a lot of sanding, but take care when starting out as you can do some damage with an electric sander if you fit the wrong paper or go too hard! Be careful not to sand across the grain, and make sure you press down on it evenly but without too much pressure or you'll get furrows appearing in your surface. There are several types:

- Orbital sander—turns a felt or rubber sanding pad in small circles (or orbits). There are clamps on the end of the pad, or a Velcro base, that hold the sandpaper in place. Used for smoothing of wood and metal and polishing of paint.
- Pad or palm sander—a smaller version of the orbital sander, available in models that use 1/4 or 1/3 sheets of sandpaper. Palm sanders vibrate in a slight circular pattern and you must move them in the same direction as the wood grain to avoid scratching the stock. Lightweight and very handy for small jobs.
- Reciprocal or linear sander—a sander where the pad moves back and forth in a straight line. It can be used on bare wood to produce a smooth finish. This is the slowest and least aggressive of the power sanders, and is sometimes called a finishing sander. Can be fitted with specially shaped bases for sanding along mouldings and handrails.
- Belt sander—has a pair of drums on which a seamless loop of sandpaper is mounted (imagine a conveyor belt in a factory). Used for heavy-duty sanding, long lengths of timber, and large flat areas such as table tops. Great for rapid smoothing of rough old hardwoods. Can be fitted with metal sanding belts as well. Can be mounted upside down to a workbench or sawhorse to use as a fixed unit for edge shaping and tool sharpening.

High speed router. For more advanced woodworking, it machines wood for tight-fitting joints and cuts intricate patterns and contours. Used for making decorative edges, rebates, grooves and channels. It has interchangeable bits, and the depth of the cut can be altered. Very useful bits that you'll like to have for your router include jointing bits, finishing bits, shaping bits and flush trimming bits.

Hiring tools

For many DIYers it's a wise move to hire expensive power tools—often you'll only want to use them once and it'll save you money. It's also a good way to try before you buy. But do make sure you know EXACTLY how to use them before you leave the hire shop, and be careful. Powerful electric and motorised tools can cause damage to surfaces if not used properly—and also to fingers and toes! Make sure you know what kind of fuel is required (two-stroke or unleaded) and that you have READ the safety instructions supplied. Hire outlets can supply you with the appropriate safety equipment and any consumable add-ons, such as blades or sandpapers.

The most commonly hired tools which you may like to consider are:

- angle grinders
- high-pressure water cleaners (but only if they're allowed under your water restrictions)
- air compressor powered tools—e.g. nail guns (great for a big nailing job but make sure you practise first on some old timber)
- plate compactors (used to level soil or sand before putting down pavers)
- chainsaws
- mulchers and other garden implements like rotary hoes
- jackhammers
- tile cutters and tile and paver saws
- drop saws
- nail guns
- floor sanders
- spraypainting equipment.

Looking after your tools

Where possible, hang your tools on a tool board rather than chucking them in a pile where they may get damaged. A tool rollup with pockets is a good way to store smaller tools. To look after your tools:

- Keep them clean and rust free by wiping over after each use with a coat of WD-40. (But don't put it on hammers, files or spanners!)
- Make sure your power tools are kept clean and air vents are cleared of sawdust.
- Always fully uncoil extension cables and power tool cables before use, recoil them loosely before storing, and make sure they aren't cut or split.
- Always keep them sharp—see below.

Sharpening tools

For me nothing beats the satisfaction of working with sharp tools—but that's just the kind of guy I am. They make your jobs easier and give you better, cleaner results.

The cutting edge of certain tools such as chisels and plane blades are usually made up of two bevels on the same side of the blade, known as the 'primary' and 'micro' bevels. The primary angle, usually set at about 25 degrees, is often ground mechanically. This is done with the aid of a grinder or similar. The micro bevel is the one that really brings the blade down to a fine edge; this bevel only covers the last millimetre or so of the business end of the blade and is usually finely honed by hand at about a 30 degree angle. The basic sharpening action is to rub the blade at the correct angle on an appropriate sharpening medium, or to hold it firm against a moving grinding wheel.

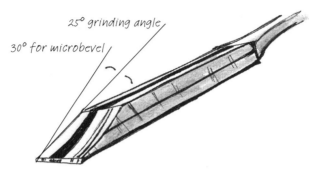

25° grinding angle

30° for microbevel

A blade bevel

The sharpening process will create a fine furry ridge along the cutting edge known as a burr; this is removed with a leather strop. Done well, this process should make a tool sharp enough to shave hairs off your arm. Once the primary angle has been made it will only need to be renewed occasionally, while the tool can be kept sharp by touching up the micro bevel.

Other tools such as knives rely on a single, very low angle bevel on each side of the blade. Knives don't need the extra fine honing of woodworking tools and actually benefit from the slightly serrated edge of grinding alone. At a microscopic level the edge of a kitchen knife actually looks like a very fine saw, which is just what you need to cut through the soft fibres of meat and vegetables.

Sharpening stones—every shed should have at least one

Sharpening stones are usually about 75 mm x 220 mm, and should be stored close at hand to constantly keep cutting tools well tuned. Use them on a stable surface so you can sharpen your tools easily and safely.

These stones are essential for keeping an edge on chisels, planes and the like. You can also use them on your knives and scissors.

TYPES OF STONES

Sharpening stones come in a variety of grades and in three basic types:

Oilstones. The most economical, but beware the cheaper ones tend to be inconsistent in their hardness and grit size. Originally all cut from natural stone, but most are artificially manufactured these days. They're used in combination with light machine oil as this lubricates the grinding action. You can even get some that are reversible, with a coarse grade on one side and fine on the other. Keep your oilstones free from dust and damage by storing them in a wooden box. Metal filings, old oil and grime can be removed by soaking them in kerosene.

Water stones. These stones, originally from Japan, have started to gain a lot more popularity due to their extremely fine-quality grades. A water stone is a natural stone consisting of microscopic particles of quartz suspended in clay, but (like oilstones) they are now being artificially manufactured. When sharpening, the clay slowly dissolves away, exposing fresh quartz. Water stones cut faster but tend to hollow out quickly and need to be reflattened by 'dressing' (i.e. rubbing) with a flat brick or stone.

Diamond stones. These are made from industrial diamonds bonded to either a steel or plastic base plate, again with different grades on either side. These stones are lubricated with water. Ranging in size from nail file size up to 250 mm x 90 mm, they can be very small convenient mini-stones that are great for tuning up the tips of power tool blades. Compared to the other stones they are expensive but will last for many years and won't hollow out—and you can't drop and break them.

GETTING THE RIGHT ANGLE
A honing guide is a very handy little device. It's a kind of locking frame that can be used with any stone to hold the tool blade at the precise angle required as it's ground on the sharpening surface.

Other ways to sharpen

Files are ideal for putting an edge of gardening tools such as spades, mattocks and axes. These types of tool should by held in a vice while you grind the edge.

A **belt sander** can be used in lieu of a bench grinder. Fit the sander with a fine, fresh metal sanding belt and clamp your belt sander upside-down onto a sturdy work surface. Use the base plate area for a flat grind or the roller end for a hollow grind. Be careful not to grind away too quickly.

Abrasive paper has become available in finer and finer grades. These superfine abrasive sheets can be used as a substitute single-use stone by spray-gluing a sheet onto a flat surface like hard plastic or wood. This is an excellent way for a beginner to sharpen without the initial expense of a high-quality stone.

Sandpaper is very useful for sharpening scissors; all you have to do is cut the sandpaper up with the scissors to sharpen them!

TEN GREAT TOOL TIPS

1. To make screwing a screw in easier, rub the screwdriver blade tip with a magnet. It will temporarily magnetise it and so keep the screwdriver connected to the screw in tough spots.

2. A mothball and some bags of silica gel thrown into your tool storage area or toolbox will absorb moisture and coat tools with camphor residue to keep rust and bugs at bay.

3. If you've broken your only small drill bit halfway through a job, you can easily substitute it with a cut nail—just snip off the head with side cutters or pliers.

4. I like to have a bunch of timber wedges around in my tool box—from them you can make your own foot lifter, door stop or door wedge.

5. If you have a metal tool that's gone stiff with rust, you can often resurrect it by soaking it overnight in metho. Then the next day you'll find you can snap the rust's grip and be able to open and close them again. Give a good spray with some WD-40, then rub down with some fine steel wool. Rub clean with a rag and then spray again.

6. Make your own rubber mallet by putting a rubber doorstop or one of those chair leg rubber cups over the head of a normal hammer.

7. Keep your hammer from slipping off nail heads as you strike them by rubbing its face on rough concrete or a piece of sandpaper to roughen up the face and create better grip.

8. Use oven cleaner to remove the build-up of pitch and wood resins from the tips of saw blades and router bits or to clean the sap from pruning saws.

9. Start a hacksaw cut or a steel tube cut without the blade slipping by making a starting notch with the edge of a triangular file.

10. Drill clean holes in sheet metal by sandwiching it between two pieces of wood and drilling through the lot. This will result in neat, clean holes without burrs.

Chapter 3
PRODUCTS AND MATERIALS

Knowing about the products you use around the house is a really important part of being a 'fix it' person. Understanding how and why they work, and what to use where (and more importantly, what not to use), can make your job so much easier. Here's a bit of information about some basic products that everyone should have in their 'shed', plus I've waxed lyrical a bit on some of my favourite ones! For information about paint, see Chapter 13, 'Painting and other finishes'.

Key ingredients

Sandpaper

To identify different types of sandpaper, look on the back of the paper; you'll find information such as the grit type and size, and whether it's suitable for use with liquids or should be used dry. Other information sometimes includes whether it's good for painted surfaces and also which direction it should run around a belt sander.

In the descriptions below, the colour given is just a guide, because colours vary from manufacturer to manufacturer; always read the back to be sure of what type of sandpaper you're selecting. The term 'grit' refers to the number of abrasive particles per inch of sandpaper; the lower the grit numbers the rougher the sandpaper and, conversely, the higher the grit number the smoother the sandpaper.

The basic sandpaper types are:

- Wet and dry—dark grey to black in colour, with silicon carbide grit on specially treated waterproof paper. Can be used for sanding with liquids such as water or oils, or used dry. Ideal for fine timber finishing, automotive repairs, fibreglassing and metal surfaces. Available grits: 60 to 2500.

- Aluminium oxide—often yellow, brown-red, pale grey (almost white) and sometimes green. The most common sandpaper used in woodworking and painting, although it's an all-purpose sandpaper that's good for not only wood but metal, plastic and fibreglass sanding and is particularly useful for removing old paint. Available grits: 36 to 400.

- Garnet paper—orange coloured. Designed for all types of bare wood sanding and finishing. This sandpaper is the traditional choice of cabinetmakers and woodworkers for producing smooth, fine finishes on bare wood, though it's not as commonly used these days. Garnet abrasive fractures during use, continually forming new cutting edges. Available grits: 40 to 220.

- Emery cloth—usually dark grey or a red-brown colour. Flexible to fit contours and corners. Used for light rust removal and cleaning of metals.

Other abrasives

Sanding screen. Black silicon carbide sanding screens (or gauze) are ideal for sanding plasterboard joints as they won't clog with material and they allow you to remove the dust with a vacuum. They're double-sided, non-loading, washable and reusable.

Sanding belt or disc. This has aluminum oxide sandpaper on a cloth backing (for belts) or on thick paper or Velcro (for discs), and is designed for use on electric sanding tools. Has general-purpose use for working with both wood and metal.

Sanding sponge. This is aluminum oxide sandpaper on a foam pad with a waterproof bonding system. Comes in a range of styles, from blocks to soft sheets. The foam construction helps eliminate finger marks and can be used wet or dry. These flexible abrasive pads enable users to sand unusually shaped surfaces.

Sanding flap wheel. This is a number of small flaps of sandpaper mounted to a central shaft designed to fit into a drill chuck. When the drill spins, the sanding flaps are rapidly dragged across a surface. Terrific for removing rust from steel or for sanding inside curved surfaces.

Nylon scourer. A synthetic abrasive pad, similar to a Scotchbrite pad. Available in a range of grades indicated by their colour. Ideal for wet use.

Steel wool. Steel wool is available in a range of grades that indicate the fineness of the fibres. Keep grade 3 for rough paint stripping and paint removal from complex surface shapes, and '00' and '0000' grade for fine finishing work and applying waxes.

Solvents

You'll need:

- Kerosene
- Methylated spirits
- Acetone (nail polish remover)
- White spirits (dry-cleaning fluid)
- Gum turpentine—a naturally occurring solvent obtained by distillation from certain pine trees. It's an artist's grade turpentine ideal for use in fine wood finishes or as a cleaner.
- Mineral turpentine—a petroleum distillate. As a cheaper substitute for gum turpentine it's ideal for most common uses such as paint thinning and brush cleaning.

Lubricants

The typical lubricants are:

- Penetrating oil—commonly known as WD-40, a brand name.
- Light machine oil—such as 3-in-1 oil or sewing machine oil.
- Petroleum jelly—often called Vaseline, another brand name.
- Graphite powder—a dry lubricant, ideal for lock mechanisms.
- Silicone spray—a dry lubricant for nylon glides, door runners and rollers.
- Paraffin wax (candle)—great for sticky wooden draw runners, doors and saw blades.

Markers

To mark your work you'll need:

- Flat carpenter's pencils—designed to not roll away when you put them down. The flat lead can be carved to shape with a sharp knife or special pencil sharpener and will hold its edge longer than a standard drawing pencil. The colour of the pencil indicates how hard the lead is: green is hard, red is soft and yellow is medium.

- Chinagraph pencils—white pencils for marking darker surfaces, as well as glass, tiles, china and all hard, glossy surfaces. Impervious to water, yet may be easily removed with a dry cloth.
- Permanent markers—always come in handy, as do paint pens.

Rags and old containers

You need lots of them. Old cotton T-shirts are very useful; in fact any non-shedding cotton fabric is great. Also, I keep all old tin cans and non-recyclable plastic containers cut down to use as disposable paint containers and the like.

Fasteners

There's a vast range of fasteners available to fix and fasten objects of all descriptions together. There are even businesses that specialise in supplying nothing but fasteners for common and specialised uses. Even around the home many different types are used for different purposes, but here are a few that are most common:

Nails

Nails are described by their dimensions in millimetres, e.g. '150 x 4' is a nail 150 mm long and 4 mm in diameter. A description of the head and finish is typically added; for example:

- Bullet head—general-purpose nail with a small head allowing it to be punched below the timber surface and then filled. Keep a few sizes handy in both bright steel (indoor use) and galvanised (outdoor use).

- Spikes—large nails usually over 100 mm are called spikes.
- Brads and pins—extra-small nails for fine interior trim work.
- Flat head—provide greater holding power than brad heads, but the flat head remains exposed. Often used for structural framing work or for attaching things like fence palings.
- Clouts—very broad-headed nails for holding thin sheet materials, and usually galvanised.
- Fibre cement nails—are much like clouts but have a blunt point to punch through the fibre cement.
- Decking nails—designed with a slightly domed head and a twisted shank. The head just penetrates the timber, leaving only the slight dome on the surface that will not catch on your feet. The twisted shank is to improve the holding power of the nail.
- Ring shank—these have ridges along the shaft for extra grip, and are used anywhere you need more holding power than a regular nail.

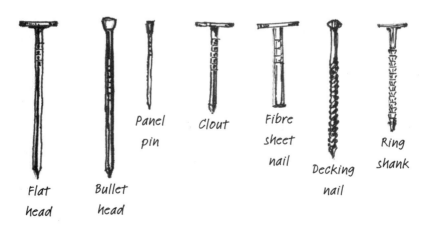

Flat head   Bullet head   Panel pin   Clout   Fibre sheet nail   Decking nail   Ring shank

Some types of nails

Screws

Once again there are many more types of screws than you're ever likely to need at home. Buy a few basic styles and a good screw sorting chest—each time you finish a job you can add the leftovers to the sorter and soon you'll have your own portable hardware supply!

Screws can be made from many types of metal, usually steel, brass or stainless steel. They may also combine steel with a special coating for particular uses, such as basic zinc plating for common indoor uses or galvanising for use outdoors or with treated pine. Stainless steel is expensive and should be saved for use in highly corrosive environments or to fix stainless steel fittings. Brass is soft and should be used for decorative work or as part of historical refitting.

Screw heads come in various types:

- Slotted, Phillips, Pozidriv—the most common styles of screwdriver designs. The head is shaped in various ways for various functions.
- Countersunk style screws—these have a downward-facing cone-shaped head designed to sit neatly into a cone-shaped recess and finish flush on top. Self-countersinking screws have a series of small ridges under the head which create their own countersink in the surface.
- Round and pan head—which have a dome-shaped head that sits on top of the material surface.

- Button head—which are large flat head screws that work like a fixed washer.
- Bugle heads—shaped like little bugles, as the name would suggest. These are found on plasterboard screws and on larger wood screws.
- Bolt or hex head—found on roofing screws that are driven with the extra force of a socket driver.

Screw threads also come in various types:
- Self-tapping thread—means that the screw cuts (or taps) its own thread groove as it's driven in.
- Self-drilling screws—available for both wood and metal drilling. These screws have a hardened drilling point that drills its own pilot hole as it's driven in. They're designed for power tool use only.
- Wood screws—the more traditional type have slightly tapered shafts and are usually not threaded all the way down.

Bolts

Most bolts for home use will be made of steel with zinc coating, galvanised or stainless steel. The three main types of bolts are:
- Hex bolts—may be fully or only partly threaded. These are used with loose nuts where two spanners are required, or are fastened into trapped nuts or a threaded hole where only one spanner will be needed.
- Carriage (or gate) bolts—have a smooth, domed head with a small square key under the head. These are used to fasten timbers together: as the nut's fastened to one side the key will pull into the timber to prevent the bolt twisting while being tightened with a single spanner.
- Coach bolts—like giant wood screws, they have a pointed tip and a wood thread. These are used, once again, to join timber by fastening into a blind hole.

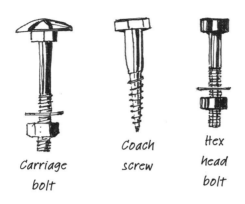

Carriage bolt

Coach screw

Hex head bolt

Some types of bolts

Wall anchors

Solid wall anchors start with your basic plastic plugs, which provide a housing for a screw or nail to be bedded into a masonry wall. They come in a range of colours that indicate their size; I always keep a few on hand in different sizes. Here are some types of wall anchors:

- Heavy-duty wall fixings, such as expanding wall anchors like Dynabolts and Loxins (brand names), are for mounting heavy items or those under load. Purchase these from job to job.
- There are special nails and screws designed to be driven directly into masonry. Ask your hardware merchant for advice on the correct type and size according to the job at hand.
- Hollow wall anchors are used for mounting or hanging items from stud frame walls clad in sheet material such as plasterboard, fibre cement, masonite or thin plywood. Once again there are various choices designed to meet different loads and other criteria.

- Screw-in anchors (such as Wall Mates) are one of my favourites as they're quick and easy to install with just a screwdriver. 'Toggle' types are better for slightly heavier loads.
- Modern stick-on anchors can be removed without damaging the wall, but they're very limited in the weight they can carry.
- A simple screw or nail will do the job if your wall is clad in timber or you can successfully locate a stud below the surface, and the object you are hanging isn't too heavy.

Glues, sealants and fillers

Glues

PVA. PVA (polyvinyl acetate) is your stock standard wood glue and probably the most common adhesive around. It's designed to work with all porous materials such as cloth, paper, leather, felt, polystyrene and even terracotta, so not only is it handy for repairing timber furniture but it's useful for craft, costume-making, bookbinding and even some masonry work. PVA is non-toxic (unless you eat it!) and water based. PVA is not a good gap filler, so the surface to be bonded should be a close fit; in woodworking, however, a little sawdust added to the glue increases its gap-filling ability. To use PVA:

1. Apply glue to only one of the surfaces to be bonded
2. Bring the two surfaces together, then apply pressure, e.g. a clamp or heavy weight
3. Leave to set. It sets best in good air circulation, at room temperature. Full strength is not achieved until about 24 hours have passed.

Two-part epoxy. Two-part epoxy adhesives (e.g. Araldite) are made for a variety of applications. They are waterproof adhesives that can be drilled, sanded or painted once set. Epoxy adhesives also have great gap-filling properties, so the two surfaces to be bonded don't need to be a close fit, and clamping isn't always required. Epoxy adhesives work on porous materials such as wood and on other materials such as glass, metal and some plastics. They're ideal for repairing items that take a lot of wear and tear or will be exposed to water, like sports equipment, tool handles, outdoor furniture or things that need to be washed regularly. To use two-part epoxy:

1. Wear disposable gloves.
2. Make sure you clean the surfaces to be glued before applying the epoxy.
3. Mix the two parts together in equal quantities. (The glue is packaged in two tubes or a double-barrelled syringe; marked part A and part B, one is the resin and the other is the hardener.) Beware —the chemical hardening process will start once the two components are mixed.
4. Apply glue to both surfaces, then bring the surfaces together.
5. Clamp or simply tape them in place until the glue has cured (up to three days).
6. Clean away any uncured glue with acetone (nail polish remover), as excess glue is difficult to remove once hardened.

Construction adhesive. Construction adhesive is a bit of a jack-of-all-trades in the building and landscaping game. Usually sold in caulking tubes, construction adhesive is thick and strong, and works with most building materials. You can use it to set stone steps onto concrete footings, for installing wallboards, gluing cork or even joining wet timbers together. One job this glue is particularly good for is applying to the underside or between the tongues and grooves of wooden floors to eliminate squeaks. To use construction adhesive:

1. Make sure surfaces to be glued are clean and free from loose surface materials. Non-porous materials such as metal should be wiped down with turpentine before applying glue.
2. With a caulking gun, apply a generous bead of glue to one of the surfaces and press the surfaces together. Use a good quality, non-drip caulking gun to gain the firm pressure required to extrude the glue from the tube and to prevent messy run-on.
3. Nail, screw or clamp the surfaces together. Once you've applied the glue you'll have up to 20 minutes to reposition the job before the glue starts to go off. Clamps should remain in place for 24 hours.
4. Clean up excess with turpentine; even cured glue spills can be softened with a turpentine-soaked rag held on the glue until it softens.

Instant bonding. Instant bonding glue such as Supa Glue is very handy to have on hand for instant repairs where immediate results are required, such as broken toys. It's very strong and sets almost instantly, but can be brittle. Ideal for non-porous surfaces such as glass, certain plastics, ceramics and metal, it can also be used to bond wood and cardboard. It can even be used in conjunction with other glues to hold surfaces together while the stronger, more appropriate adhesive has time to cure. To use instant bonding glue:

1. Make sure surfaces to be glued are close fitting and dirt free.
2. Apply glue only to one surface and simply hold the pieces together until the bond is firm. Be careful not to glue your fingers together; if you should accidentally drip some onto your skin, use nail polish remover to dissolve it.
3. Refit the lid quickly after use. The glue can be stored in the fridge.

Other glues. Here are some more that may come in handy:

- Contact cement—a pressure-sensitive glue ideal for adhering plastic laminates and vinyl flooring. And if you like a bit of cobbling, use it to re stick the soles on your shoes!
- Urethane bonds—react with atmospheric moisture to form a super-strong, shockproof, chemical-resistant and waterproof bond. Great for repairs for items used externally which require flexibility, such as exterior fabrics, canvas awnings, tents and wetsuits.
- Silicones and mastics—thick, flexible and waterproof, and they come in a range to suit different materials. Especially good for use on exteriors and wet areas.
- Hot melt glue—for instant bonding of many surfaces (great for tacking speaker wires to a skirting board, for example). Requires an applicator gun.
- Epoxy putties—available in a range of special-purpose styles. One typical product is Knead It Aqua, which is good for underwater uses such as swimming pool tile replacement or inside water features.
- Plastics glue—like Airfix glue, used in model work or for joining other plastics.

Sealants

Silicone. Silicone sealants form a tough and flexible rubber which remains flexible for years. They're designed to be used to seal out water e.g. around a bathtub, shower screen or laundry sink, or around roofs, gutters, flashing, vents, glass and even aquariums.

Co-polymer. Co-polymer sealants are highly versatile sealants which have excellent adhesion to wet and oily non-porous surfaces like roofing sheets and guttering. They dry clear and can be painted.

Polyurethane. Polyurethane sealants have long durability and are highly resilient to joint movement and exposure to harsh weather conditions. They can also be painted over, mainly with acrylic paints.

Fillers

Acrylic gap filler. Flexible gap fillers such as No More Gaps are applied to cracks and gaps between surfaces where you need to allow for movement. They're usually applied with a caulking gun and can be painted, or purchased in a pre-coloured range.

Rigid fillers. Used for filling cracks and holes in solid surfaces where a smooth, even finish is required. They're available in exterior and interior styes, some premixed but others requiring DIY mixing. A variety of types are available depending on what's to be repaired and the nature of the damage. I keep two-part polyester filler (AKA 'builder's bog') for exterior timber work and premixed cellulose filler (Spakfilla is one brand) for internal walls.

Expanding foam fillers. Foam fillers are designed for filling large irregular-shaped gaps, hollows and cavities in your home (e.g. around the pipe underneath the kitchen sink) to block draughts, dust, noise, insects, birds and so on.

Wood putty. Wood putty is available in water-based or spirit-based varieties; I prefer water based. It's available in a range of colours or in neutral, which can be mixed with stain to make your colour match. Best used before timber has been finished.

Wax putty. Wax putty is a beeswax-based filler that's available in a range of standard timber colours. It's used for making repairs to timber work that's already finished. Ideal for restoration work and maintenance.

Epoxy putty. Two-part, kneadable, fast-setting epoxy putty is ideal for repairing, rebuilding, reshaping or restoring almost anything. It can be drilled, filed, machined, screwed, sawn, sanded, stained and painted. And yes, it also tap-dances.

A BIT ABOUT CEMENT

Portland cement is the basic binding agent of concrete, and the most widely used type of cement. It's used with a variety of other ingredients to make concretes and mortars for many jobs. Buy cement as you need it in basic grey or off white, but check how long you can keep it—it does go off after a certain period of time. Old cement loses its bonding power, as I have learnt over the years to my chagrin!

Cleaners

There's a cleaner for almost every dirty job and, believe me, my daughter Hayley has put most of them to the test:

- Hand cleaner—many heavy-duty brands are available in pump packs and tubes.
- Industrial wipes—have been recently appearing in hardware stores. They are industrial-style wet towelette wipes that are simply pulled from a dispenser. They're great for cleaning greasy smears and accidental spills.
- CLR ('Calcium, Lime, Rust' remover)—a brand name product that's good for kettles, pipes and anywhere where water has left a residue.
- White vinegar—mildly acidic all-purpose wonder cleaner.
- Orange oil—for everyday cleaning of fine timber work.
- Metal polish—select a general-purpose non-abrasive metal polish such as Nevrdull.
- Goof Off—a brand name product for removing certain stains and sticky substances.
- Liquid sugar soap—for cleaning existing paint work or preparing for a paint job.
- Beeswax furniture polish—for maintaining the lustre of previously coated or raw timber and timber furniture.
- Outdoor surface cleaner—for removing moss and mildew from hard surfaces.
- Oxalic acid—a timber washing and bleaching chemical; must be used with care.
- Hydrochloric (muriatic) acid—for cleaning concrete paths and pavers and removing cement stains from bricks; must be used with care. Make sure you wear a mask and protective clothing when using it.

Tapes, strings, ropes, straps and wires

I keep the following in my shed and they seem to get me through most situations!

- Masking tape—both standard and low-tack painter's tape
- Packing tape
- Electrical insulation tape
- Gaffer tape
- Double-sided tape
- Jute twine
- Venetian blind cord
- 8 mm nylon rope
- Plastic-coated clothes line
- 2–3 ratchet straps
- Various ockie straps
- Rubber bands
- 10, 15 and 20 amp fuse wire—good for a range of little jobs in addition to repairing fuses.
- Roll of galvanised tie wire
- A few wire coathangers
- A few metres of single-core insulated electrical wire—good for binding and has the added protection of the plastic coating.

INSTANT RUBBER BANDS
An old rubber glove can be cut up with a pair of scissors to create a supply of rubber bands in different sizes. Cut across the fingers for small ones or across the hands for larger ones.

Timber and boards

Timber types is a subject I could dedicate an entire book to, but for the meantime I've listed some of the common terms you'll come across in the timberyard:

- DAR (dressed all round)—smoothed on each surface, to a range of standard dimensions.
- Rough sawn—finished with rough saw cut surfaces, to dimensions slightly larger than dressed timber.

'Dressed all round' and 'rough sawn' (the models and the wood)

- Hardwood and softwood—the difference between hardwood and softwood comes down to the cellular structure rather than the actual properties of the timber; this can be confusing as super-soft timbers such as balsa wood are actually hardwood! Essentially, flowering trees are hardwoods (e.g. eucalypts like jarrah, blackbutt and stringy-bark) and trees that produce cones are softwoods (e.g. pine, redwood, Oregon, kauri).
- Treated timbers—these have been pressure treated with a range of chemicals to give them greater resistance to rot, termites and borer.
- F grades—F numbers on timber refer to its durability grading; the higher the number the greater the durability.
- Moulding—a moulding is timber that has been machined with a decorative profile for use as trim or for decorative detailing.
- Beading—a small section of timber without the detail of moulding, used for small detail work.
- Lengths—timber lengths are stocked in increments of 300 mm (1.2 metres, 1.5 metres, 1.8 metres and so on).
- Sheet timbers—available in three main types and in a range of standard thicknesses.
- Plywood—consists of layers of thin hardwood or softwood timber joined together with glue. It's light and strong.
- MDF (medium-density fibreboard)—very fine wood dust combined with a resin bonding agent and pressed to form boards that are very flat and versatile, ideal for painted finishes. Care must be taken to control dust while using MDF.
- Chipboard—made from many fragments of timber glued and pressed together. It's great for shelving and flooring (away from water) as it remains much stiffer than MDF. It's often sold with a melamine coating for making cabinets and can be made with highly moisture-resistant adhesive, making it ideal for wet area cabinets.

Timber finishes

This is where I tend to 'wax lyrical'—one of my favourite topics! For how to apply these timber finish products, see Chapter 13, 'Painting and other finishes'.

Clear finishes

Varnish was traditionally used in furniture and oil painting; it combined drying oils and resins to form a hard, glossy, clear finish. Nowadays the word 'varnish' has become more of a generic term that refers to all hard clear finishes. Here are some of the most common clear finishes used around the home.

Oil-based urethanes. Tough, durable and water resistant, urethanes are basically a surface coating. Available in a range of gloss finishes, they tend to yellow timber straight away and get yellower with time. They're slower drying, so it'll take you longer to put down the necessary 2–3 coats. Good for surfaces that need a lot of protection like kitchen tables, vanity units, etc.

Water-based urethane (clear sealer). Quicker drying, less smelly and non-yellowing, water-based urethanes show off the real colour of timber in furniture and panelling; also easier to clean up and have less odour. Good for floors and panelling, but not as long lasting as the oil-based version.

Shellac. I'm sure I've bored many people at parties extolling the virtues of shellac. It's a natural resin secreted by the tiny lac insect (*Laccifer lacca*) found on certain trees in India and Thailand. The liquid known as French polish is simply shellac dissolved in an alcohol solvent (methylated spirits). Don't be scared off by the idea of using French polish—in many ways it's easier to use than modern polyurethane, as it dries quickly (allowing you to build up a number of coats quickly) and is easy to repair should it become damaged. Also, it comes in a range of naturally pigmented shades that perfectly complement various shades of timber colour, and it won't turn yellow with age. Shellac is a natural and comparatively non-toxic substance for use around the family home or in craft projects, children's furniture or interior timber work.

Oil finishes. There are many varieties of naturally occurring organic oils available for finishing and protective work, including tung oil. Second only to my obsession with shellac is my love for tung oil (or Chinawood oil as it's sometimes called). An organic vegetable oil extracted from the nut of the Chinese tung tree (*Aleurites fordii*), it's the world's oldest and best wood preservative.

Tung oil is classed as a drying oil—its finish cures by oxidation, not evaporation, so it doesn't give off strong fumes. It forms a non-toxic, flexible and water-resistant finish that resists abrasion, acids and alkaline, making it ideal for food contact surfaces. It's suitable for timber kitchens and all interior and exterior timber work, including floors, timber furniture, joinery and panelling.

Tung oil is now found as a key ingredient in many timber finishes, particularly for floors and decking. (It may also be added to poly-urethane to improve its flow and preservative properties.) Unlike linseed oil, tung oil doesn't hold the moisture that allows mildew to form, and won't darken with time.

Oil stains

There are a raft of oil-based stain products on the market designed specifically for enhancing and protecting exterior timbers around your home. They're called oil stains and are usually a semi-opaque finish so as not to completely hide the natural qualities of the timber as a paint would, but still offer protection from harmful ultraviolet rays. They contain tung oil and UV-protective agents, and you can get them in a range of tints to suit your timber.

Chapter 4
SAFETY WHILE YOU WORK

You'll probably all have heard some story about injuries incurred during home maintenance. People have written whole books on it! Thumbs hit with hammers, boards that fly up and hit you in the face, cuts from a Stanley knife—we've all done something stupid over the years. Well, I know I certainly have.

I recently read (on their website) some information from the Monash University Accident Research Centre: 'The leading causes of DIY injuries were grinders, lawnmowers, ladders, vehicle parts, welding equipment, power saws, vehicle parts, electrical equipment and tractors. Males were most commonly involved in DIY injury (85% of cases) . . . Injuries were most frequently to eyes and hands.' So blokes—beware!

My good party story is the time when a heavy decorative cast iron bracket fell from the top of a column and crushed my hand—ten stitches and a lot of pain later I'd learnt my lesson. I'd only put a temporary screw in to hold it in place—der! The lesson was that it's a good idea to have someone there to help you, or at least a couple of very strong clamps when you're attaching heavy items up high.

Safety is often forgotten when you're in a rush or when you don't have the correct equipment, but really it is the MOST important thing when fixing things around your home, so you don't have to end up fixing yourself!

This chapter is not about how to make your house safe to live in—there are again many publications about this, especially on childproofing a house. I'm just concentrating on how you can ensure you aren't injured when working around your home.

Number one important thing, grasshopper!

Wear safety equipment! It may not look cool and it may be uncomfortable, but it's SO important. And it's a good way to freak out the neighbours too—such a good look. Here's what you need:

■ Clothing that covers your arms and legs, and good sturdy footwear.
■ Safety goggles—adjustable lightweight plastic goggles will protect your eyes from flying chips of wood or metal. One little bit of plaster dust in your eye and you'll know it—and I'll certainly always remember the time I was cleaning a canvas awning with oxalic acid without wearing goggles. Ouch!
■ Dust mask—a lightweight disposable mask labelled as meeting the Australian Standard or WorkCover Authority specifications is vital when you're doing many DIY jobs, especially sanding jobs. We've all been alerted to the dangers of dealing with asbestos-based

products, but it's important to be aware that dust from sanding, drilling or sawing ANY product can be dangerous.

- Respirator—a mask which forms a tight seal around your mouth and nose to filter out dust, mist and fibrous materials is vital if you're doing any serious work with wood, particleboard, plaster or toxic substances. To be safe the disposable cartridge that goes in your respirator must conform to Australian Standard 1715 or 1716. You can pick these up from your local hardware shop.
- Ear muffs—very important when using power tools. Rigid plastic ear muffs with thick foam rubber inside that should seal around the out-side of your ear without being uncomfortable are the go. You can wear ear plugs as well—very useful when you're angle grinding!

The neighbours are concerned about my safety gear

Using power tools without good ear muffs can lead to permanent hearing loss. Also don't forget that children have even more sensitive hearing than adults, so either keep them away from you when you're using power tools or get ear muffs for them.

- Gloves—you'll need three sorts: there are basic leather work gloves to protect your hands from blisters, splinters and cuts (make sure they fit you properly and have no holes), and you may also need heavy-duty rubber gloves if you're working with any toxic chemicals; I also always have a box of disposable latex gloves handy for sticky or messy jobs like gluing and shellacking.

- Other safety gear if needed—a hard hat (if you're doing anything involving height or objects above you), steel-capped boots and a heavy-duty apron.

FIRST AID
Have a good first aid kit on hand. An eyewash and eyebath are particularly good things to have if you're doing a lot of work around the home.

Invisible dangers

Toxic chemicals are an invisible danger—and this means just about anything I've listed in the previous chapter (except for tung oil, shellac and beeswax—but if you ate them you'd still get pretty sick, I reckon!). It's common sense to keep any chemicals out of reach of children, with lids firmly attached. However, don't forget that when you're actually using these substances you should also protect yourself with good-quality masks and heavy-duty rubber gloves. I once ended up looking like a leopard after bleaching some furniture without wearing gloves. Plus it hurt like buggery!

Ventilation is really important. Whenever you're working with any product that has a strong smell or any kind of fumes coming from it, make sure you have windows and doors open and an extractor fan on if possible. At best, you'll get a bad headache; at worst you could cause some real damage—and this is one of those things that can really creep up on you. So be careful!

DANGEROUS DUST
When working in a roof space, beware of dust that may contain hazardous substances. Wear a mask and consider having the roof professionally vacuumed out.

Electrical safety

So now you've got a mountain of power tools and can't wait to play with your new toys. Just remember that they are potentially very dangerous toys, so please don't let your new game end in tears! Remember the following:

■ When using a powerboard (those handy multi-socket devices that most of us have under our desks or on our workbenches) make sure it has a circuit breaker fitted. Some older types don't have them—you can tell by just looking at it as there will be some kind of button, which you press to reset. For extra protection, especially when using power tools, you should also use a RCD (Residual Current Device) which can be built in to the circuit at the switchboard by an electrician, or you can buy a portable plug-in type.

■ Replace any frayed or cracked power cords on your tools—don't try to fix with electrical tape.

■ If you have a metal workbench, it's not a bad idea to get it earthed— this can be done by an electrician.

IT'S ALIVE!
Don't forget: as long as the battery is inserted in a power tool it's live. Always make sure you remove the batteries before removing or adjusting blades, and don't leave them lying around where your kids can play with them!

Fire hazards

Have a fire extinguisher and a fire blanket in your workshop, and also make sure the smoke detectors in your house work. Don't store flammable paint solvents or petrol near any flame source (like a heater) or anywhere with little ventilation.

Ladder safety

Ladders around the home are a classic disaster-looking-for-somewhere-to-happen. Here are some tips to follow:

■ Anytime you're working on a ladder higher than a metre, have a friend watch you. Never work on a ladder when you're the only one home.

■ Ladders, including stepladders, should be placed so that each side rail (or stile) is on a level and firm footing and the ladder is rigid, stable and secure.

- Ladders should not be placed in front of a door that opens towards the ladder, unless the door is locked.
- Ladders should be used at a 1:4 angle: in other words, the distance from the foot of the ladder to the structure it's resting on should be one-quarter of the length of the ladder.
- You should never work on the top two rungs of a ladder.
- When working on gutters, remain on the ladder; don't be tempted to climb onto the roof.

HOW TO NOT HIT YOUR THUMB
When hammering in small tacks or brads (i.e. pin-type nails), hold them in place with a small pair of pincer pliers or a magnetised screwdriver.

What to do about lead paint

The number one cause of lead poisoning in children in Australia is from old paint found on buildings built before 1970. It's far too easy for the DIY renovator, busily sanding or heat gunning, to poison themselves and their children or pets. It's estimated that there are at least 3.5 million homes in Australia with lead-based paint, and it's not possible to identify it by its 'look'. Lead paint is often sweet tasting and therefore children will pick at it and eat it, and animals will lick it. When this paint is sanded or scraped, or is peeling, it creates a dangerous lead dust that's easily inhaled or swallowed. This dust also enters soil where it can be accessed by children or animals. The big problem is that lead does not break down; it remains toxic, and unless dealt with safely it will not go away.

You can get a simple lead testing kit from any hardware or paint store. Follow the instructions on the pack and make sure you test all the layers of paint—not just the surface layer. It's the lower layers of paint that are likely to be a worry, and some old paints contained up to 50 per cent lead. If lead is present in your peeling paint you'll need to work out the best and safest method of removing it or covering it:

- When removing old paint always protect yourself with a dual filter respirator, gloves and overalls.
- Don't work near children or animals.
- Place a plastic drop sheet below your work area to gather the old paint up for safe disposal.
- Try to avoid dry sanding, and if you do have to create dust, organise a dust extractor system fitted with HEPA filters. These also can be hired and are the only filtration recommended for fine lead dust and fume removal from extracted air.

There are many professional 'lead safe' removers who can do the job for you.

How to remove it: chemical or physical?

There are special paint systems available, such as Peel Away and Let's Clean, for the removal of multiple layers of all types of old paints. Peel Away is particularly suited to removing lead-based paints and recommended by the EPA (Environment Protection Authority) as an approved method of lead paint removal. It's a smooth alkaline paste that's applied with a spatula or by brush or roller. The paste is then covered with a laminated cover and peeled away, taking the paint with it.

Chemical solutions may not be appropriate for timber in houses, as you'll be left with chemical residue and excess moisture in your wood. There are new infrared heat tools now available to remove most kinds of paint and varnish from timber. Infrared heat is a low-temperature deep heat that penetrates the wood and draws the moisture and resins in the wood to the surface, enabling the removal of multiple layers at a time. Infrared heat works fast and doesn't create the high temperatures that release lead fumes.

Disposal of any chemical waste from domestic homes is a problematic issue. Some regions have household chemical clean up days (limited to 20 litres/kilos) but for more information contact your local council or environmental protection authority.

Chapter 5
MAKING YOUR HOME MORE ENERGY EFFICIENT

Making your house more 'energy efficient' is something that everyone can do. Here are some ideas on how to save yourself money in the long term by making your house easier to cool and heat, and use less fuel in the process. It's not an exhaustive list, and with new energy-saving initiatives and products arriving every day it's a booming subject. There's going to be heaps more information available for the proactive 'fixer' hell bent on becoming a carbon credit tycoon!

Installing or updating your insulation

Insulation will significantly reduce the amount of heat that escapes *from* your house in winter, and comes *into* your house in summer. It's also great for reducing noise problems. The important thing to remember when selecting insulation is comparing the R-values (the measure of thermal resistance) of each type.

If your home is already insulated, check the condition of the insulation to see if it's performing to maximum capacity. Insulation can be affected by moisture, by vermin (including possums) or simply by becoming compressed with age and settling.

Ensure corners of ceilings, walls and floors are properly insulated— this is often where heat leaks are found. Also avoid leaving gaps between sections of insulation.

INSTALL A WHIRLY BIRD
Often the problem with homes in Australia is not how to keep them warm, but how to keep them cool. Excess heat and humidity builds up in the roof spaces of homes, and if not removed this heat has nowhere to go but back down into your living space. Installing a 'whirly bird' exhaust fan will solve the heat problem, and by removing excess humidity will also help prevent mildew and the rotting of roof timbers. As whirly birds operate purely on the flow of air from convection and natural breezes, they'll cost you nothing other than the initial installation cost.

A rather large 'whirly bird' for a very big shed

Draught-proofing your house

Cracks and gaps occur in many places around the house. It's a good idea to get rid of them as they'll really increase your heating costs, and in summer they let in hot air and dust. And it's not only the strong winds of winter forcing air through gaps in your home that will cause draughts. The warm air rising and escaping from a heated room will draw cold air into the room through the openings around doors and windows and even through spaces between joints and floorboards.

Sometimes gaps are obvious, but if you suspect there's a gap but can't see it, light a candle or incense stick and place it by the suspected gap—movement in the smoke will let you know if there's an air leak.

Most cracks and gaps, including around skirting boards, architraves and cornices, can be filled with a caulking compound, like an acrylic gap filler. Best to apply with a caulking gun, but caulking compound is also sold in applicator tubes. There's a wide range of coloured caulking products available at the hardware store; you should find one to match the colour of your paint or timber work. To apply the caulking compound:

1. Hold the applicator at 45 degrees and push it away from you as you run a bead along the gap. This will help force the filler deeper into the gap.
2. As you finish each section, clean up the bead by wiping away the excess; the best tool for this job is a basic one, your finger.

Doors

With doors there are two areas to tackle: the gap at the bottom of the door and the spaces on the sides between the door and the frame. To fix gaps on the sides of a door:

1. Get some self-adhesive weather strips, available from most hardware stores. They're made of rubber, foam or even plastic; choose the one that best suits the size and shape of your door and jamb.
2. Make sure the surface you're sticking it to is properly cleaned and dry before you start, so that the adhesive works best.

WERE YOU BORN IN A TENT?
Consider fitting an automatic door closer. A seal around the frame won't help much if the door is left open!

3. Unroll the weather strips and lay them in the sun for five minutes or so to soften before starting, as this will make them easier to work with.

4. Seal the space around the door's perimeter with the strips by pushing them into the rebate that you are sealing, and trimming off any excess at the corners. In some cases a small frame of timber beading with a rubber seal insert in it can be fitted around the inside of the door jamb.

At the bottom of the door you can use a draught excluder. There are many styles to suit different types of doors and frame constructions. Most of them are easy to fit and usually come in a kit that will include all the hardware and instructions needed. Take careful note of how your door works and all the measurements before heading off to the hardware store.

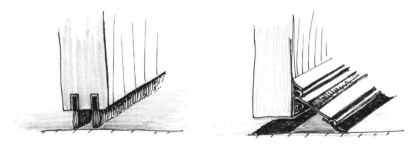

A couple of kinds of draught excluders for doors

Windows

If your curtains are flapping in the breeze even when the window is shut, or if there's wind whistling or windowframes rattling on breezy days, then you need to address some window problems:

- Seal most windows with the same weather strip used around doors.
- Sliding and sash windows (and doors) are a little more difficult because the sliding action of the frames will tend to drag on a rubber seal. In new windows these gaps are usually sealed with a brush strip which allows the frame to slide freely (much like a broom over a wooden floor). If you have old sash windows, fitting brush strips is not a difficult exercise as they're available in adhesive-backed lengths.
- Replacing cracked or broken windowpanes is also really important. For safety reasons this is a job I recommend be left to a professional glazier.

Reducing heat gain through windows

You can reduce your cooling costs by reducing the amount of heat coming into your house through your windows.

One of my least favourite DIY jobs is covering my daughter's schoolbooks with contact. I wish someone would write a book on how to do this without getting air bubbles in the rotten stuff! Having said this, I'd still recommend installing tinted window films in your house. If you have your car windows tinted then you'll know how much cooler a car with tinted windows can be—the same goes for your house. There are numerous DIY window film systems, or you can have them professionally installed. Either way you'll stop between 70 and 80 per cent solar energy coming through the glazing in the form of heat and glare and up to 99 per cent of the UV light that fades your curtains and furniture, without detracting from your view.

To further decrease the amount of heat entering via windows, install awnings or even shutters. Or simply follow in the footsteps of our clever colonial forebears and build a decent verandah!

DIY double glazing

Double glazing is normally a task requiring the complete replacement of windows with new double glazed units, consisting of two sheets of thermo-efficient glass fitted into a windowframe with a narrow gap between the two sheets. The gap is then filled with an inert gas. This assembly creates an insulating effect to reduce the amount of noise and heat travelling through the window.

It's possible, however, to achieve a simple DIY double glazing effect on your windows by installing an acrylic panel over the existing windows. You stick a Velcro border around the windowframe, which in turn holds the framed acrylic panel in place, creating an air space between it and the existing window and thereby producing an insulating barrier. There are also commercial versions of this system available.

Although not as effective as full double glazing, these panels are a fraction of the price and ideal if you have historic feature windows, such as lead lighting, you don't want to replace.

See Chapter 8, 'Doors and windows', for more draught-busting solutions.

Floorboards

See Chapter 7, 'Floors . . . and what's underneath', for ways to fix draughts coming through floorboards.

Refrigerators

With the fridge accounting for up to 10 per cent of our energy usage it's worthwhile checking that it's working to maximum efficiency, and considering if you really need that second (beer) fridge in the garage.

Check the seal for any splits and tears, and if it's damaged replace it. Here's how:

1. Check with local appliance outlets or the manufacturer to locate a replacement seal before removing the old one.
2. Remove the fridge door and lay it flat.
3. The seal is held in place by the inner door panel, which is held by a series of screws hidden under the rubber seal itself. Peel the seal back enough to reveal the screws and remove them.
4. Take a careful note of the positioning of the old seal before removing it completely.
5. The new seal may be a bit kinked, stiff and difficult to position. Soak it in some hot water for a few minutes or even throw it in a clothes drier for a minute. The heat will remove the kinks and make it a bit more pliable for fitting into position.

6. When fitting the new one, work your way around the perimeter fitting the screws loosely and then go around again to tighten them evenly, but not so tight as to crack the edge of the plastic panel.
7. Refit the door and check the seal all round by placing a sheet of paper between the seal and the fridge. If you can pull the paper out easily once the door is closed, the door may need adjusting to make a firmer seal.

Another important job is to pull the fridge out from the wall and vacuum all the dust away from the coils. Excess dust will be making the fridge motor work much harder and hotter than it needs to. Also remove and wash the drip tray.

Air conditioning

Keeping the filters clean on your air conditioner will help it to run more efficiently and last longer. Allow for adequate air flow to the unit by cleaning the surrounding area, removing any debris, and trimming foliage back at least 600 mm. Keep the condensation line free of mould and mildew by pouring in a small amount of bleach.

On standby

Would you believe that leaving appliances such as televisions, DVD players, stereos and computers running on standby could actually be increasing your electricity usage by as much as 10 per cent?

If you have trouble remembering to turn them off, connect an inexpensive plug-in timer to do it for you. Some can be set to match your lifestyle patterns but it's still important to turn your TV off with the remote control rather than rely on the timer to do it for you. Note, though, that the clock function will lose its setting when turned off at the wall.

See Chapter 12, 'Plumbing and electrical', for info on energy-saving lightbulbs.

OTHER TIPS FOR STAYING WARM EFFICIENTLY
- Use timers on electric oil or water circulation heaters so they turn themselves off at bedtime and come back on an hour before you get up, rather than leaving them on all night. Other types of electric heaters can be dangerous if left on anyway, so shut them down while you sleep.
- Install ceiling fans with a reverse function; this will distribute the hot air that has risen to the ceiling back down into the living spaces.

Reducing energy used for hot water

For most households, hot water is the second largest cause of greenhouse gas emissions. Water heating accounts for about 30 per cent of an average Australian household's energy usage. To help reduce this, ensure that the temperature gauge on your hot water systems is set at 60°C. If you have small children you should have a temperature-limiting valve fitted to your hot water system—this limits the maximum temperature coming from the taps to 50°C.

One project you can attempt yourself is insulating hot water pipes. Low-density closed-cell foam tubes with a split down the side can be purchased for a few dollars a metre from any hardware store. By cutting lengths of this to size with a utility knife and slipping it over any exposed hot water pipes, particularly the first few metres of pipe running from a hot water tank, you'll prevent excess heat loss, helping your hot water system to run more efficiently.

If you're putting a new bath in your house you can also put fibreglass batt insulation in the space beneath the bath to help maintain the water temperature.

Saving water

Much has been written about things you can do to save water around your house. Here's a brief refresher:

- Don't run taps while you're cleaning your teeth or washing your face or hands.
- Fill a sink to wash your hands or face rather use running water.
- Even while gardening you can half fill a bucket to wash your hands while you go.
- Minimise the length of showers—Australians tend to average seven to eight minutes in the shower when five is probably enough.
- Don't shave in the shower; shave your face or your legs (or whatever you like to shave) in a small amount of water before showering.
- Never run your dishwasher or washingmachine without a full load.
- Minimise flushes of the toilet.
- Tissues and dead insects can go in the bin rather than in the toilet.
- Replace old garden hoses and add trigger-release nozzles.

- Never use your hose to clean paths and driveways—a broom will do.
- Install a water tank and a grey water diverter.
- Keep the garden beds well mulched.
- Only ever wash the car from a bucket.
- Cover pools when not in use to prevent excess evaporation.
- A product that's worthwhile keeping handy is a can of spray-on leak stopper. If a drain pipe or air conditioner hose develops a leak, a blast with this stuff will seal it up until you have time to call in a plumber to fix it properly.
- Check for leaks: they not only waste many litres of water but could also be causing damage to your property. The way to be sure is to check your meter; before you go out for the day, check that water-using devices and taps are turned off properly and then make a note of your meter reading on the way out. When you return home the reading should be the same. If not, there's probably a leak that will need to be tracked down and repaired.
- Install water-efficient taps or tap aerators. There are some items, like tap aerators and AAA-rated showerheads, you can install yourself. They simply screw onto the end of existing outlets. AAA-rated shower-heads can reduce consumption from 24 to nine litres per minute—that's a massive 105 litres for your average seven-minute shower.
- If installing a new toilet is out of the question, consider fitting a flush minimisation devise like Water Wizz or Flexiflush instead. These assist you to regulate the amount of water being expelled by the cistern by only allowing water to release while you hold down the button.
- Even if you don't have a tank, downpipe water diverters are a great way to use rainwater coming from your roof. These simple devices are easily fitted to your downpipes. The next time it rains you can divert the water running off your roof to top up your swimming pool or increase the rain that goes into your garden.

■ Drip irrigation systems use less water than hoses and sprinklers because they deliver controlled amounts of water directly to where the plants need it most. A common problem with watering systems, however, including water-efficient drip irrigation, is that they switch on even when it rains. A rain sensor will turn your electronic controller off when it rains, as will a soil moisture sensor. These detect moisture and switch off your watering system controller when your garden has sufficient water.

WELS WATER
As of 1 July 2006, the government has implemented the Water Efficiency Labelling and Standards (WELS) Scheme. This rating system requires all manufacturers to display a water rating label on their products, much the same as the energy rating stickers we've seen on fridges, washingmachines and dryers for years. The more stars, the more water efficient the device is. You don't have to worry about the look of your bathroom for the sake of water efficiency, as all the big manufacturers of taps, toilets and shower fitting are using the WELS system standards for their designer ranges now. You'll need a plumber to connect most of these fittings.

Chapter 6
WALLS AND CEILINGS

In this chapter I've tried to look at some of the most common things that may need fixing on walls and ceilings. I've also included some interesting DIY projects you might like to attempt to improve the look or practicality of your home. The most common wall and ceiling cladding in modern homes these days is plasterboard (often referred to as Gyprock—a brand name), so I'll start by looking at some simple repairs to this versatile, easy-to-work material.

Repairing plasterboard

Fixing holes in plasterboard walls

It's fairly easy to knock a hole in a plasterboard wall (or ceiling for that matter). I know—I've managed to do it several times. Fortunately it's a pretty easy thing to fix! Basically you need to put something behind the patch so the joint compound doesn't just fall through the hole into the wall cavity.

 WHAT YOU NEED

- piece of plasterboard roughly twice the size of the hole
- jointing compound
- sandpaper—medium and fine
- plasterboard screws
- touch-up paint
- cordless drill
- keyhole saw (the pointy saw blade on a handle)
- sharp utility knife
- plastic broadknife (wide plastic plaster applicator)
- paintbrush
- dust mask and safety goggles.

 WHAT TO DO

1. Make sure you wear a mask and goggles whenever working with plasterboard as it's very dusty material.
2. Cut a square patch of plasterboard with a utility knife or saw, a fraction larger than the hole in the wall.
3. Use the patch as a template to mark around the damaged part of the wall, then use the keyhole saw to remove that area—you are, at this stage, making the hole bigger. Using your knife, cut a bevel around the front edge of the hole (a bevel is a 45 degree angle) and also around the front edge of the patch.

4. The patch won't stay in the hole on its own, so we'll create a backer board to attach it to. To do this, cut another piece of plasterboard (or you can use plywood) roughly the same shape as your patch but about 3 cm bigger across one axis. Drill a hole in the centre for your finger to fit through.
5. Pass this backer board into the hole and hold it in place with your finger in the hole. Using a couple of plasterboard screws, screw through the wall into the backer board to hold it in place.
6. Then, using the patch of plasterboard, fill the hole and screw the patch to the backer board; the two bevels come together here creating a 'V' groove around the edge of your patch which will be filled with jointing compound. Spread the compound across the entire repair with a plastic broadknife, covering the seams, screw heads and any unevenness.
7. Once dry, use sand paper (medium) over a block to sand it all flat. Unless you've done 'A levels' at the University of Plaster Repair (right next door to the School of Hard Knocks), you're probably going to need to go over it again and fill in some imperfections. Wait for it to dry before applying a second coat.

BUST THAT DUST
When you're doing any cutting, drilling or sanding on walls have a 'helper' standing by with the vacuum cleaner so that the dust is vacuumed up straight away.

Get a helper on the vacuuming job whenever you do dusty drilling

Re-taping plasterboard that's come unstuck

Plasterboard sheets are held together with tape covered with jointing compound. Sometimes if damp has permeated the join the tape starts to lift. To fix this:

1. Cut the loose section of tape with a utility knife and then remove all loose tape with a spatula.
2. Sand away loose tape and rough edges.
3. Apply a new strip of self-adhesive gauze jointing tape.
4. Apply two thin coats of jointing cement over the tape, feathering the edges (not some kind of tribal initiation—this is smoothing it away from the repair to blend with the surrounding area). Allow enough time for the first coat to dry before applying the second.
5. Leave to dry, then sand smooth and paint.

Flattening a popped nail in your plasterboard walls

If your timber framing is shrinking you may find that some of the nails that were used to fasten your plasterboard onto the framing have popped out. To fix this:

1. Drive a plasterboard screw into the stud 20 mm below the popped nail, sinking the head just below the surface.
2. Scrape away the loose paint and filler and drive the popped nail back into place.
3. Finish by covering the screw head and the nail head with premixed cellulose filler (e.g. Spakfilla), sand smooth and then paint.

CUTTING PLASTERBOARD

To cut through a piece of plasterboard with a utility knife simply cut deep enough to get through the layer of surface paper, place the board over the edge of a length of timber and then snap the board to get through the plaster layer; the break will follow the cut line. Finish by cutting through the remaining paper layer with the knife.

Fixing corner chips on masonry walls

The corners of our house cop a beating from various kids' bikes, trolleys and bits of furniture being dragged too close. To fix chips on corners of plastered or rendered masonry walls:

1. Use a bricklayer's float as formwork.
2. Hold it even with the side of the corner and fill in the area on the other side with cornice cement or a plaster topping compound (not

Spakfilla) with a trowel, as these compounds can easily be sanded into a neat new corner without it crumbling away.

3. Slide the trowel to one side; be careful not to lift it until it's away from the patched bit.

You could even use two-part kneadable fast-setting epoxy putty if it's a very high traffic area and bumps are likely to happen again. By kneading it before you use it, you ensure the hardener is blended with the putty, setting up the process. Shape it before it dries as it's difficult to sand once dry.

Repairing holes in masonry walls

You may have small holes in your masonry walls where a picture hook or screw has been removed—easy one to fix! You can also use this method on small holes in plasterboard or even painted timber walls.

 WHAT YOU NEED

- cellulose filler (e.g. Spakfilla)
- putty knife
- sandpaper.

 WHAT TO DO

1. Clean out the hole really well—any crumbly remains will mean the filler won't stick.

2. Do a little light sanding to tidy up the area.
3. Mix up a small paste of cellulose filler (you can also get it premixed) and slightly overfill the hole with your putty knife. When it's dry, a light sand will make it flush and smooth again.

Fixing cracks in rendered walls

The most common cause of cracks in your walls is the change of moisture level in the ground below the house, causing the soil to shrink or swell—soils with high clay content are particularly reactive. Brick and concrete homes are too stiff to flex with this movement so they crack in the weakest places, which is usually around windows and doors. The loss of in-ground moisture due to our prolonged drought conditions has seen many new cracks appear in houses, or old ones widen. Sometimes when there's rain a lot of these cracks start to close again.

It's a good idea to find out what is causing the problem in case there's something sinister happening under your house. Other causes of cracking include poor design and construction, vibration, extreme temperature changes, invasive tree roots, subsidence, earth tremors and wind loads, or the deterioration of building materials such as rusting lintels.

The good news is that most cracks are only superficial and are easy to repair. Usually there's no cause for concern other than aesthetics, although a few hundred dollars spent on an engineer's report may well be a worthwhile investment before making good the cracking.

 WHAT YOU NEED

- scraper
- small screwdriver
- sponge
- flexible gap filler* (e.g. No More Gaps)
- good-quality caulking gun
- some touch-up paint
- vacuum cleaner.

* For this job I would go for acrylic gap filler as standard plaster fillers tend to be brittle when dry, so if the crack opens or closes any more the filler will crack as well. Acrylic fillers are flexible and will expand and contract with the wall to a certain extent.

 WHAT TO DO

1. Use the tip of the screwdriver or the corner of the scraper blade to scrape away loose material from cracks. Scrape out the inside of the crack as well, removing loose sand or plaster and slightly widening the crack to allow more filler in.

2. Use a vacuum cleaner to suck up any loose material. It's important to remove all dust and debris, or the patching material won't bond with the wall and will fall out.

3. Slightly dampen the crack with the sponge to help slow and even out the drying time of the filler material.
4. Apply the filler using the caulking gun.
5. Make sure the surface is smoothed off before the filler dries, as acrylic filler cannot be sanded flat once it dries. Use your scraper to clean away excess and then use the damp sponge to clean the walls on either side of the repair, but be careful not to wipe the filler out of the crack. You can also use the sponge to dab the acrylic filler to create a slight texture to match the surrounding wall surface if necessary.
6. In a few hours the repair can be touched up; apply a coat of primer first and then your topcoat. Use a small paint roller to apply the top-coat, as brush marks won't match the surrounding surface—thus highlighting the repair rather than camouflaging it!

Fixing timber-lined homes

Some houses are lined with tongue and groove timber boards. If you have a problem with one of the boards (some wood rot or a split perhaps) then it's possible to replace it. See 'Fixing a damaged tongue and groove floorboard' in Chapter 7, 'Floors . . . and what's underneath'—it's more or less the same method.

Removing wallpaper

Here's how to remove wallpaper from your walls. Not a fun job but some-times it just has to be done!

WHAT YOU NEED

- bucket and warm water
- large sponge or paint roller
- dropsheets (waterproof ones if you have carpet)
- wide stripping knife (like a wide paint scraper)
- wallpaper scorer or utility knife
- wallpaper paste
- detergent
- steam stripper (optional).

 WHAT TO DO

1. Make sure you cover the floor before you start—it's a very messy job.
2. Score (scratch) the surface of the wallpaper (only 1 mm deep) all over with the scorer or blade. This is to open up the surface so water can penetrate.
3. Put a small amount of wallpaper paste and a squirt of detergent into the warm water. Wet the whole wall, using the sponge or paint roller to apply the water. Only do one wall at a time. Leave it to soak in for up to ten minutes.
4. You'll know it's ready to be stripped if, when you slide the scraper in at a seam or edge, it wrinkles and lifts easily. You may need to add more water until it does.

If this is all too hard, you can hire a stream stripper, which will make the job a lot easier and quicker!

Soundproofing your house

Suffering from noisy neighbours, a four-lane highway out the front door or airport runway fallout? Or maybe you just like the idea of a sound-proof booth? Well, there are many ways to reduce the amount of sound coming into (or out of) your house. I've covered it in Chapter 5, 'Making your home more energy efficient', but you can also make some changes to your walls and ceiling which will help keep down the racket. Some of these things also help with reducing the sound travelling between rooms within your house or between apartments with adjoining walls.

Insulate your ceiling

Good old ordinary thermal insulation in your ceiling will not only reduce your heating costs but dampen sound travelling in from the outside and reduce the travel of sound from room to room via the roof cavity. I'd recommend installing rock wool insulation; this is made from melted volcanic rock (basalt) that's spun into fibres. These are then formed into batts or blankets or further processed to form loose fill granules. Its high density makes it an excellent sound as well as a thermal insulator. Next best would be polyester insulation, as it's very easy to work with, is hypo-allergenic and won't attract vermin. It comes in rolls or batts and is simply cut with large scissors to fit neatly between the ceiling joists.

Install acoustic matting

If you have excessive overhead noise you can take this to the next level by rolling out a layer of a special acoustic vinyl matt know as Wavebar acoustic barrier. Lay it over the top of the joists and insulation.

Add an additional lining to your walls

Barrierboard is one of several special wall panelling products designed to reduce sound travel. It consists of two sheets of differing thickness plasterboards separated by an insulating layer. Soundproofing panels are available in a number of standard sizes up to 35 mm thick.

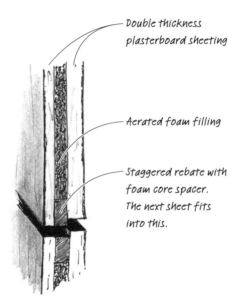

Double thickness plasterboard sheeting

Aerated foam filling

Staggered rebate with foam core spacer. The next sheet fits into this.

Cross-section of Barrierboard

If you don't have much room to spare, acoustic plasterboard can be glued and screwed directly to your existing wall surfaces to give you a sound reduction of up to 50 per cent. The effectiveness of the acoustic plasterboards themselves can be increased to 75 per cent by gluing and screwing a series of 45 mm x 45 mm timber battens to the old wall surface and filling the space in between these with some more of your polyester insulation material before attaching the board over the battens. Then let the rock band loose!

> **SUCK UP THE SOUND**
> Don't forget that hard surfaces such as timber and tiled floors, or granite and stainless steel bench tops, reflect noise, while carpet, curtains and upholstered furniture will make a room much quieter. A good rule of thumb is to have at least 25 per cent of these soft, sound-absorbing surfaces in a room.

For more info on how to keep your house warm and cool, check out Chapter 5, 'Making your home more energy efficient'.

Dealing with damp

If any of these things are occurring, you've got damp problems:

- A musty smell in the house—this is an obvious sign of 'rising damp'.
- Paint and wallpaper may start to lift from the wall surface.
- Brown stains start to appear on the wall.
- Plaster becomes flaky and soft and starts to fall away.
- White powdery or crystalline substances form on surfaces, and timber skirting boards and floorboards start to rot.
- Outside the house, symptoms such as stains and powdery deposits or mortar starting to fall out from between bricks.

What is rising damp?

Rising damp is the result of salt-containing groundwater rising up masonry walls by capillary action (i.e. the porous masonry draws moisture into it). Building design usually allows for this natural action by putting a moisture barrier or 'dampcourse' between bricks or blocks just above ground level to stop the water rising. However, if this has deteriorated due to age (or was never installed in the first place) or has been bridged by internal concrete floors, renders or external paths and earth levels, it won't work. The moisture will continue to move up the wall and leach out of the surface, causing health problems for both you and your house. Timber homes can also suffer damp rising up brick chimneys and then affecting the surrounding timbers. If you try to hide the results of rising damp by covering walls with waterproof render or panelling, you'll only end up forcing moisture further up the walls. You need to fix the problem!

Falling damp

The moisture may also be coming from above or horizontally through your wall, this is known as (wait for it . . .) 'falling damp'. It's usually caused by leaking or inadequate roof drainage. Overflowing gutters or leaking downpipes spill water onto brick walls, making them saturated with moisture, which then works its way through walls to the inside of your home.

Another cause of 'damp'

If your house smells musty but you can't see any visual signs in your walls, you might have a build-up of excessive humidity under the floor area due to a lack of sub-floor ventilation, or if the soil underneath is damp due to poor drainage. The timber floorboards swell or bulge and so damp, musty air is trapped underneath. For solving subfloor ventilation problems see Chapter 7, 'Floors . . . and what's underneath'.

Identifying damp

You can buy a relatively inexpensive moisture meter which will give you a better idea of the presence of excessive moisture, or you can hire a more sophisticated unit from an instrument hire specialist. Drill or punch a couple of small holes through any render in order for the instrument to read levels in the brick below.

If your damp walls are below ground level (e.g. a basement or garage) it may be because ground water is being forced through them, especially if the drainage behind the wall is inadequate. Or it may be condensation from inside due to poor ventilation, as mentioned above. You can know for sure by performing the following test:

- Tape a 30 mm square piece of aluminium foil to the wall, with all four sides of the foil airtight.
- Keep the foil on the wall for a couple of days, then remove and examine it. If the outside of the foil is moist, the problem is condensation. If, on the other hand, the foil that was facing the wall is wet, the problem is water penetration.

Some solutions for damp

These depend on the cause and seriousness of the problem.

IF POOR DRAINAGE IS THE ISSUE

Inadequate, poorly built or poorly maintained drainage may be allowing stormwater to accumulate near or under your house. Raised garden beds built right next to the walls may also be bridging the dampcourse. You need to change your drainage around the house; you could try laying 'ag' drain (a perforated flexible pipe) on the outside of the wall under the surface of the soil to take excess moisture away from the wall. You may need to consult a plumber to get this right, but the very least you can do is keep drains clean and clear. Move any garden beds and other possible moisture bridges away from your walls.

Now, inside your home, the solution can be found in a paint can: waterproofing paint is formulated to be painted directly onto masonry walls and resist water pressure of up to 32 psi coming through. But you must attack the problem from inside AND outside to really solve it.

DAMPCOURSING—PROFESSIONAL REPAIRS

If, after several months, these initial steps have made little or no difference you may need a new dampcourse. Professional installation of a new plastic barrier is the most effective resolution but it's also the most expensive. A whole course of bricks is removed one section at time to allow for the installation of the new barrier. Another professional treatment involves a chemical treatment where a series of holes are drilled in a brick course and a special chemical compound is injected into the brick under pressure.

DIY DAMP COURSING

You can attempt chemical dampcoursing yourself using nothing more than a hammer drill. It involves the same type of chemical fed into the brickwork with the aid of gravity; you can purchase a special kit for doing this (see useful info at the back of the book). Once you're purchased your kit:

1. Drill a series of holes, starting in the mortar line but at a downward angle towards and into the brick.
2. Place a series of specially designed feeder tubes (from the kit) into the holes and then fill with the chemical.
3. After an hour or so the chemical should have soaked down into the brick, where it will form a permanent waterproof course of brick.

A cream version of this chemical treatment, which is ideal for smaller jobs such as a chimney, is also available. The holes for the cream need only be drilled into a line of mortar and the cream is then injected with a standard caulking gun.

After a rising damp treatment has been completed you'll need to wait several months for the existing water in the wall to come to the surface and evaporate before refinishing.

FALLING DAMP

Exposed brick walls, particularly on the cooler, moister, south side of your home, may simply become saturated from direct rain. If this is the case, the wall needs to be covered with a protective coating of waterproof render, paint or even a clear coat if you don't want to lose the brick look. You should clean gutters and downpipes and repair or replace them if needed (see 'Cleaning and fixing gutters' in Chapter 14, 'The outside bits—your home's exterior').

Hanging pictures on your walls

A poorly hung picture draws the eye, but not in a good way. Hanging pictures properly and securely is not a difficult job, but it's always a good idea to have another set of hands and eyes there to help.

The first decision is what picture to hang where, whether to form some kind of arrangement, hang them individually or hang them in a row and how high they should go. Some of these decisions come down to personal taste and the nature of the pieces, but there are a few general rules and tips I can share with you to assist.

How to decide what to hang where

Most galleries hang work with the centre 1500 mm from the ground. This is considered to be an average adult eye height. You'll have to consider the height of furniture and position of windows. Whatever height you decide to go with, it's important to be consistent: in each room make the centre line the same for every picture.

If you're arranging a group of pictures together, consider the whole group as one and work out your centre from there. It may be helpful to cut out some paper rectangles that match the size of your frames and use these to help you make your arrangement (stick on temporarily with Blu-Tack and stand across the other side of the room to see if you like the arrangement). If you're arranging your pictures in a row or individually around the house, set them all out on the floor first until you're happy with the positions before starting to install.

Never hang artwork in direct sunlight—even with protective UV-blocking glass, prolonged exposure will fade images. Also, don't hang artwork above sources of heat—temperature swings can cause condensation to form inside a frame, damaging the image, and smoke from fireplaces will stain them.

GET YOURSELF A LASER LEVEL

If you find yourself hanging a lot of pictures, shelves or even the occasional plasma TV on walls, you may consider buying a laser level. They're very handy and will give you extremely good accuracy across long distances. Many are designed for wall work and can be attached to the wall, where it will project a long level line of light for you to work with and give you both hands free for other tasks. There are a great range of DIY quality laser levels available—you'll pick one up for well under a hundred dollars at any hardware store. Some also double as a stud finder, which is very useful for hanging anything heavy, and some will warn you of live wires or pipes lurking behind.

Choosing the fixings

Choosing the right fixings for a picture is a difficult task, so you need to make a good assessment of the job at hand:

1. Examine the picture to be hung—what type of hanging device it's attached to, its weight and size.
2. Examine the wall where it's to be hung, and determine what material it's constructed from, its thickness and surface type.
3. If it's a stud frame wall, try to locate the studs and see if they coincide with your hanging position.

All of this information will help you (and the hardware sales assistant) choose the right fixings. The few main types I come back to again and again are as follows:

Masonry walls. Use plastic expanding plugs. Red or green plugs will be strong enough for most works. Fit the right-sized masonry drill bit into your hammer drill and make a hole the correct depth, clean out the dust and tap in the plug. If there's any excess protruding, cut it off with a sharp chisel before driving in a screw.

Plasterboard walls. Mostly pieces can be hung from screw-in plaster-board wall anchors, like Wall Mates. These are inserted with a screw-driver or cordless drill and have a three-pronged end on them that pierces the wall and then a deep open-threaded shaft that imbeds itself into the plasterboard. Once screwed into the wall, an ordinary pan head or button head screw can be inserted into the centre of the anchor to hang from. These types of anchors will hold up to 10 kg each—one or two is plenty for most jobs. If you're lucky enough to have a stud in the right position, just the wood screw will do; use a minimum 45 mm #8 gauge.

Plasterboard with wallpaper. If the plasterboard has a wallpaper sur-face I'd consider using some angle drive picture hooks as these are metal surface hooks with a pair of pre-positioned nails that drive into the wall at a downward angle. These will minimise damage to the surface and will also hold 10 kg each.

Plywood or thin fibre cement. If your walls are made of thin fibre cement or plywood, try sticking to the stud positions. If the studs don't work out and you have to hang from the board, use a toggle-type anchor. These require a hole to be drilled first (beware of asbestos) and the toggle device is then pushed through the hole. Once into the cavity the toggle will either drop or spring open (depending on type chosen). The screw at the front of the toggle is then tightened to clamp the device either side of the wall surface.

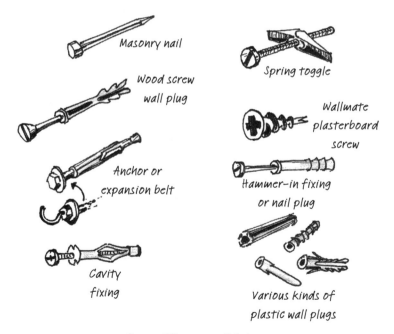

Some different wall fixings

Installing shelves on your walls

Installing a simple shelf would have to be one of the most common jobs tackled by novice and experienced DIYers alike.

The usual approach

The usual approach would be to measure up the position, make a level line on the wall and then attach a row of brackets before placing the shelf on top. This method does require a fair degree of accuracy if all the brackets are to fit snugly in place under the shelf.

My alternative

The alternative technique I've adopted over the years is a little different:
1. Place just one bracket on the wall at the correct height.
2. Secure the rest of the brackets to the underside of the shelf.
3. Lift the shelf onto the one wall-mounted bracket and level it.
4. Screw the remaining brackets into place.

There are a couple of things to remember along the way:

- The weight of objects on a shelf, combined with the shape of the average bracket, will create leverage that pulls the fixing away from the wall rather than pushing down, so you need to think about this when choosing the right fixing hardware.
- If your shelf is to be installed on a stud frame wall, try to measure your bracket spacing to match the stud positions for maximum strength.

Other options

There are other shelving systems that are easy to install at home:

Slotted angle. Slotted angle shelving systems are most often seen in warehouses and are incredibly strong and versatile. If you enjoyed Meccano as a child you'll love this; it's made up of lengths of steel angle with elongated holes, brackets, shelves and bolts. All you need is a spanner, and then you pick and choose the pieces you need and bolt together whatever configuration of shelf is required.

Strip shelving. Although rarely very attractive, this stuff is certainly very practical. It's a shelving system that operates by attaching a series of slotted metal channels to a wall and fitting metal brackets into the slots to support the shelves. They vary in their strength and load rating, so make sure you get the correct type for your job— the heavy-duty stuff is distinguished by the double row of slots on the wall channel and the double brackets to match. You must make sure the strips are connected to strong points on the wall, and make sure the slots are all lined up and level. When setting out, it's worthwhile identifying where the wall studs are and marking the positions down the wall surface (the strips will cover these marks anyway). Make sure all the strips are the same way up and make a level line across the vertical marks that will correspond with one set of screw holes in the strips.

Hanging mirrors

Framed mirrors can be very heavy. The glass, frame and a timber backing board all combine to make a mirror a hanging challenge. Talk about seven years' bad luck! To try to hang a mirror from a single hook with a single strand of wire can be fraught with danger. The solution is to spread that weight over several hanging points with at least one of those fixed into a strong point on the wall.

The use of a split baton is a technique preferred by professionals to hang any number of heavy items from vertical surfaces. A split baton is made up of two interlocking bars, one attached to the back of the mirror frame and the other secured to the wall. When the mirror is lifted into place the bar on the frame is housed into the one on the wall. This creates strong positive support that's unlikely to fail and will help keep the mirror perfectly vertical rather than letting it lean forwards, where it reflects only an image of the floor.

To make a split baton:

1. Set your electric saw to cut at a 45 degree angle and cut a strip of plywood or MDF down its length, creating two separate and equal parts.
2. Attach one part to the frame. This part should have the angled cut pointing down and away from the frame.
3. Attach the other part to the wall, level and with the angle pointing up and away.
4. Fit the two parts together, making a long horizontal picture hook.

5. Secure each part (one on the wall and one on the frame) with several screws before fitting the mirror into place.

If using an electric saw is not an option, the two parts of the baton can be shaped with a hand plane, or you could exchange a timber baton with some aluminium gutter channel, which has a 'J' shaped profile. Two sections of this gutter channel will interlock in much the same way as the parts of a timber baton.

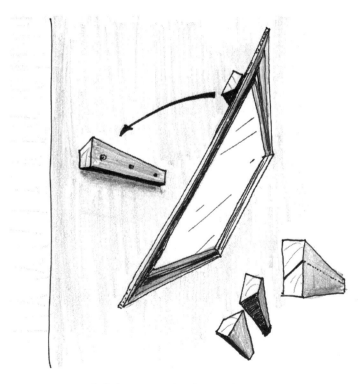

Split baton used to hang a large mirror

Repairing or installing a new cornice

Cornices can sometimes show signs of damage, and it's possible for the home DIYer to repair them. Damage can come from a leaking roof (NOTE—fix the roof leak first!), or perhaps it's just come unstuck with age. The most important thing is to find the exact match for your existing cornice—take photos, measurements and drawings with you and/or a piece of the existing cornice if it's already fallen off.

You can also install a new cornice if your room has none, and you can even put a new decorative one over the standard old basic 55 mm cove cornice (the curved concave trim found in many new houses), as many of these decorative profiles are designed to fit right over the top. Check out some of the options at a plastering trade centre or log on to a plasterboard manufacturer's website.

Once you've selected your new bit of cornice, here's what to do:

 WHAT YOU NEED

- mitre box
- old fine-toothed woodsaw*
- 100 mm plastic broadknife
- plasterer's small tool
- utility knife
- tape measure
- cornice cement
- drop sheets
- mixing bucket

- sponge
- cleats
- hammer

* It's best not to use a new, sharp woodsaw for this job as cutting plaster will make it blunt.

 WHAT TO DO

1. If you're simply repairing a section, remove the damaged part, being careful to leave a neat edge where you cut it off from the intact section.
2. If you're installing a new cornice, start by drawing a pencil line along the wall and ceiling to indicate where the edges of it will sit.
3. Do this by cutting a small piece of the cornice from a length and holding it in place with the pencil held at the base. Slide the piece of cornice and the pencil along to make the mark. If you're only replacing a section, there'll probably be an existing outline from the old piece you can follow.
4. Partly tap a few nails into the wall along the bottom pencil line, about 1800 mm apart. These will help hold the cornice in position while the cement dries.
5. Measure and mark the position to be cut on the cornice. Remember to take your measurements from the wall surface and then mark these on the edge of the cornice that will be on the wall. Make careful note of whether you'll be cutting for inside corners or outside corners and indicate the direction of your mitre cut at the ends.
6. Place the cornice piece in the mitre box to make the cut. Be sure to support the rest of the length that protrudes from either side of the mitre box with some blocks of wood.

7. Alternatively, you can use a simple plastic guide (available from plaster suppliers) that fits over the cornice to help angle your cuts. Cut the mitres with the fine-toothed saw and then lift each piece into position to check the size.
8. Once you're sure the piece fits, mix some cornice cement. Just mix enough to install a few pieces at a time.
9. Apply a generous 10–15 mm thick bead of cement along each edge of the cornice and then lift and push it into place until excess cement squeezes out.
10. Where the corners meet, some more cornice cement can be applied to fill any gaps. A plasterer's small tool is a small metal plastering knife with a flat pointed tip on one end and a small square tip at the other; it's ideal for shaping and neatening the cornice cement to match the face of the cornice.
11. After about 20 minutes you can remove the positioning nails and wipe away excess cement with the broadknife.
12. Tidy and smooth out the finish with a damp sponge. Wait 24 hours and then you can paint your cornice.

Attaching a new ceiling rose

There's nothing better than lying in bed (or on a sofa, or on the floor) and contemplating a ceiling rose—as an alternative to your navel.

In the 60s and 70s home decorators went mad with modernising their homes. Many Victorian and Federation homes were stripped of their original fittings. Ceiling roses, cornices, picture rails, etc, were all taken to the tip to be replaced with snazzy metallic wallpaper and stick-on mirrors. Those were the days.

You may have bought one of these homes, or you may just have had damp problems in your ceiling which have meant that over the years the ceiling rose has fallen off or decayed. But it's not too difficult a job to replace it.

The most difficult thing will be to decide which one to attach. Then basically use the same technique for attaching the cornice. Use a length of timber with a rag on top as a prop to support the rose until the cement has started to cure.

FIXING CHIPS
If you just have some chips or dings in your cornice or ceiling rose you can try to repair them. Mix a stiff mixture of Plaster of Paris and apply with a brush or plasterer's small tool—remember it dries quickly but can be easily shaped by chiselling and sanding back to shape.

Chapter 7
FLOORS . . . AND WHAT'S UNDERNEATH

Floors don't usually give the home handyperson too much trouble—it's what's underneath them where problems can arise. If there are serious concerns with your foundations then it's time to call in a professional tradesperson, but there are some jobs you can do yourself. Some issues that arise with floors are basically to do with their appearance, and there are also a few 'preventative measures' I can suggest to look after your floors so small problems don't turn into large ones!

Fixing creaky floorboards

If you have teenage children, you may like the fact that you have creaky timber floorboards—they're very good alarm system for past-curfew arrivals! However, most people would like to get rid of their creaks (and I'm only talking floors here—not your ageing joints!).

Creaks and squeaks in the floor are caused by friction—when you put your weight on the offending spot different surfaces rub together to make the noise. The friction can be floorboards moving up and down on nail shafts or the edges of boards rubbing together, or it can be coming from below the surface, caused by movement in the sub-floor. And that's a good place to start, if you can get under the house and under the offending floorboards.

If you CAN get under the floorboards

Once you get down under the floorboards:

1. Check the bearers and floor joists for rot or evidence of pests. Joists are the timbers which rest across (and at right angles to) the bearers under your floor. Your floorboards are nailed to these joists. You also have joists in your ceiling which rest on the wall plates. See later in this chapter for what to do about floor pests.
2. Check that the bearers are firmly resting on the foundations and/or piers; pack any small gaps with fibre cement off-cuts to re-support the bearer and create a firm base for the floor framework. Sometimes you can solve the problem by simply running a bead of construction adhesive along the seam either side of the joist edge where it meets the floorboard. Grab a caulking gun and a few tubes of liquid nails and apply a fairly generous bead, forcing it into any gaps as you go.

If you're a little more serious about doing the job properly, cleats may be the go. Cleats are short lengths of timber fixed to a board or other object for the purpose of hanging or fixing the object to another object—for example, a cleat may be used inside the corners of a wooden box to affix one side to another.

In this situation you'll be using the cleat to fix the floorboard to the joist from underneath. Glue (with construction adhesive) and screw '2 by 2' (42 x 42 mm) timbers along the top of the joists as close as possible to the board and then run another screw in upward through the timbers into each floorboard. A few tips:

- Make sure you drill clearance holes for the screws before driving them in. A clearance hole is a hole that's slightly larger than the shaft of your screw and runs right through the cleat, so the screw should slip through the hole without resistance and then screw into the timber below. This will ensure that the contact between the timber surfaces will be tight.

- Use plenty of that construction adhesive when you install the cleats; you'll need a bead along the side that contacts the joist and another along the surface that contacts the underside of the floor.

- Be very sure you're using the correct length screws; the last thing you want to do is come in and find you've screwed all the furniture down!

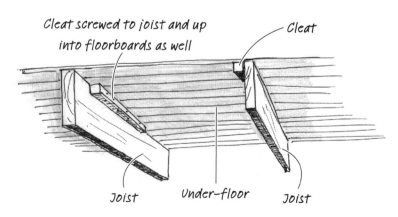

Timber cleat used under-floor to attach joist to board

If you CAN'T get under the floor

If you can't get access to under the floor you have a few different options:

- The easiest fix of all involves some loud music. And no—not just to drown out the sound of the creaking floors! First, sprinkle a generous amount of talcum powder over the squeaky area, then place one of your loudspeakers face down on the powder and play something very loud. I would choose Beethoven, but you may want to try Metallica. The vibrations from the music will work the powder down between the boards and the powder will lubricate those rubbing surfaces!

Sprinkle the talcum and pump up the volume

- Screwing boards down is very effective but you'll have to plug (or fill) the holes and touch up the finish afterwards. Once again, a clearance hole is important, as is a countersink in that hole to house the head of the screw and a plug hole at the top—sounds complicated but believe it or not you can purchase a special drill bit that will make all of these in one action. While you're at it, pick up a packet of timber plugs to match; you may not find them in the right colour for your floor, so you'd better get a little stain as well.
- An easier but less effective fix is re-nailing: first try re-punching the existing nails; if this only works for a short time you'll need to add some more nails. Pre-drill your nail holes at slight angles so they skew towards each other at the point, hammer them until the head only protrudes a couple of millimetres, then punch them below the surface. Fill holes with tinted repair wax.
- If the loose board is under the carpet then use your trusty stud finder to find the floor joist. Part the carpet fibres and push the point of a 65 mm bullet head nail through the carpet and underlay, then drive in the nail—but be aware that if it goes in too easily you may have missed the joist. When you know for sure you've got the nail going all the way in, drive a couple more in at slightly skewed angles and punch the nail head through the carpet and into the floorboard.

Fixing creaky timber stairs

Just like creaking floorboards, squeaky stairs are usually caused by timbers which have become loose, rubbing together whenever somebody steps on them. Stairs are built from three basic components: the tread, the riser and the stringer (the side piece). Usually it's a tread rubbing against a riser or stringer that cases squeaks. Treads can become loose because the timber has shrunk or the supporting blocks or nails have loosened. Stopping the movement is the solution to stopping the noise.

First, identify where the noise is coming from. If you can get underneath the staircase, have someone else walk on the offending step. If the noise comes from the spot where the foot meets the tread, concentrate your repair efforts there. If the noise comes from one side when you step in the centre or if it comes from the rear of the tread when you step at the front, the chances are pretty good that the entire tread is moving.

Noise at the front of a step is the most common and easiest to fix. If you're under the steps the join between step and riser simply needs securing with some timber cleats.

If you CAN get under-stair access

 WHAT YOU NEED

- length of 2 x 2 (42 mm x 42 mm) pine for the cleats (the amount of this depends on how many treads you have to fix)
- drill with 6 mm drill bit
- construction adhesive glue
- screws

 WHAT TO DO

1. Cut 100 mm timber cleats from the length of pine.
2. Drill a pair of holes through each axis of the block of wood (offsetting the holes so they don't intersect) and countersink them so the head of the screw doesn't split your small cleat when it's screwed into place. To gain maximum tension drill these holes with a 6 mm bit so that the screws can slide clearly through them.

3. Glue the block with construction adhesive.
4. Screw it to the top of the riser first, leaving a couple of millimetres' clearance between the top of the block and the underside of the tread. When you screw the block to the tread, this little gap will allow the tread to be pulled down tightly against the riser. Be sure not to use screws that are so long that they break out through the top surfaces.
5. Traditionally built stairs will have a set of wedges driven into the housings at the end of each tread. If these are loose they should be removed, sanded and then reinserted with a fresh coating of glue. If the stairs don't use wedges just repeat the block mounting process.

If you CAN'T get under-stair access

 WHAT YOU NEED

In addition to the above, you'll need some timber plugs to hide the screws. Ready-made timber plugs are available at any hardware store in a variety of sizes; 8 mm should do for this job, plus an 8mm brad point drill. You won't need the length of timber as you won't be able to use cleats.

 WHAT TO DO

1. Start by determining the centre position of the riser in relation to the tread, and draw a pencil line along it.
2. Drill the plugholes along this line 100–150 mm apart.
3. Use an 8 mm brad point drill to drill the plug holes around 6 mm deep.
4. Through the bottom of these holes drill a pilot hole, then drive the screws in.

5. Coat the timber plugs with construction adhesive and tap them in to hide the screws.
6. Once the glue dries, cut the top of the plug off with a sharp chisel and then sand flush before touching up the finish.

Fixing gaps in floorboards

Many older homes have gaps between the timber floorboards—these gaps can be part of the charm of the house and allow for expansion and contraction of the boards in different humidity. However, they also allow for a loss of heat, let draughts in, and can be unsightly if they're uneven or too wide.

It's possible to fill the gaps, but you need to do this as part of the floor sanding and finishing process, not after the floor has been polished. There are a few options to try:

- Use wood putty to fill the cracks—though this may crack and fall out with time.
- A traditional method is to make up a filler paste by mixing sawdust with PVA glue; this will be a time-consuming and messy task but the resulting putty will allow some flex as the boards expand and contract.
- Another traditional method is to painstakingly cut a series of small timber fillets to fit into the gaps; these should be glued just on one side to allow any further shrinkage to take place.
- The boards can be made to look like the timber deck of a boat by filling the spaces with sandable mastic filler. This comes in a limited range of colours but I've seen a floor filled with black mastic to great effect; this works best if the spaces are even.

- Gaps can also be filled with acrylic gap filling compound such as No More Gaps if you plan to paint your floor rather than clear finish it.

Fixing a damaged tongue and groove floorboard

This will require a bit of care and accuracy (see also 'Repairing decking boards' in Chapter 14, 'The outside bits—your home's exterior').

 WHAT YOU NEED

- carpenter's square
- keyhole saw or compass saw with spade bit, or jigsaw
- drill
- sharp chisel
- small cleat or baton
- 75 mm screws
- hammer
- 60 mm bullet head nails.

 WHAT TO DO

This basically involves removing the broken board and replacing it with a full new one, or perhaps only a new section of a full board. If you're only replacing a section, then make sure the new section meets the old board over a joist, so it can be secured firmly.

1. Check the floor underneath for any services that may be attached, like electrical or telephone cables.
2. Using the carpenter's square, mark up exactly where you'll cut the old board.
3. On the inside of the broken board, drill a hole with a spade bit, big enough to insert a keyhole or compass saw, or the blade of a jigsaw.
4. Using the saw, the drill and the chisel, carefully cut and remove the old board (or section of board), remembering that you'll want to preserve the tongue and groove of the neighbouring boards if possible. Remove any remaining nails and clean up the newly exposed edges of the existing boards and the tops of exposed joists.
5. Screw a small cleat to the side of the joist, flush with the top of the joist and extending under the bottom of each neighbouring board.
6. Prepare your matching replacement board by removing the bottom lip of the groove, so that the new board fits neatly into the gap, with the tongue of the existing board supporting the replacement when it's slotted in.
7. Apply a small bead of construction adhesive to the groove of the existing board, adjacent to the repair and to the underside of the modified groove of the replacement board. Nail the replacement board to the cleat and to any exposed joists; drilling small pilot holes for the nail will prevent the new piece from splitting. Punch the nails' heads to below the surface.
8. If the new board sits slightly higher ('proud') or lower than the existing floor surface, a belt sander can be used to even it out. Finish off by hand sanding, also sanding a little of the neighbouring boards, gradually feathering off the sanded area.

9. Apply a new finish to the repaired board and over the sanded area of the neighbouring boards. As you apply a finish to the feathered-off sanded area, the new finish should be applied very sparingly with an almost dry brush. Apply extra coats of the new finish each day until a depth of colour is achieved that matches the existing floor. If the surrounding floor has darkened with age, a little bit of stain can be added to the finish to help match the colour.

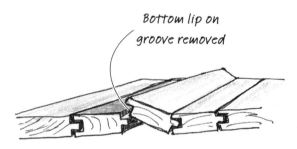

Bottom lip on groove removed

How to cut a replacement T&G board

Protecting your polished floors

I love timber floors—they're warm and create a great atmosphere in a home. But, as with anything natural, you have to look after them:

- Make sure you replace any missing rubber chair tips on metal chairs or stools.
- Add felt pads to the bottom of wooden chairs or nail-on nylon skids; you'll find these at any hardware store. They'll not only help protect your floor but make the chairs more stable.
- Put a doormat at the front and back door so grit, sand and other abrasive substances aren't walked through the house.

- For protection from staining and abrasion on oil-finished floors, applying floor wax is also worthwhile; it'll help make the floor less slippery. On the other hand, floors that have been polyurethaned should not be waxed but cleaned more regularly as they can actually become slippery with wax.
- Try not to wear your stilettos inside! (I always leave mine at the front door.)

Fixing scratches

OILED FLOORS
Wax your floor. If you're not up for a complete refinishing job, buffing the floor with a coat of wax will disguise scratches.

SCRATCH FIX PEN
If you have slightly deeper scratches in your floor, revealing the lighter colour of the timber below, a Scratch Fix pen may be the answer. These pens can be purchased from many antique dealers or furniture restoration suppliers and are like felt tip markers charged with wood stain rather than ink. Make sure you choose a colour that's lighter than your floor, and then build the colour up with several applications. Finish the repair with wax or polyurethane, depending on the floor finish.

POLYURETHANED FLOORS
Small scratches on polyurethaned floors can be touched up with more polyurethane after cleaning. Carefully apply some polyurethane to the scratches and then wipe over the repaired area with a rag lightly dampened with turps to remove the excess poly from the surface, leaving only what's sitting in the scratches.

HEAVIER SCRATCHES

For heavier scratches, the entire board or boards should be lightly sanded and then coated. If the new finish is a bit too glossy, cut it back a bit with some fine 0000 steel wool. If you don't want to repolish the whole floor and want to try fixing only the affected patches, you may find that over the years the colour of the original finish will have darkened with exposure to sunlight. You'll need to stain the floor, or the polyurethane, to match the existing colour before you apply the poly.

APPLYING/REMOVING BEESWAX

I'd highly recommend applying a wax to an oiled timber floor as the wax will act as a 'sacrificial coat' that adds shine while protecting the finish below from scuffing, minor scratches and staining. The wax can be stripped back periodically and reapplied to make your floor look like new again. The best kind of beeswax to use on floors to cover up scratches is Dark Stain beeswax, as it will help to hide the scratches well. Apply with a soft cloth and then buff off. If you're interested in waxing your entire floor there are specialty floor waxes. Gilly Stephenson make a really good floor wax which is available from hardware stores.

If you want to *remove* wax from a floor I'd recommend a mix of one-third gum turps, one-third metho and one third vinegar (shake well before and during use). This also acts as a good general cleaner for polished timber work. Store any leftovers of this blend in a cool place, as it can become a bit volatile if it overheats.

A good place to create some storage ... or hide

Pests in flooring and under the floor

Pests can affect all parts of your home, but the problems usually start
under it! There are three main kinds of pests that cause serious damage
to timber in buildings:

1. Termites—also called white ants.
2. Borers—sometimes called furniture beetle.
3. Wood decay fungi—also called wet and dry rot.

Termites

There are over 350 species of termites in Australia, of which some 20 can damage timber in houses. If you find termites are active in your area, don't panic. Don't disturb the termites by using household sprays or removing infested wood—disruption only makes identification harder and termites will abandon that particular working area for somewhere else. Presuming there's no immediate danger to your home, take time to investigate the size and nature of the problem as well as available options.

Identify the species, as many cause little damage to structural timbers and should be left alone to do their good work recycling old organic matter. Collect a few ants in a jar containing two parts metho to one part water and take the specimens to either your local pest inspector, the Forestry Commission or the CSIRO in your state for identification. Look for any other colonies in or around your property and check out any history of infestations with previous owners and neighbours.

If you do find termite activity in your house:

- It's time to call the pest inspector, as any chemical treatment must be done by a licensed operator.
- You'll need to determine the extent of the damage by doing a full investigation of concealed structural timbers.
- Repair or replace damaged timbers with pest-resistant materials.
- Plan regular inspections to make sure the problem has been eradicated.

If the colony can't be found or infestation persists after treatment, or the building structure can't be easily accessed, then consider having your pest inspector install a chemical bait or barrier system.

PREVENTING TERMITE INFESTATIONS

To help prevent infestations:

- Tidy up around the house—termites need old timber to feed on and this may include old building material, timber stacks, garden decoration, tree stumps, untreated sleepers and logs.
- Fix any leaking pipes and plug any holes, as well as the capture water from air conditioners, drains, showers and sinks, as termites like moist areas.
- Keep air under the house dry (termites also love humid conditions) by improving subfloor ventilation, fixing poor drainage and making access easy and clear.
- Ensure concrete work is properly designed, laid and cured, as termites won't chew through properly laid concrete.
- Keep edges of the house clear of clutter, vegetation and garden beds, including any bridges of material from the soil to timber sections of the house.
- Make sure all subfloor timber has the correct ant barriers and ant caps and that these can all be clearly inspected between the foundations and your sub-floor timbers.
- Arrange regular inspections—once a year in cooler areas and twice a year in warmer areas.

Borers

They come in many types—and no we're not talking about your boss at the company Christmas party. The main problem pest is a borer called furniture beetle, which leaves its calling card in timber in the form of tiny round or slightly oval holes. Most other kinds generally leave larger oval holes in the timber, and this means very little serious damage will occur, but small, closely spaced, round, unstained holes with a fine powdered wood dust present are signs of furniture beetle and they can cause substantial structural damage.

Borers mostly target pine furniture and floors and are hard to treat. Some old furniture will exhibit signs of borer damage, but the borers may be long gone. To find out if they're active in a suspect area, draw a small circle about 100 mm diameter with a permanent marker around a collection of exit holes (on the underside of the floors or furniture of course!), count the borer holes and do another recount in 12 months. Choose several areas, and if new holes are present then the infestation is still active.

TREATING BORERS
Here's how to treat these pests:

- Remove and replace infected timber boards in either autumn or winter when the beetle is inactive.
- Check that there's good under-floor ventilation and cross-breezes through the under-floor area, as they don't like the movement of air.
- Even though chemical treatment is of little value as the borer resides deep inside the timber, try injecting the pin holes with a 1:1 solution of borax and water or kerosene.
- Paint or polish the timber to prevent insect entry.
- Have furniture professionally treated; it will need to be delivered to a professional spray company.

Wet rot and dry rot
These are both types of fungi that love to grow on timber where there's a source of moisture present. The rot grows, breaking down the timber and leaving it mouldy, crazed or broken up into cubes, or spongy. Damage mostly occurs in timber in contact with:

- damp subfloor walls
- wet areas, such as around baths and showers
- soil.

To prevent rot:

- Make sure under-floor ventilation is adequate, as with rising damp.
- Allow good drainage in the subfloor area.
- Try to make sure there's a clearance of at least 450 mm from ground level to subfloor timbers, more if possible.
- Check that stormwater and paving is graded away from the house and that there are no plumbing leaks.

Rot should be treated initially by removing the source of moisture or humidity and opening up the affected area to ventilation. You'll need to remove the rotten timber and clean the immediate area, then treat with a fungicide. Have a look at 'Removing rot from outdoor timber areas' in Chapter 14, 'The outside bits—your home's exterior' for lots of information on how to replace rotten timber.

> **THE RAT (HOLE) PACK**
> If you have gaps where rats or mice are entering your home (e.g. around pipe work), steel wool makes great packing as they won't eat through it.

Under-floor ventilation problems

This can be corrected by installing a dehumidifier or by increasing the ventilation. Almost all older brick homes have inadequate subfloor ventilation and the majority of minor rising damp problems can be cured by increasing the ventilation. Here's how:

- Replace the old terracotta vents with pressed metal or woven wire units. This will increase the airflow up to twelve times, and if you double the number of vents this number can increase to thirty times.

- To remove the old vents, cut out the surrounding mortar with a grinder or dig it out with a plugging chisel.
- Mortar the new vents back into the hole.
- Under the house it may be necessary to form openings in the bases of cross walls to ensure that the entire area is ventilated and there are no dead pockets.
- Remove any old debris and building rubble which may also be obstructing the smooth flow of air.

Other types of flooring

Flaking slate floors

Slate was a very popular floor covering in the 70s and 80s, but a lot of people are finding that, several decades on, their slate floors are flaking and looking pretty ordinary. It's pretty easy to refresh your slate floor—that's if you want to keep it! (Slate is apparently making a comeback.)

The original floor would have been painted with a sealant, which is probably by now worn and peeling in patches. It's hard to know what sealant was used—a little experimentation may be needed. In an incon-spicuous spot try a little acetone (nail polish remover) to start with. This can be purchased in 1 litre bottles at hardware stores, as can commercial slate stripper. For the best advice on what type of stripper to try, I'd speak to a specialist flooring supplier.

Once the floor has been stripped, there are some choices as to what to reseal it with. Once again there are a range of commercial sealers available from hardware stores and flooring suppliers. There's also an organic product called Livos Meldos Hardening Oil, which is ideal for porous substances like slate as it's water resistant yet breathes. It's easy to apply and won't cause flaking in the future.

Removing old cork or linoleum

Removing cork or linoleum tiles may be a difficult job as they'll sometimes be glued directly to the flooring, but it's one you'll have to do if you want to replace them with an alternative floor covering. If you're lucky the cork or linoleum will actually be glued to a layer of masonite that's sitting over the original floor, and this can be torn up fairly easily taking the cork or sheet linoleum with it.

If your cork or linoleum is glued directly down to the original floor, here are some options:

- If you're dealing with vinyl sheeting, make a series of parallel cuts in it about 300 mm apart and remove one strip at a time. There's a tool known as a floor scraper that's designed to assist with this type of job. It has a 1200 mm long handle with a flat interchangeable blade at the base. Ask at a tile supplier or try a specialty hardware supplier. Another tool you might find useful is a long-handle square-mouth shovel.
- An easier plan of attack would be securing an electric floor scraping tool from an equipment hire company.
- To tackle the glue removal, try using a hot air gun to soften it before scraping. Any further residue may be softened with a solvent and scrubbed away with nylon abrasive pads. **Do not use the hot air gun and solvents together, as the fumes are poisonous and solvents are flammable**.
- If this is taking too long you could try hiring a concrete grinder, but be prepared for a lot of dust and noise!

Repairing damaged vinyl flooring

If you have a damaged area on your vinyl floor and don't want to replace the entire floor, it can be patched. You may be lucky and have some spare pieces of your vinyl hanging around (my motto is never throw anything away, you might want it one day—you should see my sheds!). If not, find a suitable matching piece of vinyl to make your repair. If your local flooring shop can't help, try looking under the dishwasher or similar area to find a piece and cut it free. Make sure the piece you cut contains the same pattern as the area you're replacing. Another option is contrasting vinyl patches, which are available from hardware stores and flooring specialists in various sizes and colours. You could add several contrasting patches in an interesting pattern to your vinyl as a way of repairing one problem area.

 WHAT YOU NEED
- sharp utility knife
- piece of matching replacement vinyl (or contrasting squares)
- metal straight edge
- putty knife or scraper
- turpentine
- acrylic adhesive
- liquid seam sealer.

 WHAT TO DO
1. Lay the patch over the damaged section so the pattern is aligned with the floor below, then tape it in place.
2. Use a metal straight edge and utility knife to cut through both the patch piece and the old vinyl beneath; if there are obvious lines in the design of your vinyl, use these as the edge of your patch to make the repair less visible.
3. Set the patch aside and remove the damaged section. If the section has firm adhesive behind it, you may need to scrape it away from the sub-

floor. If adhesive remains, soften its hold with turps and scrape again to create a clean, level surface for the replacement patch. Thoroughly clean away any turps residue and allow the area to dry completely.

4. With a scraper, apply a thin, even coat of water-based vinyl adhesive to the subfloor. Install the patch and smooth with a clean damp sponge. If any adhesive oozes out the sides, wipe it off immediately. Once you have it seated perfectly, cover it with a layer of baking paper and place something flat and heavy over the top, such as some phone books.

5. Allow the patch to dry for at least 24 hours. Then apply a thin line of liquid seam sealer (available from vinyl flooring suppliers) to the edges to keep the corners flat and to make the patch merge with the rest of the floor.

Replacing vinyl or linoleum tiles

For vinyl or linoleum tiles, replacements are made by first removing the damaged tile by cutting it with an 'x' pattern from corner to corner and then scraping it out from the centre. Once removed, follow the repair process described above.

Ceramic tiles

For information on how to regrout your tiles, and replace a cracked tile, see Chapter 11, 'Wet areas'.

Carpet

Fixing snags in carpet

Do you have a running snag (a long, loose but not broken thread) in your looped carpet? Here's how to fix it:

WHAT YOU NEED

- nail punch
- carpet seam adhesive
- masking tape and scissors.

WHAT TO DO

1. Count the number of loops it will take to fill the run on both sides of the pulled strand.
2. Count the curls in the yarn and cut it where it'll provide the right amount of yarn for both sides of the run.
3. Protect the surrounding area of carpet with masking tape.
4. Squeeze a heavy bead of carpet seam adhesive into the run.
5. Use a nail punch to press each 'scab' (spot where the original adhesive clings to the yarn) down into the carpet's backing until the re-established loop is at the correct height.

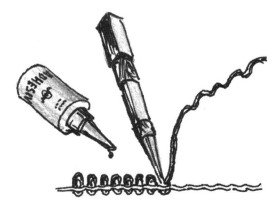

Repair a snag in a carpet by re-looping the loose thread

Removing furniture indentations from your carpet

To remove those annoying indentations in your carpet after you've rearranged your room:

- Spray the flattened area with a little bit of water.
- Use a fork to prise the squashed carpet fibres up and lift the pile.
- Use a hairdryer to dry the carpet back into shape (gently!).

Fixing a small damaged spot like a burn hole, or impossible stains

For fiddly jobs like this:

- Cut the ruined piece out carefully with a sharp utility knife, making the cut as neat as possible and making a note of the pattern and shape of carpet weave and pile.
- Save it as a template or cut a piece of cardboard exactly the same size as the hole to mark onto a matching scrap to create a replacement plug. If you have no scraps left from the carpet, you can steal a piece from a hidden area, e.g. inside a built-in wardrobe.
- Dab adhesive onto the plug and edge of existing carpet, align the plug with the weave and pile of the surrounding carpet, and set it in place.

Chapter 8
DOORS AND WINDOWS

It's always the moving parts in any machine that wear out first, and it's the same with houses. Doors and windows and their frames are constantly in use, and so they're often the first up on the 'fix it' radar. I know in our house they cop a beating—kids climbing in and out, doors being slammed and swung on—you name it, it happens! Old houses have their own peculiar problems—windows stick, doors don't close properly, hinges come loose, handles are wobbly and jam. But newer homes are not perfect either—the natural settling-in process or cheaper materials that are often used gives rise to many a fix-it challenge. Doors first, then I'll move on to windows.

Fixing a rattling door

Often a door is rattling because the latch is no longer fitting as snugly as it should into the striker plate and cavity. To ascertain this you have a look in through the crack between the door and the jamb with a torch to see if the latch is sitting outside or to the top or bottom of the cavity. To fix it you may need to:

- File out the cavity a little to make it fit more snugly.
- Or adjust the plate, either by pushing the striker plate closer to the rebate or slightly bending the 'tang' (the small piece of metal that's bent into the housing) outwards with the tip of a screwdriver.
- Or remove some timber from behind the striker cavity with a chisel so the striker goes in completely once it's reinstalled.
- Or simply tighten the screws (as with the hinges, see below).

Fixing doors that won't close properly

Do you have a door that doesn't close properly? This is probably because it's moved out of alignment due to:

- a hinge or striker plate pulling away from the frame
- the house moving
- doors warping or swelling.

Fixing hinges

When a hinge pulls away from the door or doorframe, the screws holding it in lose their grip. The timber on the inside of the screw hole has been stripped away by the weight of the door and possibly by the screws being over-tightened. The easy fix simply involves removing the screws, filling in the holes and replacing the screws so they regain their tight fit.

WHAT YOU NEED

- matches
- PVA glue
- screwdriver suitable for your screws.

WHAT TO DO

1. Remove a couple of screws at a time so the whole door doesn't have to come down.
2. Dip a couple of matches into the glue and push them into the holes.
3. Snap off any excess and then, once the glue is dry, drive the screws back into the hole.

You'll find the screws now work with renewed purpose and will pull the hinge back in tight, solving the door latch problem.

Hinges that are hard to remove

If your door hinges are covered in a lot of paint, it can be tricky to remove them. To solve this problem:

1. Place just one tip of the screwdriver into one end of the slot, with the screwdriver angled away in line with the slot. Gently tap the handle of the screwdriver with a hammer so that the point pushes along the slot, removing the paint as it goes.
2. Next, straighten the screwdriver up and place it firmly in the slot and give the handle one firm blow; this will help break the grip of any rust on the screw.
3. If the screws are still stiff, a spanner or locking pliers can be fitted around the shaft of the screwdriver to give some extra twisting leverage.

Houses moving

Sometime new houses take a while to settle in, and with the passing of a few seasons you may find things shift about a bit. Same when there's extreme weather like a drought. If you have a door that goes out of alignment, be patient and wait to see if it all moves back after a few months. If you're concerned that there may be a major structural problem, however, you should get an engineer's report. If there are no major problems and it appears you're going to be stuck with a door that isn't closing, you may need to change the shape of the door or the door jamb.

DOORS STICKING AT THE BOTTOM OR SIDE

If the door is sticking just a little, first try lubricating it by rubbing candle wax along the edge. If it's jamming at a point of contact, you'll need to remove some of the door edge by sanding, or planing a couple of millimetres off. If the door is sticking on the bottom:

- Take the door off its hinges to sand or plane it.
- Dry the bottom of the door thoroughly—it may be sticking due to moisture penetration causing it to swell.
- Once dry, planed and sanded, seal the bottom of the door with primer and a coat or two of paint. When planing, make sure you plane in from the edge towards the centre so you don't breakout the edge of the timber. A belt sander can also be handy to remove a millimetre or two in this situation.

Straightening a warped or swollen door

If your door is not closing properly because it's bowed, you can try straightening it:

1. Remove the door and place the ends on a pair of sawhorses with the bow facing upwards.
2. Make sure the sawhorses are sitting on flat, level ground. If you don't have any sawhorses, just lay a pair of timbers across the ground.
3. Place some old towels or cardboard on the surface to protect it, then stack some weights, such as bricks or a bag of sand, on the centre of the bow. Cover the door with a tarp to protect it from any rain.
4. Remove the weights every few days and use a straight edge to check if the door is straightening.

If you can keep the door attached to the jamb but out of service for a while, you can try screwing a length of timber across the frame with the door shut to push the door back into place, but you'll have to fill the screw holes once you've removed the timber.

If it's a tin shed door that has warped then it may be fixed almost instantly by removing the diagonal cross-braces, placing the door on a flat surface and weighing it down before refitting the braces.

Restoring door furniture

The term 'door furniture' refers to things such as locks, latches and knockers. Believe it or not, you can update the look of your whole house by changing or restoring the door furniture!

How to remove it

Most are held on with simple screws, but sometimes even when the screws are removed the old fitting remains stuck in place. If this happens, you can prise them free by placing a screwdriver under the edge and gently tapping.

How to recycle it

The original furniture from your door may be worth restoring and recycling (even if you're replacing the actual door). You can strip any paint and lacquer from it with paint stripper or a bath of caustic soda and water, then polish it up with a good-quality, non-abrasive metal polish such as the ones found in motor vehicle accessory shops. You can use these compounds not only on brass but also copper, chrome, pewter and even silver and gold, and it's gentler on plated metals than abrasive cleaners.

Once you've achieved a fresh new shine, you can keep it by protecting the surface with a fresh coat of lacquer. Metal lacquer, such as Incralac (an acrylic-based clear coating) is available in pressure pack cans for spraying onto metal fittings or in cans for dipping items into.

INSTANT ANTIQUE!

If you have brand new shiny brass door furniture in your home and you'd like to give it a more antique patina, ageing is not a difficult process. This also works for brass fittings such as lamps and reproduction luggage racks.

Basically you'll need to apply paint stripper to remove the lacquer that will have been applied to the fitting and then apply brass blacking solution, available from some antique dealers, hobby stores or traditional hardware merchants.

To achieve an authentic antique look, gently rub back the blackened surface with a little steel wool in the areas that would normally receive the most wear and then protect the surface with a coat of beeswax furniture polish.

Locks

Most cylinder locks will need light lubricating on a semi-regular basis. Graphite powder is best as oil in the keyhole will tend to attract dust, which will clog up the holes. Graphite power is a dry lubricant that comes in a small bottle with puffer spout to blow the graphite deep into the mechanism.

But for older-style rim or simple mortice latch locks (i.e. those with larger moving parts inside) you can spray an aerosol lubricant (e.g. WD-40) using the narrow straw-like applicator that comes with it through the latch, bolt and keyhole. If this doesn't do the trick, you'll need to remove the lock from the door, open up the mechanism and lightly grease the workings.

HOW TO CHANGE OR TIGHTEN A LOCK CYLINDER

Sometimes the cylinder (the part that the key goes into) becomes loose on a deadlock or night latch and will need to be tightened. Or you may want to change the keying of your lock without changing the whole lock mechanism, so you'll need to change the cylinder over. Here's how to do it:

Front and back of a cylinder lock being adjusted

- First, take the latch mechanism off to reveal the cylinder.
- The cylinder is held in place with a plate, which is held by two screws running from the latch to the rear of the cylinder face. Locate these screws, and if you're tightening the lock, simply tighten the screws then replace the latch mechanism.
- To swap over the cylinder, undo the screws and remove the cylinder— the protruding, flat connecting bar will come too.
- Take the cylinder to a locksmith to get a replacement with matching keys.
- You may need to trim the connecting bar on the new cylinder so it matches the bar on your old cylinder—you can snap it off with multi-grips and pliers or maybe a hacksaw. It needs to be the same as the old one so it fits back into the original latch when the cylinder is in place.
- Insert the new cylinder into the hole and make sure the handle of the lock connects with the bar. Tighten the screws.

Door handles

Door handles that lead between internal doors in your home are called 'entry sets', and maintenance is quite simple.

MODERN KNOB-TYPE HANDLES

If you have a squeaky or loose door handle, remove the handles by backing off the small grub screw that's located on the underside of the stem of the handle. A grub screw, also called a set screw, is a screw without a head that simply has a screwdriver slot or Allen key housing cut directly into the top of the threaded shaft. Twist this anti-clockwise to loosen, then remove the handle.

Many modern entry sets are held in place by a pair of screws that run directly from the circular base plate under one handle right through to the other. Sometimes these screws may be hidden under a decorative cover plate that you'll need to unthread first. Other designs use a pin that can be released by pushing the tip of a small screwdriver into a small hole located on the stem. The square steel rod that's now exposed is called the spindle; it will come out with the opposite handle still attached. Wipe the mechanism clean with a cloth or a cotton bud to get into the small crevices to remove dust and gunk, then lubricate with graphite powder. Finally, return the spindle through the square hole in the centre and replace the opposite handle; push it on firmly before retightening the grub screw. It should now feel tight and be squeak free.

OLD-STYLE ROUND BRASS KNOB/LEVER HANDLES

Many older homes have round brass or steel knobs, often as part of an old rim lock mechanism, which over time will become loose. It's pretty easy to fix them when you know how.

These knobs are held onto a square steel spindle with a short grub screw. Remove this screw and the knob will slide off the spindle. There's usually a series of holes in this shaft that will allow you to move the screw to a position where the knob sits firmly. Or you may need to remove the screws.

A small washer placed between the knob and the face plate (or the lock mechanism) may also help to close the space between the knob and the backing plate and be enough to improve the looseness of the handle.

Other door furniture

You may also consider:

- Fitting a push plate (a plate that goes under the door handle to protect the door) and/or a kick plate (ditto on the bottom) to your doors. These fittings simply screw on.

- Installing a peephole by drilling a 10 mm hole through the door and inserting the main barrel of the peephole device through it, then screwing the cover plate onto the other side.

> **BANGING DOORS**
> To reduce the noise of a banging door, put a couple of spots of silicone sealer on the inside edge of the door jamb. Keep it open until completely dry!

Fixing dents on door and window frames

Do you have dings and chips in your timber door surrounds? This problem is relevant to both door and windowframes, but it's really the poor doorframes that cop a beating—kids running in and out and not quite making the turn, blokes carrying in toolboxes or misjudging the opening after a big night, dogs having a chew—after a few years most doorways sport a few bingles.

The edges of timber are certainly more challenging to fill and repair than holes in the face, as there's less surface area for the fillers to grip, so your repair patches tend to be easily knocked off again. Sometimes it may be necessary to initially make the dents deeper with a small chisel or a drill before filling them to increase the gripping area.

 WHAT YOU NEED
- two-part polyester filler (e.g. builder's bog)*
- chisel

- file
- sander or sanding paper.

* This is a lot harder than standard wood putties

 WHAT TO DO

1. Only mix and use small quantities of the two-part polyester filler and then mix more as needed.
2. About a golf-ball-sized ball of filler to a pea-sized ball of hardener is usually a good ratio, and you can add a little wood stain or coloured oxide powder if you need to match a timber colour. Some experimentation may be required to create a good colour match. The stain should be added to the polyester base to match the timber colour before adding the hardener.
3. To form a new sharply angled edge on the door, try overfilling the dent. Then wait for the filler to go off (i.e. harden) and about ten or fifteen minutes later before it goes really hard you can cut and carve the filler with a sharp chisel to match the original edge.
4. Later, when the filler has fully hardened, use a file and a sander to fine-tune the edge before painting. And then tell the kids to slow down!

Repairing a mullion or a muntin

What is a mullion and what is a muntin, I hear you ask? If you have timber-framed glass doors or windows that have timber frames within them—e.g. panelled windows or French doors—then you have mullions and muntins. The difference between the two is that a mullion is larger and divides two separate windows, while a muntin (also called a glazing bar) is the thin strip of wood or other material which divides the panes of glass. If nothing else, this information will be useful next time you play Scrabble!

Mullions and muntins are often damaged by pets (trying to get in or out) and children—or burglars. Note that I don't put these two groups in exactly the same barrel. Here's how to fix them:

- If damage is only shallow, then you can use ordinary wood putty. Sand away any remaining finish before filling. The wood filler can be applied with a putty knife and should be applied in layers in the deeper holes. Once dry, the filler can be sanded smooth before refinishing.
- If the damage is a bit more extensive, then use a tough two-part polyester filler in exactly the same way.
- If the damaged timber has a decorative profile, then you'll have to shape the filler to match. Make a scraper to match the profile by tracing the profile onto a piece of thin metal and then cutting the shape out with tin snips. Use the shaped metal to scrape the filler into shape while it's still soft.
- Finish the repair with tough polyurethane or enamel paint to help keep future damage to a minimum. (And maybe put in a doggy door.)

Repairing a broken door or doorframe

If your door or doorframe has been splintered or broken in a forced entry situation, then try to locate all the sections of timber that have been broken or split from the area. Reset the jigsaw puzzle of pieces with two-part epoxy glue. You can use a glue syringe to squeeze the glue into the area, then clamp the re-glued repair for a few hours to set firm. Make sure you wipe off the excess glue with acetone while it's still wet. Epoxy is very strong and will also fill in any areas where splinters of timber are missing.

Protecting doorframes from damage

If you have a particularly high-traffic doorway or special circumstances such as a wheelchair user in your home, you might like to reinforce the doorframes to protect them. This is a very good idea if your architraves are made of MDF or some other soft composite rather than hardwood. MDF is more easily damaged, and, to make matters worse, once the surface is damaged the MDF will absorb moisture and tend to swell around the damaged areas.

You could consider replacing the frame with a solid timber like meranti, but even this will not resist everything.

A better solution may be to repair the existing frame with polyester filler (as described above) and then reinforce the edges of the frame with some pieces of aluminium angle. The aluminium angle can be purchased in a range of dimensions to suit and then glued to the bottom of the frame with construction adhesive. You can then paint it to match the frame.

REDUCING NOISE
If you want to reduce noise travelling through your house, consider replacing your hollow doors with solid core ones and fitting door seals to close any gaps, especially at the bottom.

Fixing sliding doors

Sliding doors can be a real asset to any house—space saving, attractive and easy to use—that is until the rollers stick. My family has witnessed, to my shame, a number of tantrums over the years caused by non-rolling sliding doors, especially those pesky multi-panelled glass shower screen doors!

The answer to this issue is, of course, maintenance. I know we'd all rather wait to fix something until it's well and truly broken, but really in the case of sliding doors a bit of TLC before things go completely 'off the rails' will save you time, money and blood pressure issues in the future.

As soon as you notice that your sliding doors don't roll back and forth as easily, check out the condition and cleanliness of the tracks. If this doesn't solve the problem you may need a new set of rollers—most sliding doors and windows rely on some sort of rollers or glides to make them work and, like any friction-bearing device, these will eventually wear. Whether it's big access doors on the exterior of your home, smaller internal doors, shower screens or even built-in wardrobe doors, keep an eye out for the following telltale signs:

- They become stiff and don't slide freely.
- They jam and won't open or close at all.
- They create excessive noise or grinding sounds when moved.
- There is extensive wear and tear on the tracks.
- They feel bumpy when sliding.

External door rollers

To replace the rollers on an external door:

1. Wind the roller adjusting screw to its loosest point.
2. Lift the door off its track high enough to clear the tracks and pull it out from the base. If the door is large or has glass in it, grab a mate to give you a hand.
3. Once the door is clear, lay it on its side so you can see what's happening. The door can be held securely with the aid of a door brace made by cutting a slot about 50–60 mm wide across the side of a length of

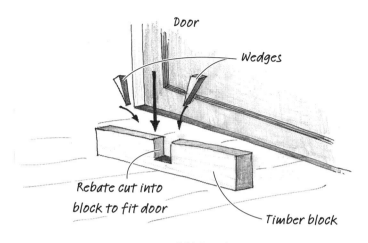

Door

Wedges

Rebate cut into
block to fit door

Timber block

DIY door brace

90 x 45 mm timber, placing the edge of the door into the brace slot and tapping in a timber wedge to hold the door firmly in place.

4. If the roller assemblies appear in good condition, give them a good clean and spray with dry silicone lubricant to help the rollers last longer.

5. If the rollers need to be replaced, then release the old roller assembly by removing the holding screws. You'll need to take it to the hardware store to make sure you get the correct replacement.

6. If you can't find the one to match yours exactly at the hardware, try the manufacturers directly. It's not a bad idea to upgrade to a new stainless steel set, especially if you live near the coast or your doors are exposed to a bit of weather.

7. Before inserting the new rollers, tidy up the bottom of the door by sanding. Use this opportunity to treat it with a timber preservative; also polish the tracks with a bit of metal polish and then spray them with some of that silicone lubricant.

8. Insert the new roller into position and screw it in firmly. Most of these types of assemblies have an adjustment screw that moves the roller up and down, so, before refitting the door, wind the roller to its minimum extension. Once the door has been repositioned, the adjustment screw will still be accessible from the side and you can now adjust the door up to the correct position.

ALUMINIUM DOORS
If you have aluminium doors, stick to the original style roller assembly; mixing metals will only cause greater corrosion problems.

Sliding wardrobe doors

Most sliding wardrobe doors have rollers that run in a track at the top and small plastic glides at the base to keep the doors in line. As with external doors, you may find the roller bracket needs adjustment or the rollers have worn.

Without removing the doors, check for the adjustment screw on the roller bracket; when tweaked, this will raise and lower the door. Raise the door slightly and test if this helps the movement.

If, after raising the doors, they're still stiff or bumping along the track like a red rattler, the rollers may need replacing. Follow the instructions above to do this.

Another problem with sliding wardrobe doors (and some sliding screen doors) is that the actual metal track along the bottom of the door has become damaged—bent or split. You may be able to repair it, or you can remove the entire track profile with a screwdriver and replace it without too much difficulty.

See Chapter 11, 'Wet areas', for info on fixing sliding glass shower screens.

Maintaining sash windows

OK, now let's have a look at windows. One of the most common window problems in old houses are sash windows that won't open, or stay open. I know in our house we had several sash windows propped open with rulers, old sticks and library books for years until I finally got around to fixing them.

Fully functioning sash or double-hung windows allow for good ventilation and are well suited to a warm climate. By opening both sashes the same amount an air current is formed, with cooler air entering from the bottom as hot air is allowed to escape from the top.

More modern double-hung sash windows use spring-loaded spiral balances to support the sashes, but traditionally metal counterweights held in boxes either side of the window were used. These weights are attached to the sashes using braided cords fed over pulleys at the top of the frame.

Both types require some periodic maintenance to keep them functioning efficiently.

Windows stuck shut with paint

This is one of the most common problems with sash windows (and many other types of old windows). Try this solution:

1. Carefully cut through the layers of offending paint with a sharp utility knife, making sure you cut every edge that's painted shut.
2. Once the seal has been cut, prise the window open with the blade of a large chisel. You may need to gently tap on a block of timber as you slide the chisel round the sash frame to help free it up. Proceed very carefully with this process to avoid cracking a windowpane.

3. You may need to clean and lubricate the top pulleys and sash cord to get it all working again.
4. Once the sashes are moving again, scrape away excess paint before priming and repainting the timber frame; this time, be careful not to stick the window closed! (See Chapter 13, 'Painting and other finishes', for how to 'cut in' correctly, to avoid this problem.)

Windows nailed closed

Sometimes you'll find an old sash window has been nailed closed at some stage, usually as a form of makeshift security or because the window has stopped working correctly. Often these nails have been covered with subsequent layers of paint and will be difficult to locate. Here's what to do:

1. Remove the outer timber beading, called the 'stop bead', which holds the sash in place. This is often easier to remove by punching the small nails that hold it right through the timber rather then prising it free.
2. Fit a blade into a handy hacksaw; this is just a simple handle that clamps onto the end of a hacksaw blade to give you a safe grip if using the blade in a tight spot.
3. Slide the end of the blade down between the sash and the frame. It should travel freely down these gaps but if it hits something along the way it's probably the offending nail, which can then be cut with the end of the blade.

Lubricating your sash windows

If you can open your windows but they're a bit sticky, try adding a bit of lubrication in the form of wax or soap. Rub inside the channels on each side of the frame with a candle or some soap. Avoid silicone-based lubricants for this job as silicone residue will make it very difficult to paint the windows in the future.

Replacing broken sash cords

Broken sash cords are the usual failing of the older-style box frame sash windows, but replacing the cords will usually return them to full working order. Replacing the cords is a job best tackled only by an advanced DIYer or a professional window restorer. Describing the process properly here would no doubt fill this whole page, but if you're keen to try this yourself most companies that sell the spare parts for traditional sash windows can also supply you with an illustrated instruction sheet on how to tackle this project. It will involve dismantling the window to gain access to the weights, so if you take on this job be sure to replace all four cords and not just the broken one.

BALANCING SASH WINDOWS

An important thing to watch for with sash windows is that you have the correct balances to suit the size and weight of your sashes. It may seem logical to simply buy identical balances to the old ones, but if the glass in the sash has been replaced at some time you may find that the new modern glass is a little heavier than the original and the extra weight will have to be countered by a stronger balance.

To check this, you'll have to remove the sash from the frame and weigh it on some scales. Also make a note of the dimensions of the frame and the diameter of the channel that houses the balance. A specialist supplier will identify and supply the correct balance for your window.

Replacing spiral balances

If your windows are like mine and are controlled by more modern spiral balances, then you'll find their replacement a much simpler process. It's very important to make sure you buy the correct replacements to suit the size and weight of your window. Try your local hardware or contact a specialist supplier; you may like to take the old one with you, as well as the measurements of your window.

WHAT YOU NEED
- replacement spiral balances
- screwdriver
- something to prop the window open (not your head).

WHAT TO DO
1. Remove the old balance. The lower sash should be raised to its highest position and then propped in place. The metal hook at the bottom of the balance, known as the 'shoe', is removed first. Be careful, as there will still be some tension in the spring that may cause the shoe to spin as it's freed. The screw at the top of the balance can then be backed out and the old balance removed.
2, To fit the new balances, start with the set for the top sash. Position them and fasten the top screw. Next fit the balances for the bottom sash in the same way.
3. Adjust the balances, starting with the bottom sash. Lift it to its highest position and prop it open, wind the spiral mechanism gently up until the foot meets the bottom of the sash and then add some tension by pulling the foot down and giving it three extra twists. Temporarily fasten the foot to the underside of the sash frame and repeat the same process for the other side.
4. Once both are fastened, you can test the tension by lowering and raising the sash frame. If the frame fails to stay all the way up, some extra twists of the foot may be required, but no more than six in total. If the window is difficult to pull down, then some tension should be released instead.

5. Once the lower sash is working, correctly repeat the adjustment process for the top one.

It's possible to retrofit spiral balances to old box frame sash windows but it's not a simple task as you'll have to remove the sashes and cut a housing for the balance with a router along each side of the frame. Going to this much trouble will make you wonder why you didn't just repair the original mechanism; done properly, it will last many years.

Replacing putty around glass in your windows

If there are a few pieces of putty missing from around the glass in your old windows, it's easy to replace them—and a good idea before things go too far and the glass falls out! Window putty is simply a combination of linseed oil and whiting (chalk) and can be bought from any hardware outlet.

 WHAT YOU NEED
- window putty
- linseed oil
- putty knife.

 WHAT TO DO
1. Before replacing missing pieces, paint the surrounding putty and exposed timber below the missing pieces with linseed oil. This will

recondition the old putty and nourish the exposed timber. It will also slow the drying process of the new putty so it will harden without becoming brittle.

2. Roll a piece of new putty into a small roll, push it into position then shape it with your finger tips to fit; just prepare a bit at a time so it doesn't dry out.

3. Smooth the surface with a putty knife which has been dipped in more linseed oil to prevent it sticking.

You'll find more useful information on windows in Chapter 5, 'Making your home more energy efficient', especially things like sealing gaps around windows.

SCRATCHED, BROKEN OR CRACKED GLASS
To remove shallow scratches from glass in your windows, use Brasso or jeweller's rouge applied with a soft rag and LOTS of elbow grease.

If you do crack or break some glass, I'd recommend having it replaced professionally. Not only is fitting new glass a potentially hazardous job but some special skills are required to properly apply window putty to an entire windowframe. You can save some money by removing the sash or hinges from the frame and taking it to the glazier rather than have a glazier come to you.

Fitting locks on your windows

Unfortunately modern life has resulted in a society where we all feel we need to lock our windows and doors to keep us safe from the world outside.

Over 60 per cent of all break-ins are made through windows, especially ground-floor windows at the back of a house. Breaking the glass and opening a window is pretty simple. One solution is to fit window locks— well, at least it will keep your insurance company happy. Fit them to all ground-floor windows and to any windows accessible via drainpipes or flat roofs. Of course they can still smash the glass and climb through— so many people resort to metal grilles over their windows, but that's another story.

There's a wide range of locks available to suit all types of sliding or hinged wood or metal windows. There are different versions for wood-framed and metal-framed windows, so take care when choosing. Some even lock automatically when the window is closed or can be used to lock the window into a slightly open position for both ventilation and security.

 WHAT YOU NEED

■ Most window locks can be fitted easily with only a drill and screw-driver.

 WHAT TO DO—HINGED WINDOWS

A basic lock for a hinged window works in a similar way to a door lock: the part with the bolt is fixed to the window and the second part that receives the bolt is fitted to the frame. It's important to fit enough locks to make the window resistant to force from the outside.

1. Mark the position of the locks. If the window swings sideways, one lock near the top edge and one near the bottom will provide the strongest option. Put one on each side (left and right) if the window swings upwards.

2. Mark the positions for the screw holes on the opening window by holding the lock in position and pushing a pointed object through the holes to make a small dent in the timber. I use an awl, but if you don't have one of these just use a screw or large nail.
3. Remove the lock and drill a pair of small pilot holes using the little dents as a starting point.
4. IMPORTANT: the screws that come with the locks are special security screws that can only be screwed inwards with a standard screwdriver and then can't be removed without a special tool. So it's a good idea to use some standard screws first to be sure everything is in the right position before exchanging them for the one-way screws.
5. Now mark the position of the catch and repeat the process.
6. Close the window and check that the mechanism works smoothly. Once you're happy with the way it's working you can safely exchange the screws.

Instead of fitting a lock on your hinged window, you can fit a wind-out window stay with a lock. This will allow you to wind the window open and closed and lock it any position.

 WHAT TO DO—SASH WINDOWS

You can secure a sash window by fitting a locking bolt that runs through the timber frame of one of the sliding sashes into the timber of the other. These are even easier to fit than the hinged window locks.

1. Close the windows and fit the bolt-locking mechanisms to the inner frame using the technique described above. It's particularly important to use regular Phillips head screws for the first stage here as you'll need to remove the lock for drilling the bolt holes.

2. Fit a bit to your drill that's slightly narrower than the locking bolt and then run it through the hole in the mechanism that the bolt would normally fit into. This will start your hole in the correct position. Remove the lock and fit a new drill bit, this time slightly larger than the bolt. Drill this into the timber to the required depth.
3. Refit the lock with the security screws and slide in the bolt.

If you drill a second hole slightly further up the top sash frame you'll be able to secure the window in a slightly open position to allow some ventilation. You won't need to remove the lock for this—just slide the window up to start the hole the same way as before and then slide the window back down while you finish it with the larger drill bit.

SLIDING ALUMINIUM WINDOWS
There are many different styles of sliding windowframes and locks to suit. See if you can identify the original manufacturer of the windows and contact them directly, as they'll have an appropriate recommendation and may even be able to supply the locks to you. Make some careful measurements of your windowframe and note how it works and then jump on the Internet, try one of the lock manufacturing companies OR take your measurements and a photograph of one of your windows to your local locksmith, who'll be able to identify appropriate locks and order them in for you; of course they can also come and fit them.

Fixing hinges on your windows

If you have windows that are hinged, they can stiffen with age. This can result in the joints in the frame widening or cracking. To fix this problem:
1. Remove the window (fill the gap with a piece of plywood).

2. Completely remove the hinges from the window and soak them in paint stripper overnight.
3. Wash away any old paint with some warm soapy water and medium-grade steel wool. You may find they're brass under the paint, in which case they should clean up like new.
4. Use some WD-40 to free up the stiff mechanism, but not as a long-term lubricant; for this I would recommend something like high-tech motorcycle chain lubricant. If the hinges are beyond repair, seek out brass or stainless steel replacements from an architectural hardware supplier.
5. In the future, avoid painting the hinges; just reapply the lubrication from time to time.

Making and fixing flyscreens

Flyscreens are an easy and very satisfying fix-it job, especially if you have a lot of openings around your home as I do—train carriages have a LOT of windows!

Most timber windowframes will have a small rebate in the moulding to allow for the installation of screens. If not, you can install the screens flat against the outer surface of the frame. If you have sliding, sash or inward-opening windows you'll find the rebate for screens on the outside. If your windows open outwards, however, like casement or awning windows, the screens will have to be fitted on the inside. Inside screens will present you with the added complication of having to add mechanical winders to open the windows without removing the screens. For sliding aluminium windows, screens are fitted into an outer track.

It's a flyscreen meltdown!

 WHAT YOU NEED

- tape measure
- aluminium flyscreen frame (available in a range of colours to suit your windows)
- corner connectors, four per screen (plus screws to fasten these)
- fibreglass screen mesh (the most common, but there are other kinds)
- toggle clips (to hold screen in frame)
- plastic flyscreen spline (enough to match total window perimeter plus 10 per cent). Flyscreen spline is flexible PVC tubing with little ridges on it.

- spline roller tool
- hacksaw*
- mitre box
- utility knife
- scissors
- screwdriver
- cordless drill
- file.

* Aluminium is soft and easy to cut with just about anything; if you don't have a hacksaw a fine-toothed wood saw can be used, but spray the blade with WD-40 first.

 WHAT TO DO

1. Grab a tape measure and make a careful note of the space between the inside edges of the rebates, then allow a couple of millimetres clearance all round to determine your screen size. If the screens are to fit into aluminium tracks, the vertical measurement starts on the upper inside surface of the top track but stops on the top edge of the lower track. Subtract a further 3 mm from this measurement for tolerance and you'll have a screen size that that can be fitted by lifting it into the top track and pushing it past the edge of the lower track before dropping it into place.

2. Once you've measured all your windows, make up a quick diagram of each of the screens to be made before heading down to your hardware store for the supplies.

3. Set up a sturdy, flat work surface and then measure, mark and mitre cut the aluminium frame stock to size with the aid of the hacksaw and mitre box. Small mitre boxes specifically for this job are available for a few dollars and can be found in the same area of the hardware store as the rest of the flyscreen materials.

4. If you have a file, remove any burrs after cutting.
5. Assemble the flyscreen frame using the corner joiners. Use a piece of wood or a mallet to gently tap corners into position. When assembled, test on the window to ensure correct size. If the window or your handiwork is slightly out of square, a gentle push on the corner of your frame will adjust it.
6. Place the frame on a flat surface with the channel side up. Use the floor if your bench isn't big enough to ensure the frame is supported all the way around. Cut a piece of fibreglass mesh with a 50 mm overhang on each side. Place this piece over the frame and then diagonally cut the corners of the piece of mesh.
7. Cut a length of flyscreen spline slightly longer than required. The ridges on the flyscreen spline are designed to catch and pull the mesh into the channel. Before starting to insert the spline it can be soaked in a dish of hot water to make it more pliable.
8. Start about 100 mm from one corner and push the spline in with your finger initially, then follow through with the spline roller; this will force the spline and mesh deep into the groove. Continue this all the way round the frame. Keep a little bit of tension on the screen but not much; as you work around with the spline roller the screen will become taut.
9. Trim off any excess mesh with a sharp blade.
10. The screens can be held in place with the aid of four (two each side) small plastic toggle clips. These are secured to the surrounding windowframe with a single screw each to allow them to pivot back and forth to release the screen for future cleaning and maintenance.

Fixing old screens

If you already have screens but they're damaged, the mesh can simply be replaced in the existing frame using the technique described above.

Cleaning flyscreens

You should clean your screens thoroughly at least once a year, as dust and grime will build up quickly. You'll be amazed how much more light will come in once the screens are cleaned:

1. Remove the screens and place them on a flat surface covered with an old towel.
2. Gently scrub the screen with a soft brush and warm soapy water; when you remove the screen from the towel you'll see the old grime left behind.
3. Lean the screen on the side of a tree and then rinse with a light spray from the hose (if this is permitted under water restrictions). You could always save water by cleaning your screens in the shower while you clean yourself!

Maintaining powder-coated aluminium windows

Love 'em or hate 'em, aluminium window and door frames are everywhere. They're chosen for their ease of maintenance, but nothing lasts forever and eventually even they'll need some TLC.

Most powder-coated finishes are tougher and much more flexible than conventional solvent-based paints—they're about the same hardness as automotive paint. To clean a powder-coated surface, use the same care and methods you'd use to clean your car. Gently wash with a clean, soft cloth and a mild detergent, followed by a clear water rinse. If the colour is looking a bit dull, you could try buffing the frames with a car cutting polish.

On raw aluminium the early stages of corrosion can be removed by wiping the frames with household ammonia. Make sure you wash off any cleaners very well—if you leave them on they could cause further corrosion!

If the corrosion is a little more advanced the solution can be found at a car accessory shop in the form of a non-abrasive mag wheel cleaner or metal polish.

Non-anodised aluminium can be cut back with fine wet and dry sand-paper to remove corrosion pitting and then followed up with car cutting compound. Finishing the job with a coat of car polishing wax will help protect the surface from further weathering, although keep in mind this is only a temporary fix-it.

The other option is to paint them—after making good surface prep-aration of course! To paint powder-coated aluminium:

1. Prepare the surface by scrubbing with a scourer or fine wet and dry sandpaper dipped in turpentine.
2. Clean it again with more turps to remove loose material.
3. Prime the aluminium with a metal primer.
4. Once the primer is dry, put on a top coat of your choice.

AND FOR YOU REV-HEADS OUT THERE . . .
Car accessory shops have a great range of mag wheel cleaners that are a bit more heavy duty and are terrific for polishing the tarnish off old aluminium windowframes and other aluminium window and door fittings.

Removing old masking tape from windows

As I'm sure you know, when you're painting windows it's a very good idea to put tape on the glass so you only paint the frame and not the glass. A fiddly job, but worth it. But I'm wondering if you've ever been in the situation where you've left the masking tape on a bit too long and it's got permanently stuck. And then you've tried to scrape it off and been left with a mess of old glue, tape and paint. Luckily, there are several ways to approach the problem:

- For tape on glass, soften the glue with heat, gently applied with a hair dryer. You should be able to peel it off with your fingers.
- For tape on painted surfaces, remove the tape by steaming off the paper first by covering it with a damp cloth and applying a hot iron.
- In both cases, a plastic scraper may help but be careful not to gouge the paint surface or scratch the glass.
- If there's sticky residue left after removal, dissolve it with gum turpentine or Goof Off, which is a cleaning compound specifically designed for removing sticky substances.

Removing bubbling tint from windows

I'm having horrible flashbacks to the schoolbook contact covering here! Window films are a terrific way to keep your heating and cooling costs down, and they help make your glass more shatterproof. We all know how much cooler a car with tinted windows can be, and the same goes for a home. But eventually you may come across some film that has bubbled from age, or poor initial application. Here's how to remove the old, bubbling film.

WHAT YOU NEED
- spray bottle filled with household ammonia
- roll of plastic food wrap
- broad-bladed putty knife
- razor blade.

WHAT TO DO
1. Spray the ammonia onto the window film and immediately cover the ammonia-wet area with a layer of plastic wrap.
2. Wait for the ammonia to permeate through the film layer and break down the glue below (probably about 45 minutes).
3. Use the putty knife to remove the film. Use warm soapy water and a fresh razor blade to remove any residue.

Remember that window tinting is a huge energy-save, and not just during daylight savings. It's well worth replacing once you've removed the old film.

Chapter 9
BUILT-IN CUPBOARDS

Almost every home has some built-in cupboards and usually we want more of them! Whether it's in the kitchen, bedroom or bathroom, they're often in fairly constant use and so suffer the same wear and tear problems suffered by doors and windows. Kitchen cupboards in particular cop it from constant opening and closing (and in our case being swung on by a four-year-old) and being in contact with water and heat.

Built-in cupboards can be one of the more expensive things to call a tradesperson in to build in your home—good joinery is an art—and it's a good idea not to scrimp on the materials and construction costs initially as they'll last longer and usually look a lot better. There are, however, some jobs the average DIYer can do around the house to fix up problems and update the look of their built-ins.

Kitchen cupboard doors that no longer line up

Over time, cupboard doors tend to sag, especially the ones that get used all the time. About once a year I have to take a screwdriver to the cupboard door hinges and fine-tune them in order to keep the doors aligned.

Most doors are designed to be adjusted quickly and easily with nothing more than a screwdriver, as most kitchens built in the last 25 years or so have concealed, adjustable hinges. Typically these hinges have four adjusting screws, allowing you to make three basic adjustments:

- Lateral—the front grub screw (or set screw) adjustment allows the door to be moved side to side.
- Depth—loosening the back screw allows the door to be moved in or out.
- Vertical—the two top and bottom screws allow for adjustment of the door in an up or down direction.

Corner cupboard adjustable hinge

You'll need to experiment with the readjusting to obtain perfect alignment, but you'll soon get the hang of it. It's worth noting that most of these types of hinges are manufactured in Europe and will probably have Pozidriv screws in them (see Chapter 2, 'Tools', for info on this).

Fixing sagging corner cupboard doors

The curse of many built-in kitchens is the corner cupboard. It always end up a black hole where you can't find anything that's pushed up the back, and the doors, being double sectioned, often sag and eventually fall off.

This type of hinged door is a lot heavier than your regular cupboard door, as the hinges on the cabinet have to carry the combined weight of both doors. In order to counter this extra weight and open the gap between the top of the folding door and the adjacent door, you should compensate by overadjusting not only the hinges that attach the doors to the cabinet but also the hinges that join the two doors together. Both hinges will have an adjustment screw that fits through a slotted hole, usually at the back of the hinge assembly (see above). Loosen this screw slightly and then push the two parts of the hinge closer together before retightening. It may take a couple of attempts to get the doors to sit where you want them.

Fixing swinging wardrobe doors

Swinging doors on most professionally built wardrobes will be installed with the same type of concealed hinges you find in your kitchen cupboards (as described above), although more of them are used per door and sometimes they're larger. These are adjusted in the same way. Fixing sliding doors on wardrobes is covered in Chapter 8, 'Doors and windows'.

Fixing drawers

Just like the rollers on sliding doors, rollers on drawer runners can become worn or damaged. Replacing the inexpensive runners or slides will have the drawers rolling like new again and is a pretty straight-forward operation:

1. Pull the drawer forward and lift the front to remove it from the cabinet. This will give you access to both parts of the roller assembly.
2. Removing just a few screws will free up the old mechanism. Once again, a decent hardware store should have an exact matching assembly; if not, try cabinetmakers' supplies in the phonebook.
3. These are usually sold in pairs and you should replace both sides of your drawer at once. You'll only need a screwdriver to replace the old screws into the original screw holes.

Sometimes with excess pulling and overloaded drawers (or perhaps if the runners were broken), drawer fronts can become loose and pull away from the rest of the drawer. If this is happening to yours:

1. Remove the drawers and clamp the front back into position.
2. Add some small metal 90 degree angle brackets to the inside of the drawer before it comes apart completely.

Another common complaint is the collapse of the thin baseboard in the drawer. This will often happen because the drawer has been overloaded.

The base is only held in place by a shallow groove that runs around the sides and front of the drawer, and it's tacked into the back with small nails. The weight pushes these back nails out and then the base panel flexes and pops out of the channel. To fix it:

1. Flip the drawer over and slide the base panel back into position.
2. Tack it back down at the back with some new flat head nails.
3. Place a couple of small 90 degree brackets over the back edge. These can be screwed into the back of the drawer with 12 mm button head screws.

Shelf supports

Missing shelf support lugs can be replaced; you'll find an assortment of styles at any hardware store. (They're the little round removable plastic things that are used in modern built-in wardrobes to support shelving.) Sometimes, though, the lugs go missing because the lugholes have worn and become loose. The best solution might be to swap the shelf positions in order to utilise a new set of holes, but if you're stuck with the layout you have, a quick, easy repair can be done by replacing the lugs with some 20 mm #8 gauge pan head screws. Replace all four at once and just leave the screw heads sitting 6–7 mm proud of the surface to support the shelf. You can even paint them (or use Liquid Paper) to match the interior.

BUILDING A FLAT-PACK BUILT-IN CUPBOARD
It's possible for the home handyperson to create their own built-in cupboards—although not a job for the beginner. You could think about starting with a ready-made flat pack cupboard unit which you just assemble

and fit. You need only minimal skill with tools to create professional and accurate cabinets, as all components arrive cut to size, edged, pre-drilled and labelled for easy identification and assembly. Manufactured from HMR (highly moisture resistant) board, they usually even come with a warranty.

Make sure you measure up the space carefully and do a drawing. Also make sure you get the benchtop a bit longer than the required finished dimension, as you may find that your walls aren't quite square. Cut a template from the cardboard packaging to get the correct shape and size required of the benchtop.

Looking after and updating your laminate kitchen

Many kitchens feature a laminated benchtop and/or cupboards (you probably refer to it as Formica or Laminex, which are brand names). These surfaces are basically a heat-resistant, wipe-clean plastic laminate of paper or fabric with melamine resin. They're relatively inexpensive and come in a great range of colours and textures. Here are some tips for looking after it:

- Don't use abrasive cleaners (even cream cleanser) or scouring pads—you'll scratch the surface. Best to use warm soapy water or spray cleansers.
- Laminate will withstand fairly high temperatures, but it's possible to scorch it if you don't use a protective mat, e.g. when you take a saucepan from a hotplate or a casserole from the oven. To remove a scorch mark, you can try a mild abrasive such as toothpaste and a soft toothbrush or cloth, but be warned—go gently here as you may cause more damage than you fix!

- Laminates are pretty tough but they can be damaged by chopping and cutting, so always use a chopping board. If there are some scratches in your laminate you can try using car polish to hide them. Laminex also sell a filling kit with matching colours for their brand to fill severe cuts and scratches as well as joins.
- If you spill any kind of glue on your laminate, or you have a painting accident and spill some enamel paint, you can remove it with the appropriate solvent. Metho, turps and acetone can be used sparingly, but don't use paint stripper. On metallic-look laminates don't use ANY sort of solvent.
- Laminates are resistant to many spills, but in some cases you should clean them up immediately or they'll stain, e.g. beetroot juice, tea, red wine and berry juices.

If your kitchen is ten-plus years old, chances are the cupboard doors and benches are starting to look a little shabby and possibly a bit dated (there still seems to be a fair bit of lime green 70s laminate around!). If the kitchen is still structurally sound and the layout is workable, it's possible to update your laminate kitchen without spending a fortune.

Inside the cupboards

You can use tile and laminate cleaner to clean the inside of the cupboards, and if the inside shelf edges are chipped or have fallen off you can replace the laminate edging fairly easily:

1. Remove the old edge strips from the cabinets. Apply some heat with a hot air gun or iron to soften the old hot-melt glue that holds them on, then just slide a scraper under one end and work along the strip.
2. You can purchase rolls of replacement edging at any hardware store. This is also coated with hot-melt glue on one side and so needs heat to apply it. This heat is applied with an iron. Cut pieces slightly longer

than required and then iron them into place, leaving a small overhang on all edges. While the glue is still soft, slide a small strip of wood up and down your new edge while tapping it with a hammer as you go to help create good adhesion.

3. Trim the excess from the ends with a sharp chisel or utility knife, but to trim the edges use a fine flat file and work it at 45 degrees across the edge.

GAPS IN YOUR BENCHTOP

If a small gap has opened up between your benchtop and the splashback, fill with silicone sealant. Once it's in place, spray the sealant with a light spray of window cleaner and glide the tip of your latex-glove-covered finger over it, making sure any joins are smooth.

Updating cupboard doors

The cheapest option for a kitchen facelift is to paint the cupboard doors. First give them a good clean with tile and laminate cleaner, followed by the matching primer and then laminate paint, which is a high-performance enamel paint. The benefit of these laminate paints is that they have a much smoother finish than regular paints and tend not to show brush marks. They're also formulated to be very tough and resist scratching and everyday bumps and knocks. See Chapter 13, 'Painting and other finishes', for tips on painting with enamels.

A more complicated and costly option, which will undoubtedly give you a longer-lasting result, is to replace the cupboard doors. From $30 to $40 a door it's still a much cheaper option than a new kitchen. Many small kitchen manufacturers and timber panel companies offer to manufacture new doors and cover panels to match your old ones. Take your old doors to them and they'll cut new ones to size, drill the hinge holes and apply the edging. One big advantage is that you can specify to have tough 2 mm edging applied to your new doors. Another option is to have your new doors cut from plywood or inexpensive MDF and then finish them with a hand-applied coating or a fancy painted finish.

Laminate benchtops

The tile and laminate paints currently available on the market are good enough for cupboards doors, but don't use them for benchtops—they just aren't tough enough and will scratch with heavy-duty family use. I've heard of some people having success painting their benchtops using tile and tub paint, which is designed for painting baths, but if you have a textured benchtop it may not bond well.

If you decide to try the painting option, add a couple of coats of polyurethane over the paint to increase the durability, but personally I'd consider replacing the benchtops. It's not an extremely expensive exercise and will do wonders for your existing kitchen. If you have square edges on your existing bench tops, then another option is to lay a new laminate straight over the old one.

CUTTING LAMINATE
To cut laminated materials like a benchtop it's better to work with the bottom facing up when using a circular saw or jigsaw; this way the upward cutting action of the circular saw blade won't tear up the laminate on the edge of the cut. Laminate or fine-toothed blades are available for these saws.

Timber benchtops

I think a solid timber bench top in a kitchen looks terrific, but it can cop a real beating from the cook and his or her helpers; timber is probably the most vulnerable of all benchtop materials. If yours is looking shabby, here's how to give it a makeover:

1. Remove or cover any fixtures in the surface, such as sinks, before beginning.
2. Sand the surface; start with a coarse 80 grit sandpaper to first remove any remnant of the old finish and sand away stains and damage, then move through a series of progressively finer grades, say 120 and then 180.
3. Once the surface is sanded, remove all dust—vacuum it off and wipe with a cloth slightly dampened with methylated spirits.
4. Consider applying a natural non-toxic finish like tung oil; this will also make the surface water resistant yet allow the timber to breathe. Try to apply about five coats for a kitchen benchtop and refresh with a new coat every now and then. Make sure you apply a coat to the underside of the bench as well, as it helps stop long-term cracking or warping of the timber.

See Chapter 13, 'Painting and other finishes', and Chapter 3, 'Products and materials', for more information about applying tung oil.

Other benchtops

Stone, granite and marble

Cracks, chips and scratches in these materials are not easy to fix. I'd recommend a professional repairer, who may be able to fill deep damage in situ with an epoxy and then repolish the surface to make the repair almost invisible.

Tiles

See 'Replacing a cracked or damaged tile' in Chapter 11, 'Wet areas'. You'll also find info there on regrouting.

Replacing cupboard door handles

Selecting beautiful new handles for your kitchen doors is another secret to updating your kitchen. You can always just go to the local hardware or kitchen shop, but architectural hardware outlets will give you a bigger choice.

It's important to be accurate when drilling holes to fit new handles. Remember it's easier to fit the handles *before* you re-hang the doors. Try the following method to help you get all the handles fitted accurately:

1. Place a strip of masking tape on the door approximately where the new handle will fit.
2. With a fine line marker, mark the position of the handle's screw holes, in from the edge and down from the top of the door, on the blade of a tri-square.
3. Set and lock the blade and then transfer the position of the holes onto the masking tape using the marks on the blade as a guide.
4. Keep your square locked in this position, so you can make all the door markings identical.
5. Drill some 2 mm guide holes first and then re-drill with a 5 mm bit to house the 4 mm screws before removing the tape.

Note that it's always wise to test this marking system on a scrap of timber first to check your accuracy.

A MODERN TOUCH

To give your kitchen a modern feel, add some soft close fittings which make your doors close gently. These can be retrofitted to any kitchen by simply peeling off some backing paper from the double-sided tape they come with and placing them inside the top edge of the cabinet on the hinge side. Test them and then permanently fix them with a single screw.

Chapter 10
FURNITURE

In these days of disposable everything, it seems that we're much more inclined to throw things away than fix them. Being a bit of a bargain hunter, I'm often seen scouting around on 'dry rubbish' day in my street, and I'm always amazed at what people throw away. Certainly there's always plenty of el cheapo stuff that isn't worth the trouble of repairs, but for the good stuff there's a lot you can do to save, restore and protect your furniture.

Fixing dents and scratches in timber furniture

Most minor damage to stained, varnished or waxed timber furniture can be easily repaired. If you're feeling a bit nervous, best to test your resuscitation techniques on a part of the furniture that's not in public view. Here's a range of techniques to try.

Scuffs and scratches

Often minor scuffs and small scratches will disappear with the application of a fresh coat of furniture wax. A good-quality polish will contain a blend of beeswax, carnauba wax, oils and gum turpentine. Apply the wax with a very fine 0000 steel wool in small circular actions and then buff with a soft cloth in the direction of the wood grain.

Light-coloured scratches on darker stained furniture can be disguised by dabbing on a little black coffee or rubbing in some matching coloured shoe polish. Build up the colour with several applications rather than trying to nail it first time.

One of my favourite trade secrets is the Scratch Fix pen. It comes in five common timber colours and looks like a regular felt tip marker but actually contains wood stain. Just choose the right shade and colour in the scratches, wiping off any excess straight away. You can buy these pens individually as you need them or, if you want to get serious about furniture repairs, collect a whole set as part of a home furniture repair kit which would also contain some oils, waxes and polishing cloths.

Another great solution for slightly more serious dings and gouges are beeswax putty sticks. They're available in a range of shades to suit most timber colours either individually or as a set to add to your repair kit. To use one, heat a putty knife by dipping it in boiling water and then use the heated blade to scrape off a small section of the stick and wipe it into the damage. As the wax hardens again, scrape off any excess with the edge of a plastic scraper (or an old credit card) and then apply some furniture wax over the repair.

Dents and depressions in timber

Small dents and depressions can be steamed out if the timber fibres haven't been torn. Make a number of small pin holes in the dent, put a drop of water in the indentation and allow it to soak in, cover it with a cloth and apply heat using an iron. The moisture will swell the timber in the dent, filling it out. Be careful, as this excess heat may affect some timber finishes.

Major dings and dents in timber

Depending on the type of finish and texture of your timber, it's possible to fill deep dents with a mixture of two-part polyester filler (builder's bog), mixed with stain or oxide to match the surrounding timber. Make sure you test the colour on a less noticeable patch first!

REMOVING ANIMAL HAIRS FROM YOUR FURNITURE!
Now this is really more of a cleaning tip, but it involves recycling tools so I'm including it! Simply wrap masking tape around your old paint roller with the sticky side out. Then you can use the roller to pick up hairs and fluff from around the house. Then just pull (or cut) off the tape and you can reuse the roller later with a new layer of tape.

Build up of dirt on timber

When an old piece of furniture is just looking dull or grotty, an application of orange oil will not only remove years of built-up grime but nourish the timber and leave the piece looking and smelling fresh.

All sorts of marks and scratches can be removed with an antique cleaning blend such as Rotheraines Reviver, which cleans the surface and restores the old finish in one step. Or you can make your own: one part vinegar, one part methylated spirits, one part gum turpentine and a dash of boiled linseed oil. This concoction is flammable, so you should store it in a safe place. Shake before and during use. The blend of mild acid and solvents dissolve the damaged layers of old finishes and rejuvenate surfaces ready for a fresh coat of polish.

Removing white heat rings from timber

The milky-coloured heat rings that sometimes appear on timber surfaces form when excessive heat allows moisture to penetrate the surface of the finish and form a cloudy stain.

There are plenty of home remedies for these marks around; each of these solutions may work to varying degrees but they're all based on the same principle, combining oil and a fine abrasive. The oil will work its way into the surface and force out any moisture and the abrasive polishes the surface. Here's what to do:

1. Try applying some cooking oil to the mark and massage it into the timber with your finger tips for a few minutes; you may have to rub vigorously to build up a little heat.
2. If this doesn't work straight away, you may have to use some super fine 0000 steel wool and work the oil in. Make sure you rub with the direction of the grain and gently apply a little extra heat with a hair dryer.
3. If this solution hasn't worked for you, it may mean the damage has penetrated a little too deeply into the finish. A product such as Liberon Ring Remover may be worth trying before considering a refinish on the table.
4. Once the mark is removed, you'll need to wax to return a sheen to the tabletop.

Restoring timber furniture

In my opinion, there's nothing more satisfying than seeing an old piece of timber furniture brought back to its former glory through restoration. Here's a step-by-step guide to how to do it.

These instructions assume your furniture is solid, the joints are firm and no parts are missing—if you do have problems in this area, the answer may be found elsewhere in this chapter. Usually, most old timber furniture has been painted or varnished, so you'll need to remove this first. If your piece has no coating at all, count yourself lucky!

My main piece of advice is don't be too heavy handed. An old piece that's been completely stripped, sanded and refinished will often come up looking like it's brand new—but what's the point? If this is the look you're after you may as well save yourself the time and trouble and buy new furniture. The secret is retaining the history—that's what makes old furniture interesting.

Which solvent to use?

You may have to test a few solvents to see what type of stripping chemical will be required:

- Traditional old shellac is easily removed with the aid of methylated spirits. Apply the metho with fine steel wool or a synthetic abrasive pad; some gentle rubbing will soon soften and dissolve it.

- Nitrocellulose lacquers were popular with furniture manufacturers in the middle part of the twentieth century; for these you'll need to use a lacquer thinner in much the same way as metho on shellac.
- For thick coatings of shellac or nitrocellulose lacquer and for most other finishes a paint stripper may be required—this is painted on with a brush and left to react for about ten minutes before scraping off the excess and scrubbing away the residue with steel wool soaked in metho, or on bigger jobs metho mixed with warm soapy water.

 WHAT YOU NEED

- appropriate solvent (if the piece has paint or varnish on it)
- old paintbrush (it's OK to use one that's gone a bit stiff)*
- paint scrapers—standard and profile
- medium and fine steel wool
- methylated spirits
- bucket of warm soapy water
- rags
- medium and fine wet and dry sandpaper
- electric sander if you like.

* I always have a couple of paintbrushes that have gone a bit stiff lying around, so I'll use one of these to paint on the stripper and that way I'll soften and save the brush as well.

 WHAT TO DO

1. Remove any existing paint or vanish with the appropriate solvent—make sure you wear protective gloves for this. If there's inadequate ventilation where you are working make sure you wear a respirator.

In the case of paint stripper, make sure you let it soak in and do its job; don't be tempted to take it off as soon as you see the old coatings bubble, but don't leave it on the job too long.

2. Time for some scraping. For flat surfaces like tabletops and square stool legs, use a standard straight-edged scraper. Starting at one edge, carefully scrape away the stripper (and old paint or varnish). Keep the scraper at a maximum 45 degree angle and make sure you use a smooth continuous movement so you don't scratch your timber. Wipe the paint scrapings onto a piece of old newspaper for easy disposal.

3. Use a profile scraper (which has a point sticking out sideways at the top and concave semi-circle on the side) for corners, curved sections and hard-to-get-at details. Spray the scraper with cooking oil before starting for easier removal. If you tilt the semi-circled part of the scraper at an angle it can be made to fit a range of outwardly curved shapes. Again, be careful not to jab or press too hard. Another handy tool for hard-to-get-at spots can be made from a small section cut from a wire brush.

4. After you've removed what you can with the scrapers, the remaining stripper and old finish can be removed with a pad of 00 grade steel

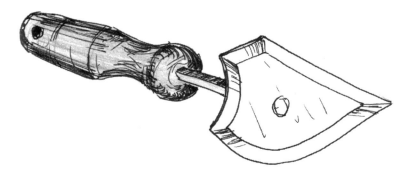

A profile scraper

wool soaked in metho. (For big jobs like a wardrobe or dining table you can use coarser steel wool like grade 1 and a mix of metho and warm, slightly soapy water.) Mix up half a bucket full of water and half a litre of metho and use the steel wool to scrub away the residue of the old finish, wiping off the excess with a rag while it's still wet.

5. You'll most likely find a few spots that will need an extra application of stripper. If there's still paint and varnish on the piece once you've been over it with the scraper, you may need to repeat the process, but only on the stubborn bits of the old finish.

6. Once the timber dries, any remaining dark spots can be removed with sanding, but don't get too carried away—you don't want to remove ALL the little stains and dings! The idea is that if you've done a good job stripping, then you only need to do a fine smoothing sand (no coarser than about 220 grit), avoiding the dangerous scratches you can get from coarse sandpaper. There's a great range of soft sanding pads and sponges available at hardware stores these days that are great for sanding shapes and details. You can use an electric sander for the flat areas but remember that orbital sanders will leave pigtails (small spiral marks made by the circular motion of the sander) that have to be removed with a final hand sanding. Once you've worked your way down to the fine-grade sandpaper (400 to 600 is ideal), clean to remove all the dust.

7. There's a range of ways you can finish your furniture—the decision will be dependent upon its use. Items such as tables and benches that are used for food preparation or eating, or that cop a lot of wear and tear like drink spills, will need a protective coating such as a satin polyurethane, which will mean it's washable and reasonably spillproof while still retaining that lovely natural timber look.

Have a look at Chapter 13, 'Painting and other finishes' for info on the different types of finishes you can choose.

Fixing chairs

Each chair is different and has its own unique problems. In fact there are so many different types of chairs out there that it would be impossible to give one set of repair instructions to cover all the bases. But here's one fix-it which will be applicable to a number of chair styles.

Loose joints on timber chairs

A typical chair has at least 20 joints, and each is a potential stress point that may weaken through age and use. If a single joint becomes loose, all the others will be subjected to extra stress and will eventually become loose as well. So even if you aren't attempting a full restoration you will still need to fix joints that have come loose on a favourite chair before it really does need restoration—or collapses underneath you.

 WHAT YOU NEED

- rubber mallet
- scraper or chisel
- sandpaper
- glue
- clamp or tourniquet.

 WHAT TO DO

1. If your chair has only one or two loose joints, just pull these open for repair—don't dismantle the entire chair. You may need to tap them apart gently with a rubber mallet.

2. Remove as much of the old glue as possible before regluing. Use the edge of a blade to scrape away glue residue from the tenon; a small sharp chisel may be necessary to clean out the mortice. (The tenon is the tongue of wood in a common joint that fits into a corresponding hole, called the mortice.) Finish your glue removal with some light sanding.
3. Once the joint is cleaned it can be reglued. Grab yourself some good-quality woodworker's glue (a cross-linking PVA or 'yellow' glue is good as it will retain some flexibility once dry). Apply the glue to both the mortice and the tenon and spread it before pushing the parts back together and clamping tight.
4. If you don't have clamps, a simple tourniquet clamp will do the job very nicely. It consists of a piece of soft rope-like sash cord and a short stick. This clamp will tighten all four legs at once. Wrap the cord around the legs twice, then tie it off. Slip the stick between the rope strands and slowly rotate it around in circles. Keep twisting the rope tighter and tighter until the joints on the furniture are drawn together. To prevent the rope from unwinding, rest the stick against one of the stretchers or rungs.
5. With a slightly damp rag, wipe away any glue that squeezes out of the joint. Turn the chair back onto its legs, place it on a flat surface and stack it with some heavy objects; that way the joints will dry with all the feet touching the ground. Leave it overnight to dry.

This technique can also be applied to timber beds and tables that have the wobbles.

STRAP CLAMP
A strap clamp (a more professional version of a tourniquet clamp) will set you back about $40 but it's still a lot cheaper than paying someone else to do the job. You can use strap clamps for tightening picture frames, tightening wobbly chairs and making boxes.

Using tourniquets to tighten chairs that have been glued

Fixing creaky wardrobe doors

Creaky timbers in furniture are a bit like creaky floorboards—the sounds are caused by surfaces rubbing together and the solution is to either eliminate the movement or lubricate the surfaces. Try these solutions:

■ Paraffin candle wax is an excellent lubricant to put between rubbing timber surfaces in furniture. Try rubbing a tealight candle on the edges of the doors; pull out the shelves and wax their edges, and if the drawers have timber runners then wax these as well. The wax on the drawer runners will make them slide a lot better as well. Some older wardrobes can be dismantled, so you should wax between all these joints as well.

■ If there are any joints you can't get a candle into, try working in a little talcum powder. The talcum powder is good for wooden chairs and beds as well. Just be warned that if you eliminate all of the creaks and groans you'll no longer be able to blame the wardrobe after you've been eating baked beans.

Fixing timber veneer that's lifting

If the top of your timber veneer is lifting off, squeeze PVA under the lifting laminate—you can use a syringe to get it in there—and make sure you wipe off the excess glue. Place a layer of cling wrap over the repair and then press it down overnight with some heavy books or a clamp.

A NOTE ABOUT BOOKSHELVES
A really important thing to do if you have freestanding bookshelves is to check if there's a chance that they could be unstable, especially on uneven flooring. Once fully stacked, they'll be very heavy—and heavy and unstable can be a fatal combination. Freestanding bookshelves should always be chocked under the feet to keep them level and plumb, and wherever possible tall units should be attached to the wall with one or two small metal angle brackets screwed to the wall at the top. The angle should run up the wall and out so that the unit will hide the wall-mounted part once it's repositioned. Finally, screw the other part of the angle to the top of the unit.

Cane and bamboo furniture

Give your old cane and bamboo furniture a wash with some warm soapy water and a pot scrubbing brush. Once it's dried, you can repair areas of loose reed with good-quality PVA exterior wood glue.

If you need it, replacement reed can be sourced through cane and bamboo specialists. Soak the reed in water to make it more flexible, then wrap it around joints, holding it in place with wood glue and clamps. Wood glue and clamps may also be used to repair areas of bamboo that are beginning to split.

To condition and refinish the surface without making it too glossy looking, give it a coat of tung oil mixed 50/50 with orange oil. This mix can be added to a plastic spray bottle and liberally applied to all the surfaces. Let it sit for a few minutes and then buff off any excess with a soft rag. Repeat this protective treatment from time to time to help keep it in good nick.

Bamboo structures will survive outside conditions better than cane, and their life can be extended with the application of high-quality mould and UV-inhibiting coatings such as Sikkens.

For information about fixing metal furniture, check out 'Removing rust from outdoor metal' in Chapter 15, 'Your garden and yard'.

Chapter 11
WET AREAS

I've lumped the 'wet areas' of kitchens, bathrooms and laundries together in this chapter as they do tend to suffer the same 'issues'. Hopefully you'll find an answer to your soggy problems here! For plumbing matters, see Chapter 12, 'Plumbing and electrical', as that's a whole other kettle of fish!

Tiling

Tiling is a common job to take on in the wet areas of your home and can be very challenging for even experienced DIYers. If not done well, the results can be uneven and messy, and tiles may start to come loose and fall off. Tiles can be laid over a broad range of new surfaces if the right preparations and materials are used. If you have some new surface areas that you've decided to tile yourself, seek as much advice as you can from tile and tile adhesive manufacturers about surface preparation and selecting the correct adhesives.

If your interests lie just in maintaining or improving your existing wet areas rather than extending or completely renovating them, then you may find some of the following fix-its useful.

Cleaning and repairing grout

Here's how to clean grout:

SOLUTION ONE

1. Clean it with grout cleaner and a grout brush (a stiff plastic bristled brush). Apply the cleaner, wait 20 minutes and repeat the process before rinsing.
2. Once the grout dries out, you'll have to reseal it with grout sealer; ask the hardware store for the correct sealer for your grout. You can apply the sealer with a medium-sized artist brush; once dry, the sealer will help protect the grout from staining in the future.

SOLUTION TWO

If this doesn't work or you're looking for a quick-fix solution, the grout can be painted. The special paint for the job is only available in white and comes in a 'grout pen' that looks like a marker pen. It costs around $15 from the hardware store, and you'll probably need two coats for a good result. By delivering the paint through the tip of a pen it can easily be controlled and applied to just the grout lines. The other good use for one of these pens is to touch up small chips in melamine kitchen cabinets.

SOLUTION THREE

If the grout needs replacing, here's how to do it:

1. Remove the grout from around the tiles with a grout rake (from the hardware store). A grout rake is an inexpensive little tool with a handle attached and a short blade with a coarse edge. It's designed to grind

away the old grout. This is probably the most difficult part of the job, so be patient!

2. Once you've removed all the old grout you can rub premixed acrylic-based grout into the space around the tile and shape it with a damp sponge and then leave it to dry. These products usually come in a range of colours.

3. The grout will take a couple of days to dry so try not to get it wet during this time.

4. If you've used a cement-based grout you'll need to waterproof it, so paint on some grout sealer with a small paintbrush.

ACRYLIC GROUT
Acrylic grouts with no added cement are much more flexible than standard grouts and are ideal for repairing old damaged grout (by just overcoating), or for using on tiles that have been laid directly over timber and so move more than they normally should.

Removing grout from tiles

The excess grout haze on the glazed surface of tiles is not hard to remove: just polish it off with a dry rag—old pieces of terry towelling are very effective. If the grout is thick or has become too hard, try a nylon scourer with water, followed up with the cloth. Finally, if you still have no joy, purchase a grout haze removal product like Aqua Mix phosphoric acid cleaner; you'll find it at tiling shops. Soak the affected area with water first, and then apply the mix and scrub with the nylon scourer.

Replacing a cracked or damaged tile

If the wall behind the tile is sound and has no sign of water damage, then the repair is relatively simple. Whether a tile is cracked or damaged or has come loose (or you'd just like to fit a few fancy feature tiles into an existing tiled wall), follow these steps.

 WHAT YOU NEED

- safety glasses and gloves
- grout rake (or an old hacksaw blade with a handle attached)
- power drill with masonry drill bits
- hammer
- cold chisel
- scraper
- tile spacers (or matchsticks)
- ready-mixed tile adhesive
- ready-mixed grout
- waterproofing compound
- grout sealer
- sponge
- masking tape.

 WHAT TO DO

1. Remove the grout from around the tile, as detailed above.
2. Once the grout is removed, the tile can be removed (definitely wear your safety glasses for this part of the job). Place an 'X' of masking tape over the tile (this will prevent the tip of the drill bit from slipping across the surface of the tile). Drill a series of holes along the tape through the tile. Be sure not to drill into the wall underneath. Once there are holes in the tile it will be easier to

smash up with the hammer and cold chisel for removal. When breaking up the tile, start in the middle and work your way out to the edge.

3. Prise away all the broken tile parts. Beware—these could be as sharp as broken glass.
4. Scrape out as much of the old adhesive as you can and any remaining grout and clean out the hole with a vacuum cleaner.
5. If you're working within your shower area, it would be good practice to coat the newly exposed wall area with a waterproofing solution.
6. To glue in the new tile, you'll need cement-based adhesive. The trick is to use the right amount of adhesive so the tile sits flush with the others. Apply the adhesive to the back of the new tile but not to the wall. Put a little more on than you think necessary, but only in the centre of the tile. Leave an unglued border of about 25 mm around the tile to allow the adhesive to spread once it's pushed into place.
7. Place the tile in the hole and push it in until it sits flush. Remove any adhesive that's been squeezed into the space around the tile and then push in some tile spacers to keep it in the right position. I often find that matchsticks are good for both removing extra glue and acting as spacers (just be careful not to glue them in).
8. Once you're satisfied with the position of the tile, use some masking tape to hold it in place and then leave it for the specified time for the adhesive to dry. It could take a day or so to dry properly, so if you don't have a spare bathroom you may need to tape a plastic cover over the job to protect it from the shower.
9. Once the new tile is set, the tape and spacers can be removed.
10. Now regrout the tile (see above).

There are many different types of tiles and adhesives, so check with your local tiling shop or hardware store.

Cutting tiles

Tiles can be cut with a tile scriber. Here's how:

1. On the face of the tile, mark the position of the cut then place it face up on a solid surface.
2. Place a steel rule on the tile and line up the edge with your mark.
3. When you're happy with the positioning, use the tile scriber to firmly score the tile from edge to edge.
4. Once you've scored the tile, grab a flat piece of wood (even a chopping board will do). Cut a thin stiff piece of wire from the bottom of a coathanger and place it across the board.
5. Position the tile face up onto the board, lining up the wire with the score mark on the tile. Once it's positioned correctly, apply pressure to both edges of the tile at the same time; the tile should break along the score mark, leaving a clean cut.

Remember to wear gloves while making the break, as the edges can be as sharp as broken glass.

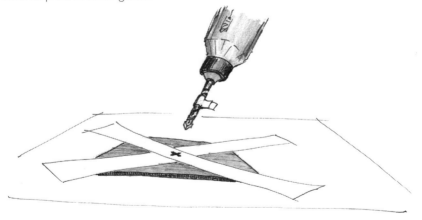

Preparing a tile for drilling

Attaching a towel rail (or other fittings) to a tiled wall

If you need to attach a towel rail in your bathroom or some hooks in your kitchen splashback, then you'll have to take care not to crack the tiles. Here's how:

1. Mark the positions of holes to be drilled and then place a cross of masking tape over the spot.
2. For most tiles a regular carbide (masonry) bit works fine, but for glass or hard ceramic tiles you'll need a special glass and tile drill bit. Do not use a hammer drill, as the rapid vibrations can crack the tile. The trick is to use a slow drilling speed and minimal pressure to carefully grind through the surface of the thin glaze. Once the bit gets into the softer core, the drill will rapidly cut through.
3. Insert the appropriate wall anchors into the holes before screwing in the mount. (See Chapter 6, 'Walls and ceilings', for information about wall anchors.) Equal care should be taken when driving in the screw: set your cordless drill onto a low torque setting or use a good old hand screwdriver and don't overtighten.

Preparing a painted surface for tiling

If you have a painted area in your bathroom, laundry or kitchen that you want to tile over, it's important to make sure your tiles are going to stick to the wall surface. First, test whether the wall has been painted with water-based or oil-based (enamel) paint and whether the paint surface is firmly adhered to the wall (see Chapter 13, 'Painting and other finishes', on how to conduct these tests).

If the existing paint is water based and in good condition, you should be able to tile straight over it.

If the paint is oil based, you'll need to make some preparations:

- On a masonry wall, removing the paint is ideal but you don't really have to remove *all* the paint. Scrape the surface as best you can to remove everything that's loose or flaking.

- The rest of the surface will need to be roughened up, or scarified, in order to create a key for tile adhesive to grab hold of. Grab yourself a scutch hammer and work over the surface of the wall until you've created a surface that's covered in little divots. Then tile over that surface.
- If the enamel-painted wall is a stud frame construction with a wall board surface (plasterboard, fibre cement, etc), you won't be wanting to bash away at it with a scutch hammer! A good base for tiling can be achieved by coating the wall with a two-part bonding primer.
- Alternatively, you can install a new surface of fibre cement over the painted wall and then tile over this. As always, it's advisable to seek a recommendation from your local tiling shop as to the best type of adhesive to use in each situation.

Tiling over tiles

New tiles can be laid directly over your old tiles provided the old ones are not drummy (i.e. when you tap them they don't sound hollow, as if they've lifted from the wall) or loose. The surface should be well cleaned and, once again, applying bonding primer is advisable. Wherever possible, try to lay the new tiles in such a way that the joins between the new tiles are not over the joins in the existing ones.

Getting rid of mildew on walls

The number one job that will make the world of difference in many bathrooms and laundries is painting out old mildew stains. These occur on the ceiling and the tops of the walls where condensation leaves the sur-

face wet after a shower. Getting rid of the mildew is a two-step process:
1. Clean off what you can and kill the spores with a bleach solution.
2. Cover the stains with a good-quality acrylic paint; use low sheen or semi-gloss and ask your paintshop for an anti-mould additive. If you want a flat finish, buy a paint that's formulated to resist mould and mildew like Zinsser.

Remember that good ventilation is important to prevent condensation and help solve the problem long term, so make sure you have an exhaust fan that works.

Replacing grubby silicone

Mildew stains can affect the silicone seals in wet areas—like where the bath meets the wall or where your kitchen bench meets the splashback. Sometimes the edges of the seal develop a little black line where moisture has obviously worked its way just under the edge of the silicone and harboured the mildew growth. The answer is to remove and replace the old silicone with a new mould-resistant one:
1. Cut away as much of the old silicone bead as you can, using a utility knife.
2. Using a scraper, apply silicone remover over the rest of the old silicone, spreading it about 5 mm thick.
3. Wait about two hours and then you can remove the now-softened old material with the scraper. Clean up the area with a cloth soaked in methylated spirits. You're now ready to apply a new seal.
4. Use a caulking gun to apply an even bead of silicone along the entire joint. Give the bead a good spray of window cleaner and then put your hand inside an old plastic bag or a latex glove before wiping away the excess with the tip of your finger. Only wipe it once. The window

cleaner on both sides of the bead will stop the silicone spreading up the wall, and the plastic bag will collect the excess for easy disposal. You can mask up with masking tape if you're concerned about getting a super-straight line, much as you would when painting. You can also wipe an ice cube along the silicone for a professional, smooth finish.

Fixing a sliding glass screen door

For one period of my life (let's call it the 'renting days'), it seemed like every house I lived in had a shower recess with one of those sliding,

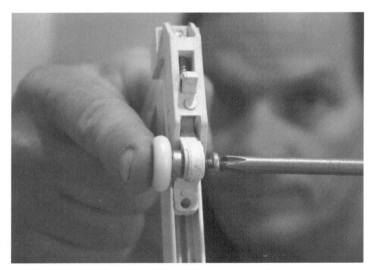

You may need to adjust the rollers on your shower screen

three-panelled glass shower screens which never actually slid. They fell off, got stuck and got very, very grubby. If you're unlucky enough to have one like that in your home, here's how to fix it!

1. Lift the doors of the sliding screen from their track and check to see if their fouled up by some kind of debris.
2. Remove the doors. These often run on rollers that run along the upper track, so to remove the screen you'll have to lift it till the roller comes free and the base can be pulled free of the bottom guide track.
3. Once both doors are removed, give all the rollers a good spray of WD-40 to loosen the adjusting screws and soften any muck. While this works its way in, give the top and bottom track a good clean and polish.
4. Clean and check the roller mechanisms for damage or corrosion and, if need be, remove and replace them. Your local hardware store or plumbing centre should be able to locate replacements for you.
5. Once the rollers have been cleaned or replaced, the doors can be lifted back and the roller mechanism adjusted so that the bottom of the doors do not drag or catch on the base track.

Rejuvenating an enamel bath

Plumbing supply specialists sell enamel repair kits if you want to have a go at fixing the chips in your bath yourself. Or you can just use an epoxy resin filler.

To resurface your entire bath (or hand basin), rub the surface smooth with fine abrasive paper and then coat the area with two coats of matching bath epoxy paint, such as Tub 'n' Tile Epoxy Enamel. This is an epoxy enamel paint that's tough enough to recolour the bath.

You can use it also on the entire surface of the grout and tiles and around a shower or bath. Use these products in combination with a grout pen to re-colour an entire tiled wall, then re-whiten the grout lines.

Rejuvenating an acrylic bath

If you have a small scratch in an acrylic bath, you can remove it by polishing with abrasive metal polish (e.g. Brasso). You can't use this on a fibreglass bath, however. If the scratch is slightly deeper, sand it out first with very fine wet and dry sandpaper, then move onto the Brasso.

TREATING TIMBER SURFACES IN WET AREAS
If you have a timber vanity unit or kitchen bench, you'll want to make sure it's protected from water damage. I suggest sanding the timber and finishing with tung oil. You may also need the tough protection of a polyurethane coating. Apply some initial coats of tung oil diluted at least 50/50 with pure gum turps. The tung oil can be over coated with the straight polyurethane, but for a smooth, easy-to-apply finish blend some more tung oil with the polyurethane. Use straight polyurethane only for the final coat.

Chapter 12
ELECTRICAL AND PLUMBING

Electrical

It's not a good idea for the home handyperson to mess around with any major electrical job; I'd recommend that for *most* fix-its you should call a qualified electrician. There are, however, a few small things you can tackle yourself and in this chapter we'll look at these, as well as offering some 'illumination' on the area of household circuitry. Also make sure you check out Chapter 5, 'Making your home more energy efficient' for lots of proactive things you can do to reduce your electricity consumption.

About circuits, watts, amps, fuses and your fusebox

I'm always surprised how few people know how the electrical system in their house works, so (with apologies to those of you who *do* know) here's a brief rundown.

Many houses have several 10 amp or 15 amp circuits, and each circuit may service several power outlets. If a circuit is 10 amp, you can run no more than 2400 watts on that circuit. If you exceed 2400 watts on one (240 volt) 10 amp circuit, you'll trip circuit-breakers, blow fuses or, worse, start a fire inside the walls. If you have 15 amp circuits you can increase the load to 3600 watts. If you're having problems with your fuses, or constantly setting off the circuit-breaker, you may have too many appliances plugged into the one circuit; alternatively, it may be a faulty appliance or the wiring itself may have a fault—namely a short-circuit.

Fixing a blown fuse

If you haven't already, find your fuse box and have a good look inside it! If your fuse box still contains the old ceramic or wire fuses, plan to upgrade to the newer circuit-breaker style of box. In the meantime be sure you have some spare fuse wire, a small flat head screwdriver, a torch and a pair of wire cutters stored in the fuse box for repairs. To repair the fuse box:

1. Turn off the main switch.
2. Pull out the fuse that has the melted or burnt wire.

3. Remove the old wire.
4. Look at the fuse rating on the front of the fuse holder; it will be in amps. Only use the right thickness of wire for that fuse.
5. Secure the end of the new piece of wire around one terminal screw; it should be wrapped around in a clockwise direction so that the screw tightens the wire as it's tightened.
6. Feed the wire through the hole in the centre of the ceramic fuse block and secure the other end to the other terminal screw.
7. Put the fuse block back in and turn the main switch back on.

Never be tempted to use a fuse wire that's thicker than specified for each fuse block or you may be at risk of causing a fire.

BETTER SWITCHES
If you can't afford to have the old ceramic fuses replaced with professionally installed modern safety switches, the ceramic fuse blocks can at least be replaced with plug-in breaker switches, available from the hardware store. These are designed to be slotted into the existing ceramic block mounting.

For some extra back-up, try to use powerboards with special safety features like a breaker switch. Some new powerboards, like the HPM child-safe powerboard, have the added feature of covers that prevent children inserting objects into unused sockets.

If you have circuit-breakers in your fuse box you can't replace the fuses, and in fact you don't need to (because if there's an overload on the system a switch will be tripped off, rather than the fuse burning through). However, you should test the circuit-breakers occasionally to ensure they're functioning correctly. There should be a test button in the fuse box that will set the breaker off when depressed; if it doesn't work, it'll need to be checked by a licensed electrician.

If a fuse keeps tripping or blowing, you could have a faulty appliance or a damaged circuit wire. Different parts of the house and different appliances are controlled by different circuits or fuses; they should be marked in the fuse box (e.g. 'power kitchen', 'lights kitchen'). Look at the appliances that are plugged into the circuit that keeps tripping, and by a process of elimination you should be able to find the offending item and remove it. If the circuit continues to trip after testing all the appliances, you know who to call.

Illumination

Or . . . how many DIYers does it take to change a lightbulb?

Answer: depends on the lightbulb. It may be obvious, but there are three important things when changing a lightbulb:

- Make sure the power is turned off before touching the fitting.
- Make sure you have the correct type of fitting before you start, with the appropriate wattage, i.e. is it a screw-in bulb or bayonet fitting, frosted or clear, 60W or 20W?
- If it's a light fitting high up, stand on something stable and make sure someone else is there to take the old globe from you and secure whatever it is you're standing on!

Types of bulbs

Traditionally all our homes featured incandescent lightbulbs with the odd old fluoro tube thrown in. Because of their relatively poor luminous efficacy, incandescent lightbulbs are gradually being replaced by more compact stylish fluorescent lights—either energy-saving CFLs (compact fluorescent lightbulbs), halogen lights or LEDs. Your average incandescent lightbulb uses only 10 per cent of the power it consumes in making light; the other 90 per cent is used up in heat output!

HALOGEN LAMPS

Halogen lamps are bulbs where a tungsten filament is sealed into a small envelope filled with halogen gas. They last roughly twice as long as incandescent bulbs and prices are coming down. Some halogen lights can be run from the full 240 voltage of your home's lighting circuits, but most common are the low 12-volt style, which use a transformer to convert the full power down to 12 volt. Transformers are often plugged in and then the 12 volt output from there is safely handled by a DIYer, which makes these systems possible to install yourself once an electrician has supplied the initial outlet. Most outdoor and garden lighting systems use low-voltage halogens, making them terrific DIY projects.

CFLs

By changing to low-energy bulbs you not only save on lighting power but also on cooling power! Some people believe that the power needed to turn on a fluorescent light exceeds the power to run it for a long period of time. This is a myth—it's best to always turn off lights that aren't needed.

It's also believed that CFLs can't be run in fittings with a dimmer switch. In fact some new CFLs can be run on dimmers but not all, so check the label before fitting. The other complaint is about the cold ghostly light these things give out, but they're now available in 'warm white' varieties. There are now even CFLs designed to replace the halogen downlights in low-voltage units. All manner of shapes and sizes of

Now here's a bright (CFL) idea!

CFLs are becoming available in the US and will soon be available here as incandescent lightbulbs are gradually phased out.

LEDs

LED lights are known as solid-state lighting (SSL). They are moderately efficient, have a long lifetime but are relatively expensive and not widely available. Technological advances mean that they will soon increase in efficiency and decrease in cost. Watch this space.

Removing a broken lightbulb

Lightbulbs can be accidentally smashed, sometimes the glass comes away when you're trying to change them, and sometimes they even explode—all of which leave you with the tricky situation of having the metal base still stuck in the light fitting. To deal with this:

- Be sure to not only turn off the switch but disconnect the power, or turn it off at the fuse box.
- Wear protective gloves and safety glasses if working on a ceiling light.
- Try to insert a rubber ball to get a grip on the base and twist it out.
- If this fails, a pair of insulated pliers should be used. Standard pliers can be pushed into the fitting and then the handles spread to grip the inside of the fitting, or needle-nosed pliers can be fed down one edge of the bulb base to grip it.
- Twist it out carefully; don't force it.
- If the base has become stuck, it will need to be jiggled loose rather than broken with force.
- When a new bulb is fitted, a little spray of WD-40 on the fitting will make it easier to remove next time.

Changing a 'starter' and tube on a fluorescent light

Fluorescents also have their tricks of the trade:

- As always, turn the light off before replacing anything.

- Remove the tube by holding the ends of it and rotating it roughly 90 degrees or until the end of the tube can be pulled down and away from the fitting.
- You'll notice the pair of pins on the end of the tube will have aligned with a little slot in the mounting to allow the tube to come free.
- Under the tube in the metal casing of the light you'll notice a small plastic cylinder inserted into a hole. This is the starter; the end of this must be gripped and twisted about 40 degrees in an anti-clockwise direction to remove it.
- Any hardware store or supermarket will have replacement tubes and starters. Reverse the process to fit the new ones, being sure not to over-twist the tube when it's replaced or it may come right back out again.
- It's good practice to replace both the tube and starter at once for trouble-free, energy-efficient lighting.

Plumbing

I've always fancied myself as a bit of an amateur plumber—the underground maze of poly, PVC and galvanised pipes at my weekender in Mudgee attests to this. But the reality is that most plumbing jobs should be left for a qualified plumber—I've certainly learnt my lesson over the years when I've tried to do something myself and ended up having to sheepishly explain to our bemused plumber about the mess I've made.

These days the traditional domain of the DIYer is being eroded by new regulations and more complex fittings, and in the case of changing a washer or fixing a leaky toilet cistern and many other potential DIY plumbing jobs it's now regulation that it be left to the plumber to handle. I've included these and some other simple processes purely for those who are interested to know how it's done.

Scott and some of the more practical plumbing installations at Ruwenzori

Dripping taps

It may sound obvious, but it's likely you just need to change the washer:
1. Turn off the water at the mains tap.
2. Turn the tap full on and put the plug in the sink so you don't lose any 'bits'.
3. Unscrew the cover of the tap. Usually you can do this by hand but you may need to use a spanner or pipe wrench if it's stiff; be careful not to damage the surface.
4. Lift off the handle with the cover (also called the headgear).
5. Undo the headgear nut with a spanner. Don't force it if it's stiff—use penetrating oil around the joint, wait ten minutes and try again. The

jumper valve and washer will be resting on the valve seating. If there's a small nut holding the washer in place, unscrew it with a spanner. Prise off the washer from the jumper-valve plate; if the nut is fused closed you can replace the whole jumper valve and washer in one unit. After fitting the new washer, grease the threads on the base of the tap before reassembling.

6. Turn off the tap and turn on the mains supply.

Wait until the waterboard get a load of this!

Repairing leaky PVC pipes

PVC pipes are used for wastewater so any leaks should be fixed by a plumber, but you can do a temporarily fix-up using rubber inner tube wrapped around the leak held on with a hose clamp. If you have leaking copper or steel inlet pipes, call the plumber straight away and turn the water off at the inlet valve near the meter.

Another easy quick fix-it for leaking plumbing can be found in a can. Keep a can of spray-on leak stopper to stop leaks in non-pressurised pipes such as drains, under sinks, gutters and drain pipes.

FROZEN PIPES?
In spite of an increasingly warmer world there are still many parts of Australia that occasionally suffer from frozen metal water pipes. A temporary solution is to defrost them with a hairdryer. Could be time consuming, so for a more permanent thawing solution try wrapping your copper piping in fibreglass or foam rubber pipe insulation.

Water hammer

When you turn off a tap in your house do you hear a loud banging noise? This is called 'water hammer' and can be caused by loose pipework or a valve closing too quickly, or even by worn taps or tap washers. To deal with it, first have a look at as much of your pipework as you can. If any pipes are a bit loose then secure them with saddles screwed onto your bearers or joists. Then wrap tape around the section of pipe and the saddle to ensure it doesn't rattle. If this doesn't fix it or you can't get access to your pipes, call a plumber to fit a water hammer arrester.

Changing taps in your bathroom or laundry

Often a good way to update your bathroom is to change the taps. You may not need to change the entire tap; the handles alone are often interchangeable. If you do need to change the entire tap, most hardware stores carry a range of plumbing supplies and fittings to help you fit it onto the existing plumbing. A couple of tips:

- Take your old tap with you to ensure the correct fit.
- Buy some thread tape to seal your joins.
- When changing a tap, always ensure that you renew the red fibre washer that sits in the groove of the tap connector. The old one may not be recognisable as a washer, so just make sure the groove is clear and clean (use a sharp-pointed object to clean it out), then insert a new one.

Leaky shower recess

There could be a couple of causes for this:

- The taps could be leaking inside the wall cavity—remove the front cover of the taps and see if there's water leaking underneath. If so, you'll need to tighten the tap body with a spanner or replace the sealing ring, which is probably a job for your spanner (or the local pro).
- It the shower base is leaking, you may need to regrout. Also you can get a silicone-based grout sealing liquid which can be spread over the entire shower base to seal it.

Clearing a blocked trap

This is the curved section of pipe under your sink or the floor waste in your bathroom. It's the place you go (very quickly) when you've dropped your wedding (or nose) ring down the sink:

- If it becomes blocked, first try to unblock with a plunger (if it's a double sink make sure you close up one of the plugholes before plunging the other).
- If this doesn't work, remove the trap—you may need a plumbing wrench to loosen the plastic fitting if it hasn't been loosened for a while.
- Make sure you put a bowl or bucket underneath to catch any spills.
- Use a piece of flexible wire to clean it out, and make sure when you replace it you tighten the rings firmly.

DRAIN CLEANER
To keep your kitchen sink trap clear of soap scum, cooking fat and bits of other organic matter give it a pre-emptive shot of drain cleaner now and then. You can buy one, or send down your own brew: mix a half-cup of salt with a half-cup of baking soda in a half-cup of vinegar and pour it down; while it's still reacting, follow this with two litres of boiling water to flush it out.

Fixing a leaky loo

Often cisterns leak at an imperceptibly slow rate, not quite enough water for you to see clearly with the naked eye, but still many litres an hour. To check, add a coloured disinfectant tablet or even some food colouring to the water in the cistern, but don't flush the toilet for an hour or two. You'll be able to see if the water in the pan changes colour. If so, you have a leak!

The actual workings of cisterns vary a lot. If you go to your local plumbing trade outlet, rather than just a hardware store, you'll be able to get not only expert advice but any replacement parts required.

If you can't solve the issue yourself, it's well worth the cost of having a plumber come and look at it rather than waste thousands of litres of water every week. Make the most of their visit and have any old tap washers replaced at the same time.

MINERAL BUILD-UP
Minerals can build up in your shower head and tap aerators. To fix this, remove them and soak in white vinegar for a short while and use an old toothbrush and sharp toothpick to clean out any material still stuck in the spray holes.

Looking after your hot water system

If you live in an area with a lot of sediment in the water, you should flush out your hot water system once a year. If you have a gas hot water heater, make sure you check the flue pipe for leaks or blockages and ensure that the pilot light is clean and free from fluff. Every six months you should operate the pressure relief valve to make sure it's working properly.

Cleaning a pilot light

If your pilot light won't light, it might need cleaning:

- Turn off the gas and the electricity to the appliance.
- Remove the access panel after the unit has cooled down.
- Unscrew the bracket which holds the pilot light, then dismantle and clean with a cotton wool bud.
- Reassemble it. If it's still not working, call a plumber/gasfitter.

Also check out Chapter 5, 'Making your home more energy efficient' to see lots of good ways to reduce your water bills.

Chapter 13

PAINTING AND OTHER FINISHES

Painting is one of the main DIY jobs we do at home. It's a vast subject to talk about; just looking at the variety on the shelves of the average hardware shop is pretty daunting. Volumes have been written on the art of house painting, not to mention whole books on different fancy paint finishes. I'm going to focus on some of the main points to consider, and touch on some of my favourite painting and finishing tasks and tips.

Paintbrushes and rollers

Brushes

Always buy the best brush you can afford; buying cheap brushes is a false economy as they'll be more difficult to use, will tend to drop a lot of hairs in the paint, and simply won't give you very good coverage. Good-quality brushes give you a thicker, smoother finish of paint with fewer brush marks, and will last for years.

Generally brushes are available in two basic types:

- Traditional natural-bristle brushes are best for traditional oil-based paints (the bristles are porous and so tend to soak up water and swell).
- Synthetic-bristle brushes should be used to apply acrylic paints, but can also be used with oil-based products.

I suggest that a few high-quality synthetic brushes are all you will need for most paint jobs; here's a starter kit:

- 50 mm trim brush—for detail work
- 38 mm sash brush—these are angled at the tip for ease of cutting in
- 100 mm flat brush—for quick general wall coverage
- a fitch—a very small brush used for details and tight spaces between mouldings.

Rollers

As with brushes, it's worthwhile buying good-quality rollers as they'll hold more paint and give you better, smoother coverage. They also hold their shape from job to job, don't have obvious seams that will leave track marks in the paint surface, and don't have many loose fibres.

When selecting a roller you need to consider the size of the surface you're painting, the texture, and the type of paint you want to apply:

- Use only synthetic roller covers for acrylic paint—there's no need to splash out on lamb's wool sleeves for general household walls.
- A good general-purpose sized roller would be 270 mm, although 180 mm is useful for smaller rooms or touch-up jobs.

Nap length (i.e. the length of the surface pile on the roller) is also important. The general rule is that the smoother the surface the shorter the nap, the rougher the surface the longer the nap. On flat sur-faces it's also important to adjust the nap length according to the gloss level of the paint being applied: longer nap for flat paints and shorter for gloss.

> **MAKE IT EASIER . . .**
> To make using a roller a bit easier, use disposable inserts in your paint roller trays. These fit inside standard trays, and once excess paint is drained you just dry them out and throw them away.

Looking after your brushes and rollers

It's important to treat your brushes and rollers properly—here's some tips to follow:

- When you buy a new brush or roller, condition it before using it by flicking it across your hand a few times to loosen the bristles and then give it a clean with warm water and mild soap. Hang it out to dry.
- Just before using a brush, dampen it with whatever solvent matches the paint you'll be using. This means turpentine for enamel paint or water for acrylic paints.
- Never dip the brush more than about 2/3 of the bristle length into the paint.
- If you're painting with acrylic on a hot day, keep two brushes going at once; keep one soaking in water and every half an hour or so swap. This will prevent paint drying on the brush before you finish the job.
- When brushes are soaked they should be suspended and not allowed to rest on the tips of the bristles. An easy way to do this is to place an elastic band on a stick placed across the rim of the water bucket; when you want to suspend the brush simply feed the handle under the elastic.

How to hang a brush so you don't bend the bristles

- Clean brushes and rollers as soon as you've finished. Never leave them soaking in solvent for an extended period of time.
- Rollers should have all excess paint scraped off; you can purchase a special tool for this job from any paint store. You can also pick up a simple roller washing device that attaches to a hose and uses the water pressure to spin the roller—quickly and effectively washing the paint from a roller using the minimum amount of water. Make sure you collect the water in a bucket.
- Once all the paint has been rinsed from the brush or roller, it should once again be washed with some mild hand soap to remove all residues. Even brushes that have been washed in turps require a wash with soap and water to remove any remaining paint-stained turps from the bristles.
- Give brushes a final rinse with fabric conditioner.

- Once dry, brushes should be wrapped in paper or foil and stored flat to keep the bristle in shape. Place roller covers in a plastic bag and hang them up rather than letting them sit and develop a flat spot.

BRUSH REVIVER
If your brushes have gone hard with paint, you may be able to revive them by soaking in paint stripper until soft, rinsing in water and/or turps (using a brush comb or wire brush to scrape out the old paint if necessary) and then finishing with a good wash in warm, soapy water.

Types of paint

There are many types of paint—here are the basics.

Primers, sealers and primer-sealers
These coatings are applied over raw surfaces to prepare them for the finish coats of paint or clear finishes.

Primers are necessary to ensure better adhesion by sticking well to the surface and providing a 'tooth' for the subsequent layers of paint. They ensure longer-lasting and more durable topcoats and help reduce peeling and premature paint failure.

Sealers are designed to seal or hold moisture out of absorbent/porous surfaces such as timber, concrete or plaster. They're also used to block off stains from water, crayon, smoke, soot, ink and the tannins from woods that will bleed through a paint coating, e.g. cedar or knotty pine.

Primer-sealers are a combination product and are common as they combine the benefits of both primer and sealer in one product. They're necessary for preparing all porous surfaces and for previously painted surfaces that have been repaired or are in poor condition—flaking or peeling.

Undercoats

Undercoats are the layers of paint applied after the primer and before the finish coat. They're matt with a high content of pigment and extender. They have many functions—such as increasing the thickness of the overall film or hiding the colour of the primer or the previous layer on the existing surface—and they're generally tinted in a similar colour range as the topcoat.

Finish/topcoat paints

There are two main types of paints commonly used: acrylic and enamel. Acrylic paint is water based, whereas enamel paint is also known as oil-based paint.

ACRYLIC PAINTS:

- Are easy to use and give excellent, smooth results, particularly on expansive surfaces such as walls and ceilings.
- Have the advantage of clean-up with soap and water.
- Dry quickly, have less odour, are non-flammable and are easy to touch up.
- Remain more flexible and allow moisture to evaporate through the film, thus reducing blistering, cracking and peeling.

ENAMEL PAINTS:

- Are tough and hardwearing; they're intended for use in areas with higher levels of wear and tear, such as doors and skirting boards.

- Require a little more care in their application but can provide results and gloss levels superior to that of acrylics.
- Use strong solvent bases, which give off a lot of gases as they dry; they therefore should be well ventilated while wet.
- Take longer to dry and require paint thinners or turpentine for clean-up.
- Require extra care to store, as they're flammable.

OIL OR WATER?
The term 'enamel' is normally associated with paints that are oil based but beware as it can also be used to describe water-based paints with a gloss finish.

And then there are the different finishes

Flat. Dry to a non-reflective totally matte finish which is sophisticated and helps hide surface imperfections. They're normally used for ceilings and walls in areas not subjected to a lot of wear and tear, such as dining rooms and bedrooms. They're not the best paints if you have young kids, but certain brands boast that they're easy to keep clean.

Low-sheen. Also known as 'low-lustre' or even 'eggshell finish', they provide a soft sheen finish similar to that of an eggshell. A low-sheen finish provides a harder, more wash-and-wear kind of surface than a flat finish. This extra durability makes low-sheen paint a good choice for walls in children's rooms, hallways, stairways and family rooms.

Semi-gloss (or satin). These are very durable and even easier to clean and more stain resistant than low-sheen paints. Semi-gloss paints are most often used on heavier wear surfaces or areas that are frequently cleaned, such as kitchens and bathrooms, and also used on wood trim and cabinets.

Gloss. The hardest, most durable and stain resistant of paint finishes. It's the easiest to clean of all the paint finishes, but makes surface imperfections more noticeable. Gloss finishes are the best choice for the heaviest of wear areas such as furniture and cabinets, floors, stairs, handrails, doors and trim, and they provide a pronounced feature where desired.

Paint additives

Various additives can be mixed with paint to change or enhance its performance. Some common additives include:

- Mould inhibitor—to slow the growth of mildew in damp conditions such as bathrooms.
- Penetrating oils—which increase the bonding and coating ability of enamel paints and slow down the drying time in hot conditions.
- Emulsions—to help acrylic paints stick to dry and chalky surfaces.
- Flowing agents—to slow down the drying time of acrylic paint and make it easier to spread.

Others worth knowing about are: odour eliminators, fire retardants, non-slip granules, insulating additives and special effect mediums such as crackle medium.

Specialty paints

There are numerous specialty paints and other coatings for specific effects, but I don't have the pages to go into to detail. Here are some of my favourites.

Milk paint. Traditional milk paint is popular for its subtle colours and slightly mottled finish. It uses the protein (casein) in the milk as a natural binder.

Distemper. One of the simplest, most traditional interior paints, made by binding powdered chalk and pigments (it was originally bound with animal glue). Distemper dries to a soft, velvet-like texture that's dead flat and chalky in appearance.

Lime wash. A unique lime-based coating specifically designed to age with time to create a soft, weathered patina reminiscent of the houses of the Mediterranean and Tuscany.

Cement paint. A cement-based coating made from Portland cement designed to be very hard wearing and weather resistant, while at the same time creating a soft, mottled finish.

Metal effect paints. There are a number of liquid metal paints around, including copper and iron, designed to give a metallic finish to other surfaces. They're a special blend of heavy acrylic with pure ground metal solids suspended in a specially formulated air-curing water-base emulsion.

Black Japan. Traditional wood stain that's made from bitumen. It's a bit tricky to use but if you get it right the result is an unbeatable deep brown colour.

Painting—the basics

Preparing the surface is the key

Good surface preparation is at least 50 per cent of a quality paint job. It's also the boring, no-fun part—but really there's no gain without the pain. So make sure you *always*:

- Check the condition and bond of old paint by doing a tape test. This is done be making an X-shaped cut through the paint with a sharp utility knife and placing a piece of masking tape over it. Remove the tape straight away and then examine if paint has come away from the edges of your cuts. If it has, some extra surface preparation may be required, such as stripping or sanding.
- Clean the surface to be painted thoroughly; sugar soap is ideal for interior and exterior painted surfaces. Apply sugar soap with a sponge on interior walls; exterior walls may need the extra cleaning power of a scrubbing brush to remove dirt, moss and mildew. You may also consider using a high-pressure water cleaner on exterior walls; this will not only give the surfaces a good clean but will remove loose and flaking material (just beware if you have rendered walls that the pressure is not so high that it removes the render!). Make sure the surface is completely dry before you start painting.
- Remove or mask up any wall or ceiling fittings if possible, e.g. light fittings, light switches, powerpoint covers, and glass if you're painting windowframes.

EXTRA PROTECTION
Difficult-to-mask fittings can be protected with a coat of petroleum jelly. Simply wipe it away once the painting is over.

- Scrape and remove any remaining loose and flaking old paint from surfaces and sand, particularly if you're painting over gloss or semi-gloss paint surfaces, to ensure the new paint adheres to the old.
- Similarly, sand off any lumps or bumps.
- Fill any surface gaps or cracks, and then sand these to ensure a smooth finish. Fill any edge gaps with a flexible caulking compound.

- Remove all dust from the entire area before you start. Use a VERY slightly damp cloth to ensure every speck of dust has been removed and then wait for it to dry. Vacuum and mop the floor as well so no dust flies up and settles on your handiwork!

Pick the right weather!

The weather can make all the difference to the quality of the job:

- Don't attempt a paint job if it's very hot (over 35°C) or very cold (under 10°C), or if it's raining or super-humid.
- If you're painting outside, don't attempt it in the evenings (after dew point) as there'll be too much moisture in the air.
- If you live somewhere where it's ALWAYS hot, you can buy a hot weather additive to add to your paint which will ensure it has a slower drying time.
- Save your exterior painting for the spring or autumn months.
- Try to follow the shade; painting in the shade will be easier on your paint and easier on your body.

> STOP PAINT BUILD-UP
> To stop paint building up around the lip of the tin when you're painting, punch some small nail holes through the lip so the paint drains back into the tin. Place a layer of plastic wrap over the tin before you close it to improve the seal and make opening it easier next time.

Where to start painting

With walls and ceilings, always start your paint job by 'cutting in' around all the corners, edges, details and fittings with a brush, then finish up with a roller to cover the main flat surfaces.

PAINTING CEILINGS

Painting ceilings can be tricky, and if you're painting a whole room always start with the ceiling:

- Remove furniture from the room or cover it with drop sheets.
- Cover floors—if you have a lot of painting to tackle, purchase a good-quality canvas drop sheet. For one-off jobs inexpensive plastic drop sheet will be fine. You should use drop sheets even if you're painting walls.
- Painting overhead and on tall walls will be easier if you use a telescopic roller pole.
- Wear safety glasses to prevent paint drops from falling in your eyes; the safety glasses or your prescription specs can be protected from paint by stretching cling wrap over them. VERY attractive.
- To protect your hair from paint, wear an old hat or a disposable shower cap (even MORE attractive), and to keep paint from sticking to your hands and face rub a layer of petroleum jelly over them before you start.
- Make sure you don't answer the door looking like this.

Ceilings are often painted with white ceiling paint, although when painting new white over old white it can be difficult to see what areas you've already covered. Some new ceiling paints are pink in appearance when they're wet to assist with this, but don't worry, they dry white. An interior decorator friend of mine gave me a good tip: if you want to have pale walls and ceiling, but not stark white, choose a pale shade for the ceiling and then double strength of the same shade for the walls. Very effective.

'Horses for courses' (or understanding the surface you want to paint)

Understanding the type of surface you're attempting to paint and selecting the right equipment and paints for the job is vital. Here's the low-down on how to attack some of the more common surfaces.

MAKE YOUR OWN PAINT TIN HOLDER

If you're working high on a ladder painting, it's always a problem as to what to do with the paint tin. You make a simple holder like this:

- Take a piece of dowel or an old broomstick and put it through the top rung.
- Attach firmly with tape, rope or wire.
- Cut a small V-shaped groove into one end of the dowel.
- Put the handle of the paint tin into the groove.

A DIY paint tin holder

PAINTING PLASTERBOARD

Plasterboard (often referred to by the brand name Gyprock) or plastered walls are the most likely surface you'll find yourself painting, whether it's applying a new colour to an entire room or creating a dramatic feature wall.

Acrylic paint is the best choice for interiors, applied with a brush and roller. In most cases, interior plasterboard walls are painted with a flat or low-sheen finish. A roller cover with a 10–12 mm nap (the length of fibres) is ideal.

If the walls have been painted before, the new colour can go straight over the old (once prepared as detailed above) unless you're making a radical colour change, in which case you should apply an undercoat. Undercoats can be tinted, which will give you a better chance of getting the topcoat colour looking nice and solid. Your paint supplier can give you advice on tinting your undercoat to a shade that's right for your topcoat.

If it's new (i.e. unpainted) plasterboard work, the first coat applied should be a plasterboard sealer. The sealer evens out the porosity of the plasterboard and provides a key for subsequent paint.

Usually you'd apply two coats of paint after you've applied the sealer and/or undercoat. For very bright or dark colours you may you need three.

PAINTING TIMBER

Probably the second most common surface you may find yourself painting is timber—windowframes, doors, architraves, skirtings, floors, furniture and sometimes walls. In most situations there'll be an acrylic paint suitable for your timber, but on doors, doorframes and windowframes and areas that take a lot of knocks and bumps you still can't go past hard-wearing enamel paint. I like to apply paint to timber with a brush, as the subtle brush marks fit with the timber's grain.

If timber is unpainted:

1. Sand it smooth and clean away the dust.
2. Apply a coat of primer, such as PrepCoat. The tannins in timber knots will bleed out through your topcoat if not sealed, so use a knotting solution or coat the knots with shellac to seal them. If you're painting hardwood (usually used in floors, decking or structural timbers), which tend to be rich in tannins throughout, you'll need to seal it with an oil-based or shellac-based hardwood primer.
3. After the primer, any holes and blemishes in the timber will become more evident, so you can now fill them.
4. For internal timbers apply an undercoat and at least one topcoat. For external timbers apply at least two coats of modern exterior-grade acrylic paint, which requires no undercoating.

If timber has already been painted:

1. Work out if the original paintwork is acrylic or enamel paint. If you did not do the original paint job then this can be tricky! You need to do a test using a solvent to see what will dissolve the paint. Methylated spirits will dissolve acrylic paint but not enamel, so give the surface a good scrub with metho and see what happens. If the paint is acrylic, the paint will start to soften slightly after about a minute or so of rubbing, a small amount of it may come off on the rag or the surface will start to become slightly tacky. If the paint is enamel, neither of these things will happen.
2. If it's acrylic paint you can simply sand lightly and do any filling that's required, then paint the new coats of acrylic or enamel straight over the top. If you're sure it's enamel paint you can paint the walls again directly with enamel, but if you wish to change to an acrylic finish some precautions are necessary (see box).

Before repainting exterior timber work:

1. Remove all loose and flaking old paint.
2. Check and repair any rotten spots and fill any gaps with exterior-grade acrylic gap fillers.
3. Thoroughly clean the whole area.

PAINTING A TIMBER FENCE

I'd recommend applying a protective coating on your timber fence, either paint or oil. Without protection it will become dry and splintery or start to shrink and split, and protective coatings can also keep excess moisture out, warding off the onset of rot.

Acrylic on timber fences. Modern exterior acrylic paint formulations are so good now that priming is not necessary in most cases (though new treated pine should still be primed), and most of the best brands claim to last at least ten years. To paint an old, dried timber fence:

1. Wet the timber down. This will prevent the moisture being drawn too quickly from the new paint, though you must allow the excess water to dry off the surface before starting.
2. Use a bucket and sponge and a stiff scrubbing brush to remove any loose fibres, splinters and moss from the timber surface.
3. Dilute the first coat of paint with up to 10 per cent water to help it spread over the rough surface. Use two brushes to paint with; keep one in a bucket of water while you work with the other, and every half an hour or so swap the brushes so that the paint doesn't start to dry and harden too much in the bristles of the one you are using. Fence painting is one occasion where it's fine to use inexpensive brushes that can be disposed of when you've finished.
4. On hot sunny days, add a hot weather additive (available from paint stores) to subsequent coats to slow down the drying time.

HAVE A GOOD OLD SPRAY
For particularly large areas of fence, use an electric spray gun, which you can hire from equipment rental outlets. It's a lot easier to spray but you must protect the surrounding areas from overspray. Spread plastic sheeting over the ground and any trees or structures directly behind the fence. Practise your spraying technique on the most obscure part of the fence first. A series of short sharp bursts of the spray gun made with a horizontal sweeping action will give you better results than keeping your finger on the trigger constantly.

Oil on timber fences. Oils are easy to apply and will maintain the natural timber look. Any of the staining oil formulations that are sold for use on decks and outdoor furniture are also suitable for use on fences. Be aware, though, that the oil will burn off in the sun and will have to be applied fairly regularly to keep it at its best. If you oil an old fence that has already 'silvered off' in the sun it will turn the timber an almost black colour. To avoid this you'll have to prepare the timber with a timber wash product applied with a stiff scrubbing brush, which will help remove the old dried cells from the surface, removing the silvered layer and revealing the natural timber colour below.

PAINTING MDF OR CHIPBOARD

If you're painting composite boards such as MDF or chipboard, apply a water-based primer for the first coat to even out the porosity of the surface. Finish with two coats of your final finish paint, but sand the surface between each coat. Unframed MDF panels such as cupboard doors will tend to bow if you only paint one side, so be sure to paint both sides with an even coverage of paint.

PAINTING FLOORS

Floors sustain a lot of wear and tear, so you should choose a tough, gloss enamel paint. You can paint floors with acrylic or traditional substances like milk paint if you like, but they should then be protected with a couple of coats of a water-based urethane (see below).

PAINTING CONCRETE AND BRICKS

There are slightly different approaches required when painting masonry (e.g. concrete and bricks), depending on whether it's a horizontal surface such as a path or driveway, or a vertical surface such as a rendered wall.
    Horizontal surfaces (concrete or brick):
■   These surfaces will take a lot of wear, so you should use tough pavement paint; this is available in fast-drying enamel versions as well as acrylic.

- Wash the surface first with a stiff scrubbing brush to remove any grime, dirt and mosses; allow this to dry for at least 24 hours.
- Coating concrete or brick with white vinegar is a good trick to help the paint stick and last longer, particularly if it has a smooth surface. The acidic vinegar will slightly etch the surface of the concrete to create a better key for the paint; alternatively a mild hydrochloric acid mix can be used according to the manufacturer's instructions.
- You don't need a primer, but the first coat should be diluted by 20 per cent to help with coverage. As concrete usually has a rough surface, you'll need a roller with a longer nap.

ANTI-SLIP PAINT
When painting a horizontal area with high traffic or a lot of moisture around, be aware that it's likely to become a slip zone. You can add a non-slip additive to assist with this problem. Experiment with adding washed sharp sand to the paint; this can be purchased from a hardware store or you can go to a marine supplier or ship chandler to buy commercial non-slip additives, which may be made of crushed walnut shell.

Vertical surfaces:
- You can apply ordinary weather-resistant exterior acrylic to bricks and rendered walls.
- Once again, clean the surface thoroughly and allow to dry for 24 hours before applying two coats of paint, with the first one diluted by 10 per cent.
- Use a long nap roller to help cover the texture.

You can coat brick or concrete details such as retaining walls and fences directly with acrylic paint, but a coat or two of a bagged render finish will give you a much smoother, easier-to-paint surface. Better still, painting on thick render-style coatings will colour the surface and achieve the effect of bagging or rendering in one application. Some products give you a roll-on render effect, specifically designed for homeowners to tackle small rendering projects straight from a paint bucket. These products are usually thick enough to cover brick mortar joints.

GETTING PAINT OFF BRICKS

If the acrylic paint on the brickwork is fairly fresh, you'll probably be able to remove it by soaking it with methylated spirits and scrubbing it with a stiff-bristled brush.

If it's old paint, or oil-based paint, small amounts can be removed from bricks with simple paint stripper. Wash the final application away with some warm water and a stiff scrubbing brush. A little methylated spirits added to the water will help neutralise any remaining stripper in the surface of the porous brick.

If this gives you no joy, try one of the graffiti removal products available at most hardware stores.

For large areas of painted brick, such as entire buildings, you can try a chemical poultice system. This uses an alkaline gel that's painted on and then covered with a special plastic coating. The chemical is given time to work and then the plastic is peeled away, taking many layers (up to 30 coats!) of old paint with it.

PAINTING METAL

You'll need to prime raw metals with an appropriate primer—galvanised metal primer for galvanised metal for example, or rust-proofing primer for iron and steel work that's been affected by corrosion. Brand new steel can be primed with a product called 'Cold-Gal' paint, a zinc-rich epoxy coating. Aluminium is prepared with an etch primer.

You'll need to scrape or wire brush corroding metal surfaces before repainting. Wrought-iron features may have developed rust spots, which should be treated with rust converter before using a rust-resistant paint.

Once primed, paint the metal with a paint of your choice applied with a brush. Small metal items can be sprayed with an aerosol paint can. For an extra hardwearing protective coating, use epoxy paint or hammered metal finish paint.

PAINTING A METAL FENCE

You can use exterior acrylic paint on fences made from fibre cement, galvanised iron or even Colorbond—with the right preparation. Before painting a Colorbond or powder-coated aluminium fence, clean it with liquid sugar soap and scrub it with some large nylon scourers to slightly abrade the surface before applying high-grade exterior acrylic straight on to the surface.

PAINTING GLASS

You can achieve great tinted or frosted glass effects with spray-on glass paints. These are easy to use and require no special equipment. Just clean the glass well and let dry before you begin. Mask off the areas you don't want painted and protect them from overspray with tape and newspaper. To protect the paint from wearing off, paint the interior side of windows (not exterior) or the underside of glass tabletops (not the top). Prepare an entire pane or experiment with stencils and spray the paint on.

PAINTING LAMINATES AND TILES

In recent years, dedicated enamel laminate and tile paints have appeared on the market to allow you to recoat melamine and laminate surfaces (benchtops excluded) as well as tiled walls.

The paints are part of a system that includes a special primer that needs to be applied first. A detail roller or quality brush is good for this job, as you'll most likely be painting a series of small surfaces. Follow up with two coats of the laminate or tile paint with a light rubdown with 600 grit wet and dry between coats.

Painting with enamel paint

As I've said before, there are still certain jobs where oil-based enamel is indispensable—for example if you're painting surfaces that cop a few knocks like skirting boards, doors and architraves. If painted surfaces are exposed to heat or are likely to remain in contact with each other—like a window and its frame—acrylic paint will eventually start to stick, no matter how long you leave it to dry. This sticking problem is called 'paint blocking' and the proper use of an enamel paint will eliminate it. I also use enamel for the superior shine it gives to feature surfaces.

Here's how to get a tough, hard-wearing and easy-to-maintain finish with a gloss level that can't be matched by even the best of acrylics.

 WHAT YOU NEED
- 180 and 240 grit wet and dry sandpaper
- oil-based primer
- good-quality brushes, synthetic or natural
- wood filler if required
- undercoat
- enamel paint
- turpentine.

WHAT TO DO

1. If you're painting doors, remove them and set them up for painting horizontally in a well-ventilated area that's free from dust and any falling debris like leaves. By painting the doors horizontally you'll reduce the risk of runs and will allow the paint to settle more evenly. However, if you're only painting one door and you don't want to remove it, make sure you still paint the underside edge. An easy way to do this without removing the door is to use a piece of carpet offcut as a thin paintbrush that will just slide under the bottom of the door.

2. Sand the original surface all over with the 180 grit sandpaper; this will create a key for the paint to get a grip on the old glossy surface. Clean away any dust and debris and then wipe the surfaces down with a rag that's damp with turpentine.

3. Apply a coat of oil-based primer. The primer is especially important on fresh timber as it not only seals the timber but creates a bonding layer for the following coats.

4. Check to see if there are holes or dents that need filling—I often wait until after the primer to check for these as they'll be easier to see. If need be, fill the holes then sand and prime again.

5. After priming, I recommend using an undercoat; this can be tinted slightly to improve the opacity of your final finish. Unlike the primer, the undercoat has a fine soft texture when dry that can be sanded to a very smooth finish.

6. Once the undercoat is dry, give it another sand, this time with 240 grit wet and dry paper. This sanding procedure is the key to a really slick finish and should be repeated between every coat of paint.

7. Apply the final finish, at least two but preferably three coats. I recommend thinning the first coat down by about 5 per cent with some turpentine to improve the paint flow. You'll need some patience, as you'll have to allow each coat to dry for at least 24 hours before sanding and recoating.

If painting with enamel and you stop for a cup of tea, don't dunk your brush in turpentine as it'll dilute the paint and make a mess. Instead, place it in a container of water. The water will exclude the air from the brush so it doesn't start to dry out but will not mix with the oil paint in the bristles. When you're ready to start painting again, just give it a wipe with a rag.

If you are using acrylic, however, the brush can be wrapped with cling wrap and the tray covered in the same way.

Each night when you've finished painting, wash the brush out. If painting with enamel, use turpentine and then wash the dirty turpentine out of the brush with warm water and dishwashing liquid. If painting with acrylic, use water in a bucket and dispose of it sensibly. Try to hang the brush by the handle to dry.

Getting a good, straight edge

There are a number of products designed for obtaining good clean edges on your paintwork, such as cutter brushes and Shur-Line pads with little rollers on the side that guide your way. Another technique is to use a stiff piece of card (or hard plastic) between your brush and the edge of the architrave, moulding or cornice—you slide the card along as you brush to mask off the line.

Unless you're experienced, though, I don't think you can go past masking tape to protect your edges. Look out for special low-tack painter's masking tape; it comes in a range of colours which indicate how sticky it is and what types of surfaces it can be stuck to without causing damage when removed. Carefully apply the tape to the edge which needs protecting; if you need to protect more than just an edge, like an entire skirting board for example, use old newspaper with a line of tape along one edge. Aluminium foil can be moulded around unusually shaped objects requiring protection.

If you find it difficult to get the edge of your tape line straight, don't fret, as a straight edge and utility knife can be used to trim it in situ.

Storing and disposing of paint

Always store paint in trays, which will catch any accidental spills and leaks. Leftover paint cans should be taped closed and then stored upside down to keep air from entering and affecting the paint—and don't forget the cling wrap trick.

Old paint that has been stored a long time can become lumpy; you can strain it before use by filtering it through a piece of cheesecloth. Keeping small amounts of paint in large cans will inevitably result in the paint going off. Leftover paint should be decanted into smaller containers and then labelled with the colour (name and formulation number), date of use, manufacturer, surface sheen level and which room you used it in; this will allow you to use it for future touch-ups. Sometimes I drink more of that excellent top-shelf coffee just to get the good airtight tins it comes in for my excess paint store—extravagant, I know!

Getting rid of leftover paint

Don't wash paint into the drainage system. After scraping as much paint from the brush or roller as possible, use a two-bucket system to wash brushes. The first bucket of water will remove most of the paint;

the second bucket is for the rinse. Set the buckets of water aside for a day or so for the paint solids to settle to the bottom. The clear water from the buckets can then be poured onto the garden or lawn. The paint solids in the bottom of the bucket should be scraped onto some newspaper and disposed of in the household garbage.

A note about lead paint

You must take seriously the health dangers involved in removing lead paint. See details in Chapter 4, 'Safety while you work'.

> **REUSING OLD TURPS**
> You can recycle old turps by storing it in a safe place in an old container. Eventually the paint and the turps will separate and the paint solids will go to the bottom, leaving the rest of the turps relatively clean to be decanted and reused later. Be careful with storing this as it's a HIGHLY volatile material.

Staining timber surfaces

It's not always the go to paint your household timber. I love the natural colour and texture of timber around the home, so I suggest you think about just finishing it with a product which will let it show through. You may, however, like to change the colour of the timber before finishing it—sometimes you need to do this when you've had to replace a section of timber or made a new addition which you'd like to match with the rest of the house. Or maybe you've bought some cheap radiata or hoop pine furniture and you want to give it some more character or antiquity. The answer is to stain it.

First get the right colour!

When it comes to matching the colour of new timber work to old, rarely is a colour straight from the tin bang on. You'll need to do some blending and experimenting to mix a stain that will be an acceptable tonal match. Experiment on some offcuts from the job—with careful notes taken along the way so that the correct recipe is recorded for making up further batches.

Using traditional spirit-based stains, you can add a few dashes of different stain colours to a base (e.g. cedar) to alter it accordingly. Then apply each sample to one of the scraps and note the blend—wait for it to dry before you decide if the blend is correct!

Applying the stain

Before applying a stain to the timber (unless it's a brand-new piece), prepare it by cutting back any original finish. Have a look in Chapter 10, 'Furniture' for how to strip furniture—this also applies to any other timber around your home.

Once the timber is prepared, paint on the stain with a brush, covering one small area at a time and then rubbing off excess stain with a rag.

When staining detailed turned timbers like banister railings or turned table legs, take care not to allow too much stain to run into the details or soak into any exposed end grain. Use an almost dry brush or even a stain-soaked rag to build the colour up. You can use a small artist brush to get the stain into the recessed grooves of the detailed turnings and wipe off the excess.

On more exposed areas of the timber, apply the stain a little more liberally. Allow it a moment or two to be taken up by the timber before rubbing back. If you do overdo it with stain, the colour can be sanded back to bare timber again and a new lighter coat applied.

To achieve a depth of colour you'll probably need two thin coats of stain. It's always better to build up to the final colour with multiple coats rather than trying to nail it in one.

When staining the end grain (which is likely to be more porous), it's a good idea to dilute your stain by at least half with the appropriate thinner so it doesn't end up darker than the other areas.

HOW TO MAKE A 'FAKE' ANTIQUE
To achieve a naturally 'aged' look to a stained project, rub back some of the raised surfaces and edges of the furniture with very fine wet and dry sandpaper before applying the final clear coat. This is called 'distressing' and makes the piece look as though it's worn slightly with a hundred years of use. After clear coating, complete the illusion with an application of black furniture wax to darken and feature any scratches and depressions in the surface.

Waxing

I love to wax my furniture—the wax should be applied to small areas at a time until the surface is completed. Apply by rubbing it into the timber in a tight circular motion with some 0000 grade steel wool or a soft cloth; once it has dried a bit, buff it off with a soft rag or cheesecloth, rubbing with the grain. You can also use a soft brush wheel added to your electric drill for a final buff.

Antique furniture that has been French polished, varnished or oiled is usually finished and maintained with a light coat of wax applied with a soft cloth.

French polishing

French polishing is one of my favourite DIY projects. I'm sure I've bored many people at parties (and those joining my restoration demos at 'ladies nights' at my favourite hardware store) by extolling the virtues of shellac. You may have a small piece of timber furniture you might like to try it on, or perhaps you have a piece that's already been French polished but has seen better days and needs to be refreshed.

Shellac is easy to apply and dries quickly, so it won't become laden with dust like slow-drying polyurethane. Best of all, it won't stink your house out for days with the smell of strong solvents, and once dry it's completely non-toxic. It comes in a range of natural shades.

You don't have to do the full French polish involving hours of fine 'skinning in' using a shellac-soaked cotton pad to get a good effect— you can get a good finish easily by applying three coats of shellac with a good-quality brush. A few more coats will simply add to the lustre and the high shine French polish is famous for.

There are some very good premixed shellacs on the market, but I find the premixed stuff has a limited shelf life so I prefer to buy the flakes, which will last almost indefinitely, and mix my own as I need it.

 WHAT YOU NEED
- shellac flakes and methylated spirits,* or premixed shellac
- furniture wax
- 400 grit wet and dry sandpaper and/or fine steel wool
- good-quality paintbrush
- cheesecloth.

* Try to get industrial-grade metho if you can as it has a lower water content, which is important to help the shellac dissolve properly.

A regular buff with beeswax polish makes the trains at Ruwenzori shine!

 WHAT TO DO

1. In a large clean glass or plastic jar, tip in 250 gm of shellac flakes and add 1 litre of methylated spirits. A rough rule of thumb is to half-fill the jar with the flakes and then add the liquid until the flakes are covered.

2. Stir your mixture intermittently over a 24-hour period and you'll have your fresh French polish mixture. Tip the mixture into a storage jar, preferably a dark-coloured plastic one. Filter it through some old stocking or a piece of cheesecloth to remove any impurities.

3. Apply the shellac to the wood. Shellac can be applied with a special pad called a rubber (cotton wool covered in linen), especially if you're trying to achieve a high-gloss finish, and it can also be sprayed on. For most projects, however, using a brush is the best way to start. It is by far the easiest way to use it, but the brushing technique does vary slightly from what you may be used to with ordinary polyurethane and water-based finishes. Don't apply too much pressure; allow the mixture to flow from the tip of the brush and work in long, continuous strokes along the direction of the grain. Each new stroke should only overlap the edge of the last slightly, and once applied the polish should not be rebrushed. Specialty brushes are good because they hold a lot of the mixture and allow a lot of shellac to be applied before having to recharge the brush, though any natural fibre brush will also give you a good result.

4. The shellac dries quite quickly, and between coats it's important to give it a sand with 400 grit wet and dry sandpaper; you can use fine steel wool instead of sandpaper to cut back the detailed areas if you like.

5. To shield the shellac finish from moisture and wear and tear, you can give the piece a coat of beeswax furniture polish applied with 0000 steel wool and buffed off with cheesecloth. The wax is a 'sacrificial' coating that will further protect and waterproof the finish below, so it's important to reapply from time to time.

Applying tung oil

If you don't know what tung oil is, check out Chapter 3, 'Products and materials'. Tung oil is suitable for timber kitchens and all interior and exterior timber work, including floors, furniture, joinery and panelling. Here's how to apply it:

1. Prepare the timber surface by sanding down through the grades. For fine timber furniture I'd recommend you go down to a minimum 1200 grit, but for panelling, joinery or outdoor furniture 400 grit is sufficient.
2. Heavily dilute the initial coat of tung oil with a solvent. I usually use artist-quality gum turpentine as the solvent, but if using the oil in confined spaces or in food service areas like kitchens, chopping boards or dining tables, I use orange oil instead. Mix two parts solvent with one part tung oil.
3. Apply liberally with a brush or pad and allow 20 minutes for the mixture to be drawn into the timber's pores before rubbing off any excess with a rag.
4. Allow 24 hours' drying time before applying each successive coat. These should be blended at higher oil concentrations; the second and third coat can be mixed 50/50 and so on until the final layer almost consists of tung oil alone. This process will provide you with a durable water-resistant surface coating. The number of coats of oil to be applied is determined by the intended use of the piece. Two to four coats are enough for decorative work, panelling and moulding. Surfaces that receive moderate to heavy use, such as tables or kitchen benchtops, could need up to six coats for maximum protection.

Tung-oiled timber can be cleaned and maintained with straight orange oil and will benefit from the occasional application of beeswax. Exterior surfaces and high-wear areas like kitchen benchtops, tables and floors will require a light renewal coat of tung oil mixed 1:1 with the solvent and applied roughly once a year, or when the surface is looking worn or dry.

Applying oil-based urethane

Oil-based polyurethane can be used to seal wood before topcoating. Here's how:

1. Mix one part turpentine and two parts polyurethane. Gently stir the polyurethane in its can and then pour the quantity required into another can along with the turpentine. Stir the mixture with a flat stir stick.

2. Use a good-quality natural-bristle brush or a foam applicator to apply the polyurethane, as the split tips of synthetic brushes may introduce air bubbles into the finish. Load your brush by dipping it about 25 mm into the mixture, then brush the wood with long, even strokes from end to end. Keep a wet edge by overlapping each pass until the surface is completely coated. Catch any drips with your brush and smooth them into the surface. Before cleaning the brush up wait for five minutes then look for any further dripping.

3. Within 24 hours of applying your seal coat, brush on a coat of straight polyurethane. Spread the poly over the entire surface with long, even strokes. Don't use too much or you're likely to get runs; use just enough to get a nice, even coat without dry spots. As soon as the surface is coated, brush over it again with the grain, from end to end. Overlap your strokes to get a uniform coating; again, catch any drips, especially along the bottom edges, and wait five minutes after the first coat and inspect for drips. Let this coat dry for 24 hours.

4. Before applying the next full-strength coat, the entire project should be sanded with some 180 grit wet and dry. After sanding, wipe down all the surfaces with a rag slightly dampened with turpentine and then proceed in the same way as the previous coat.

Painting the outside of your house

Painting the entire outside of your home is an enormous task that may not be necessary. If the existing paintwork on the walls is in good condition it can be cleaned using a soft broom and a bucket of warm water mixed with liquid sugar soap. You'll also be amazed at what a difference hiring the services of a high-pressure water cleaning company can make.

Then, by repainting just the detail work such as windowframes, the front door, hand rails, the front fence and so on, the entire façade can be given a fresh new look. See info on 'Painting timber' above. If the old paint surface has a chalky look that leaves a white film on your hand when rubbed, you'll need to wash it with some coarse cloth such as hessian before coating with a sealer/binder prior to topcoating.

Traditional enamel paints are best on doors and windows to prevent them sticking to their frames, but high-quality exterior acrylics are great for other details such as fretwork, railings, banisters and front fences.

See Chapter 14, 'The outside bits—your home's exterior', for more info on repairing gutters, removing graffiti and other jobs to improve the look of your home.

EXTERIOR TIMBER

Products that form a plastic coating, such as exterior polyurethane, on an exterior timber surface provide good protection for the first couple of years, but if not properly maintained will always pose a problem when they eventually break down, as they'll have to be removed before a fresh application can go on. A good alternative is a quality oil finish for timber that's designed for harsh conditions, as it's easy to reapply without the need to strip and sand the surface. Products such as Organoil, available through most hardware stores, also contain liquefied waxes that soak into the timber and will continue to provide protection from the sun once the oil burns off. But you'll need to reapply the oil every year or so to maintain its appearance and protective qualities.

Chapter 14

THE OUTSIDE BITS—YOUR HOME'S EXTERIOR

There's no doubt the outer shell of our homes cops a beating—wind and rain, storms, trees, vandals, the kids and even boofhead DIYers all cause destruction of one kind or another. Here are some fix-its plus some other regular maintenance tasks that will help keep the outside of your home looking good and working well.

Cleaning and fixing gutters

It's important to keep your gutters in good nick—rain ending up in the wrong place can lead to extensive damage to your property, causing excessive dampness in masonry, rotting timber windowframes, facias and weatherboards, eroding garden beds and seeping into your foundations for starters. Also, if you have your gutters plumbed into a rainwater storage tank, you want to make sure it all gets there!

Cleaning gutters

Remove flammable debris from gutters regularly throughout the summer months. Wear gardening gloves and clear all debris like leaves and moss from the gutters. You can buy some purpose-made tools to assist with this job but I find it just as handy to use a pair of old kitchen tongs and cutting myself a scraping tool from a plastic ice-cream container lid to match the profile of the gutter.

Check that the wire strainers or plastic 'baskets' that fit into the openings of the downpipe spouts are in place. If any strainers are missing or broken, make sure you get some more—they're inexpensive to replace.

Once cleared, rinse with the garden hose and check if the downpipes are draining. If they seem to be blocked, flush them out with the hose. You may need to feed the hose down the pipe; if so, it's a good idea to remove the nozzle and fitting from the hose first so that it doesn't become jammed or the nozzle dislodged. Cleaning will also give you a chance to check for leaks and to see whether water is draining away properly or pooling in specific areas.

MAKE GUTTER CLEANING EASIER
An easy way to collect the gutter rubbish and dispose of it is to tie a long rope to the handle of a bucket. Tie the rope to the top of your ladder, fill the bucket with leaves and then hoist it down to a helper below for disposal.

Fixing gutters

Gutters should fall towards the downpipe at a minimum grade of 500:1. You can check if yours is still correct by taping a pair of five-cent pieces on one end of a 1200 mm spirit level. When the level sits on the coins and the vial bubble is still central then the fall is about 500:1. If the water is pooling in your gutters, the brackets may need reshaping or repositioning. This may be a simple task of repositioning the brackets that hold the gutter in place; sometimes they just need to be bent back up into position or tightened. However, you may need to call a roof plumber if the situation is more drastic.

You can fix leaking joints, cracks or tears with roof and gutter sealant. Some of these even come in colours to match your gutter.

If your gutters are rusty, scrub and sand them with a wire brush and then some wet and dry sandpaper to remove any loose material before treating with a rust converter solution. Then use an anti-rust paint, which comes in cans or aerosols.

The fastest and easiest way to fix small to medium-sized rust holes is with weatherproof flashing tape like Flashtac. It comes in rolls of various widths from any hardware store. It's self-adhesive and has a bituminous layer covered with aluminium. Just cut a right-sized piece with scissors and stick it over the hole—one on each side works best. You can then paint it to match.

If a rust hole is large, you may need to cut away a section of the gutter with a hacksaw, treat the cut ends with protective paint and fit in a new piece. Make sure the joins to each new piece step down in the direction of the gutter's fall. Apply a bead of silicone sealant inside each joint and then rivet the pieces in place, or support the joint by adding some extra brackets.

If you're confident up a ladder, you may even consider installing inflammable gutter guards. These are a great idea as they'll reduce your cleaning regime from twice or more a year to once every 4–5 years and maximise your tank water collection.

Looking after your deck

In Australia we love our outdoor living and we love our decks. But as they're usually timber, and very exposed, they need some regular TLC. Keeping wooden decks in tiptop condition requires a little maintenance from time to time:

- check for loose or damaged boards
- inspect for rot
- look out for lifting nail heads
- make sure the frame and handrails are still firm and secure.

Timbers used in decking

Many timber decks in Australia have been built using CCA (copper chromium arsenic) treated timber. While CCA-treated timber is still a good choice for many outdoor projects, it's now not to be used in areas where it's likely to come into frequent contact with the skin (e.g. playgrounds), and decking and handrail materials are no longer made in CCA at all. Don't panic if you have an old deck built from CCA; the new regulations don't require removal of existing structures.

There are other treated timber alternatives, including copper azole, ACQ (alkaline copper quaternary), Tanalised E, LOSP (light organic solvent preservative) and even boron-treated timbers. The thing to remember when selecting a treated timber is to look out for the durability rating or 'H' number, which indicates the appropriate application for the treated timber. H5 is the highest durability rating and indicates that a timber can be used underground or even in areas where it will have permanent contact with fresh water; H4 is suitable for ground contact uses such as landscaping, while H3 is only for above-ground uses such as your decking. And H2 and H1 refer to timbers used in areas protected from the weather but that still offer protection from insects. Many good hardwood decking alternatives are also available these days that offer excellent durability, especially if properly finished. Talk to your timber supplier about the most suitable types.

Replacing damaged boards

 WHAT YOU NEED

- jigsaw or keyhole saw
- drill
- pry bar
- replacement timber
- tape measure
- galvanised or stainless steel twist nails*
- cleats and construction adhesive (if only replacing part of the board)
- belt sander and appropriate finishing product (see later in chapter).

* Galvanised twist nails are designed to hold decking boards down tight and are rust-resistant.

 WHAT TO DO

1. Cut the damaged board into smaller sections. In between each row of nails drill a hole in the centre of the board. Place the blade of your jigsaw or keyhole saw into these holes and cut out the edge of the board in each direction. Remove each section of the damaged board carefully with a pry bar.
2. Measure and cut the replacement board to length. If the new board

will overhang the edge of the deck, cut the boards a few centimetres long; you can use a saw to trim the new boards flush with the rest of the decking after installation. Position the new board and drill some pilot holes for the nails over the joists. To give the nails a better grip, drive them in at a slight angle with the points skewing slightly towards each other. If you're only going to replace part of a board, make sure the section being replaced is still long enough to span across at least three joists. Cut out the section as just explained, but this time make sure the cut is up against a joist.

3. Once the section is removed, glue and nail some 90 x 45 mm timber blocks, called cleats, to the side of the exposed joists to support the ends of the new board. It's easier to fit these if you start driving the nails into them before adding construction adhesive and positioning them. Once the cleats have been fitted you can nail on the new section of deck.

4. You may find that your new board sits a little higher or lower than the rest of the deck—a quick once-over with a belt sander will soon even them out.

LET TIMBER ACCLIMATISE
For the best long-term result with any outdoor timber work I'd advise that you let the timber sit outside to acclimatise for a couple of weeks and then paint (or oil) the ends and backs of the boards before you install them. Once installed the front surface can be coated.

Re-punching nails

As wood expands and contracts, nail heads tend to 'pop' above the surface, presenting a tripping hazard. Use a hammer and flooring punch to drive them below the surface.

Tightening bolts

Often handrails and balustrades become a bit wobbly because the bolts that secure them aren't as tight as they should be. This may occur because the timber has shrunk and then, once a bit loose, the leverage of the rocking motion has pulled the joint even looser. Having the joint open up will also allow extra water to get in between the handrail post and the deck frame, and in turn this will lead to timber rot. Extending the life of your handrails can be as simple as retightening these bolts with a spanner from time to time, and a drop or two of oil on the nuts and thread will leave them serviceable for the next time they need a tweak.

Cleaning your deck

Make sure you remove the dead leaves and debris that gets caught between the decking boards; this 'mulch' will hold water and start the process of rot.

Clean with the blade of a scraper or blast the debris clear with a jet of water. Don't use a garden hose to do this—use a high-pressure water cleaner which will simultaneously remove the debris from between boards and remove any algae or mildew that may have formed on the timber surface. You can hire these, or if there are water restrictions in your area there are plenty of licensed companies who can come to do the job for you.

Removing stains

For bad stains it may be necessary to clean the timber with an oxalic acid timber wash, which is biodegradable, so any run-off from your deck cleaning will break down naturally and not kill all your plants!

Apply the mix to the surface with a stiff scrubbing brush. After about 15 minutes it will have done the job of removing dead timber cells and the residues of old oil finishes. It will have opened up the cellular structure of the timber surface ready for a fresh intake of protective oil. Wash the acid off with water, or better still with the high-pressure cleaner.

If your timber work has gone black

Many people over the years have mistakenly finished their timber decking with linseed oil, thinking it will protect the timber. But linseed oil is mildew food so when used on exterior timber and exposed to moisture it will eventually turn black. Linseed oil also offers little resistance to UV and is not particularly durable for surfaces under foot. Fixing the problem is not easy:

- Multiple applications of a commercial timber wash product may be necessary to remove many layers of built-up linseed oil, or you can make up a solution using oxalic acid flakes purchased from a hardware store. Be sure to test one or two timbers before proceeding with the whole deck.
- As a follow-up, or if your decking only requires a light treatment, you may also consider washing all the timber work with a strongly mixed oxygen bleach solution like NapiSan.
- Once the deck is washed (or if you've just laid a new deck), I'd recommend that you leave it to dry out and allow the natural mildew-killing action of the sun to work on it before applying a new finish.

BLACKENED PINE
Another cause for the blackening of timber is when treated pine has been oiled too soon and moisture has been trapped under the decking oil. The preservative treatment process involves saturating the timber with chemicals dissolved in water and it's important to allow this moisture to evaporate from the timber properly before oiling. To fix it you'll need to remove the oil finish and treat with a mild bleach, as above.

Make your decking go 'silver'

If you replace some old rotting timbers with new boards, they may not match your existing boards, which possibly will have that grey/silver look from exposure to the weather. The silvered look is a result of the natural tannins that give timber its colour leaching out and washing away, leaving the surface to become sun bleached.

If you don't finish the new boards at all, they won't take too long to silver off and be indistinguishable from the original boards. If you're in a hurry, this process can be accelerated by mopping the new boards with a mixture of baking soda and water. One box of baking soda to a half bucket of water should do it.

If you have a whole deck you want to silver, repeated treatments of an oxalic-acid-based timber wash, followed by cleaning with a high-pressure water cleaner, will help. Once the timber does form the silvered surface you're after, no further protection will be required to maintain it. In much the same way as tarnish works on metal, the silvery layer of dead timber cells provide a protective surface for the timber below. Don't be temped to oil that surface or it will just turn it black. From time to time you can reapply the timber cleaner with a stiff scrubbing brush to keep the surface from becoming too rough.

Making your silvered deck look new!

To return deck timber to its original colour, the deck can be sanded in the same way as a timber floor:

1. Make sure you clean the deck really well, and remove all the debris that's collected in the cracks.
2. Then make sure all nail heads are punched below the surface with a nail punch and hammer, or the sandpaper will catch and tear.
3. Use a belt sander if it's a small deck, or hire a floor sander if it's large. Begin sanding across the wood's grain with a coarse belt, then diagonally with a medium belt, and finish with a fine belt going with the grain.

4. Once the deck is sanded it can be left to silver off again evenly if you like that look, or you can use the opportunity to apply tinted decking oil.

Refinishing the deck

Keeping the coatings up to your deck is your best defence against its early demise. There are many choices of finish available, from clear oils to opaque acrylic paints. As you'll know by now if you've read the rest of this book, I'm a great fan of tung-oil-based products on outdoor timber as it's a natural waterproofing agent. But you should choose a product that also contains pigmentation as a UV inhibitor.

> **SAVE YOUR BACK**
> When reapplying your deck oil, use a cheap bucket and sponge mop—this will save your back and you can just throw out the disposable sponge part of the mop when you're done.

Staining a treated pine deck

Treated pine timbers can be stained, but for best results wait three months to a year after installing if you can. This allows any excess tannins and resins to leach out. The slightly faded timber will also give a more true colour to the stain you choose. Most of the timber finish companies consider the colour of raw treated pine in their colour sampling, and if you have a look at the colour swatches at a hardware store you'll see the different colours applied to treated pine. The best bet would be to test stain a few off-cuts for yourself before purchasing all the stain required.

Use a tinted decking oil rather than a straight stain; it's easy to apply and will help preserve the timbers of your new deck. It's also easy to reapply to high wear-and-tear areas, like stair treads.

An easy way to oil the deck!

Which way to lay decking timber

Grooves up or grooves down, that is the question! A question that has caused great debate over the years. I've had 'experts' emphatically argue for either direction. I really think you can choose for yourselves, here are the pluses and minuses of each:

GROOVES DOWN

Having your grooves point down will help with ventilation at the point where the decking crosses joists, to release any trapped moisture and help prevent rot in the joists. Many people also prefer the appearance of the smooth look.

GROOVES UP

Sometimes treated timber suffers from a condition called 'checking', which is a slight grain separation caused by its tendency to absorb and then lose moisture. The main purpose of the grooves was to direct this checking to the valley of the grooves, and so hide the unattractive appearance of a checked surface. Another reason for the grooves was to reduce the chance of the boards cupping, while some think that the grooves are useful to give the surface some grip.

Just as smooth boards can be slippery when wet or oily, having the grooves facing up could make the deck surface slippery as well if mould is allowed to build up. This can happen if you don't clean your deck regularly, as the grooves trap moisture and that in turn exacerbates the growth of moss and mildew, resulting in a damp slippery deck surface. In those cooler parts of the country, moisture in the grooves can also freeze, turning your deck into an ice skating rink.

Fixing outdoor timber stairs

Outdoors, stairs are exposed to the rigours of sun and rain, and as such can be affected by timber rot or excess shrinkage and twisting of timbers. If rot has set into the stringers (side pieces) then a major rebuild may be in order, but if it's just a damaged tread or two then a simple repair is possible.

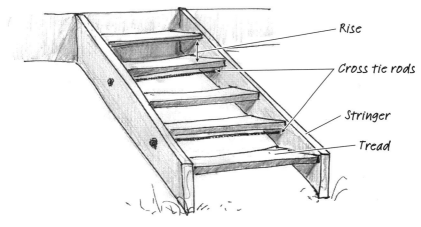

A typical step tread is 280 mm
and the rise is 170 mm

Rise

Cross tie rods

Stringer

Tread

Parts of a staircase

When open-tread outdoor stairs are constructed, the carpenter often simply assembles the stairs by driving nails or screws through the outside faces of the stringers into the end grain of each tread; this is prone to failure in time as the tread timbers dry and shrink, allowing the fasteners to become loose.

A quick fix might be to clamp the stairs together and add some new fasteners. It's better to assemble stairs with cross-tie rods that run from stringer to stringer and pull them together, permanently clamping the tread in place. If your stairs don't have these, they can be retrofitted.

Adding cross-ties to your stairs

The stringers should already be fixed at the top to a structure and at the base to the ground; this stops the stairs from spreading at these points, and it's in the middle that outward bowing of the stringers can be loosening treads so this is where a cross-tie should be installed. If the stairs have more than about ten treads then more than one cross-tie will be required:

- The cross-tie is made using a piece of galvanised threaded rod fed through a hole in the stringer set just below a tread. Drill and counterbore (see Chapter 2, 'Tools') both sides in the same position and then feed the rod through.
- Add washers and nuts to the outer ends of the tie and then tighten. The rod will function like a permanent clamp, pulling the stringers in tight. The counterbores should be large enough to house the washer and nut, so any excess rod can be cut off flush with the outer surface of the stringer.

Replacing treads

To replace warped or rotten treads in your outdoor stairs:

1. Use a handsaw to cut the old tread across the middle, then prise it out with a pry bar.
2. Remove any nails or screws, and if your stairs have cross-ties, loosen them. Replacement timber for treads is available from timberyards in both treated pine and hardwood.
3. Cut a new tread to length, but before driving it into position treat the inside of the housings and the end grain of the new tread with a brush-on wood preservative. When you're knocking the new tread in with a hammer, be sure to use a scrap piece of timber along the edge of the tread to cushion your blows. Finally, retighten the cross-ties and drive some 75 mm galvanised nails back in through the stringer into the ends of the tread.

Removing rot from outdoor timber areas

Even if the shell of your house is made of brick, timber plays a major role in the makeup of floors, roofs, doors, windows and more. Timber rot is caused by a fungus that loves moisture, so in most cases it's the presence of excessive levels of moisture that causes the rot.

Finding the rot

Inspect timber with the aid of a thin-bladed knife, as just looking is not enough. Painted surfaces may look OK but the timber underneath may be rotting. When you push the tip of the knife into timber it should only penetrate a few millimetres; if it sinks in deeply, you've got problems. Timber suffering from rot will feel spongy (even through a coat of paint) and look darker than the surrounding timber. When dry, the timber will easily crack and crumble into fine particles.

The problem may be a damaged paint finish allowing the actual timber to absorb excessive moisture, so check vulnerable areas such as windowframes and doorframes for signs of rot. The bottoms of frames are more susceptible to rot, as water can collect there. Points where timber comes in contact with the ground are another common problem area.

What to do about it

PREVENTING ROT

Removing the source of moisture is the key to rot eradication. You can also protect non-treated timber in outdoor structures with the aid of chemical treatments applied in situ. No Rot sticks (available through most hardware stores) are a good example of this type of treatment. These inserts come in the form of a small white rod, a bit like a stick of chalk. You put them into a 9 mm hole drilled in the timber, and once inserted they react with moisture to slowly release their chemical load into the surrounding timber to combat rot-causing fungi and help prevent termite attack. These can even be used where decay already exists to sterilise the timber and prevent further attack. To maintain maximum protection these sticks should be replaced every 5–10 years.

REPAIRING ROT
If you get to a rotten spot early enough it can often be repaired and patched, saving you the cost and trouble of total replacement.

 WHAT YOU NEED
- chisel
- drill
- liquid rot treatment*
- recommended matching wood filler
- sponge
- paint or other finish.

* Examples are Earl's Wood Hardener or Senseal's Multi-Primer. Rot treatments will have fillers that are recommended to go with them.

 WHAT TO DO
1. Scrape any loose and flaking material away with the aid of a chisel.
2. Drill a series of holes around and on either side of the affected area. On vertical surfaces, drill holes on a downward angle and also drill small holes into the patch area.

3. Fill all the holes with the liquid rot treatment. The liquid can be applied with a brush or sponge or even sprayed onto the surface and into the holes. The liquid will soak into the timber before hardening to not only consolidate any soft timber but also create a barrier against any future incursion of moisture into the area.
4. In a day or so, once the chemical has dried properly, you can patch and rebuild the area with wood filler. You can add wood stain to it to match your timber or leave it natural for painting over. Rebuild larger areas of missing timber with a few applications, allowing a couple of hours for each layer of filler to dry. These fillers dry rock hard, so it's easier to carefully smooth the final layer upon application of a sponge soaked in the appropriate thinner (check packing for recommendation) rather than trying to sand it smooth afterwards.
5. When the filler has dried properly, complete the transformation with a coating of paint.

IF IT'S TOO FAR GONE . . .

Sometimes the only way to effectively treat rotted timber is to cut it out and replace it. Make sure you select new replacement timber that has a high durability rating or has been appropriately treated with one of the many treatment processes. New timber in vulnerable areas should also be protected, firstly with a coat of water-repellent preservative like Cabot's Bar D-K, then with an appropriate coating of oil or paint.

Repairing cracks in brickwork

If you're feeling a little more confident in your DIY skills, you could gather the following items and have a go at fixing cracks in exposed brickwork—

Wood rot caused by a complete absence of any flashing

both inside your house and outside. It's a good idea to find out what's causing the cracks, however, as you could just be covering up a structural problem that will grow. This also applies to interior brickwork, but make sure you put down some plastic sheeting on the floor to protect from mortar spills (very bad for the shag pile, I can tell you!).

 WHAT YOU NEED

- plugging chisel
- lump hammer
- a bag of mortar mix (or make your own with cement, lime and brickie's sand)

- pointing trowel
- pointing hawk*
- screwdriver
- vacuum cleaner
- dust mask.

* You can use an old dustpan as a pointing hawk if you're just doing a one-off job.

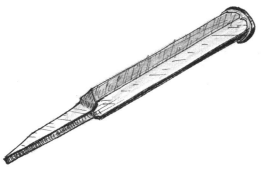

Plugging chisel

 WHAT TO DO

1. Use a plugging chisel and a lump hammer to remove the cracked and loose mortar to a depth of around 15 mm. For large jobs use an angle grinder fitted with a special cutting wheel. Brush away any dust and loose material.
2. If you're doing this indoors, use that trusty vacuum cleaner to get rid of the dust, and wear a safety dust mask.
3. The brick should be soaked so that it won't leach the water from the mortar and cause it to crumble. If you're working outside use a hose; inside use a bucket and large sponge.

4. Mix your mortar in a shallow bucket: one part cement, one part lime, six parts brickie's sand. Alternatively, you can buy a premixed mortar if the repair is small.
5. Scoop up a little bit of mortar with a pointing trowel and on the pointing hawk create a small cylindrical shape with it.
6. Hold the hawk under the groove between the bricks, slide the cylinder into the groove and press in with the trowel. Hold the hawk under the area where you're working, to catch falling mortar—it takes some practice to keep the mortar in the groove.
7. Several hours later, when the mortar has set but before it goes completely hard, use a small pointed tool like a screwdriver, or an old teaspoon that has been shaped to fit the groove, to rake out some of the mortar from the joint to match the pointing of the surrounding brickwork.

Waterproofing

Damp problems are a constant issue when it comes to home maintenance. Many of them may need professional consultation, but I can give you some advice on a few common issues.

Damp masonry walls

Exterior walls can become saturated, causing dampness and mildew to grow on the inside of the house. Step one is to try to stop the cause of saturation (see Chapter 6, 'Walls and ceilings', for advice on rising and falling damp). Once you've worked out the cause and fixed it, to prevent further problems consider the following:

- You could try rendering or bagging the exterior wall using a render mix with waterproofing agents added (see 'Bagging a wall' below).
- If you want to retain the brick surface, a paint-on raincoat may be the answer. There are penetrating clear coat paints that can be rollered straight from the can onto the wall (Concoat, for example). They'll penetrate the masonry and chemically react with it to create a waterproof surface.
- If the wall is already painted, or you'd prefer a painted finish, try using a product like Super-Prime. This can be applied directly to a number of surfaces, including bricks, render or already painted surfaces. It will form a raincoat layer that can then be painted over with your favourite exterior paint colour.

Sealing small cracks with waterproof cement paint

In a bucket, add one part Silasec (see below), five parts water, seven parts fresh cement (standard GP Portland cement) and mix together. For the first coat you can also add one part Bondcrete to help adhesion.

Mix up the slurry of waterproof cement paint and brush it on. One coat will cover any hairline cracks but three coats should fix any problems. If you like you can add oxides to your final coat mix for colour.

Filling larger cracks with waterproof repair putty

If it's a more substantial crack, mix up a cement-based putty to repair it first and then brush on the slurry. In a container add one part Silasec and two parts fresh cement and mix vigorously with a gloved hand.

When the mix is moist and putty-like you can remove it and begin to knead it. When the mix starts to become hot and while it's still soft, commence repairing the hole/crack by pushing in the putty until it becomes hard. For large repairs you may need to repeat the process.

Patching damaged render

Here's how to fix small holes or cracks in your render.

 WHAT YOU NEED

- premixed cement render
- binding agent
- wire brush
- renderer's trowel
- sponge.

 WHAT TO DO

1. Mix a small batch of premixed cement render in a barrow or on a scrap of plywood.
2. Add a dash (according to manufacturer's recommendation) of a bonding agent like Bondcrete to the water; mix the render before adding it to the dry mix.

3. Clean any loose pieces of damaged render away from the hole and then brush some of the water and bonding agent mix to the inside of the hole.
4. Use a renderer's trowel, which has a flat rectangular steel base with a handle on top, to apply a layer of render mix to the base of the hole, but only half-fill the hole with the first application.
5. Once the base coat of render has started to cure (dry), use the corner of the trowel to make a series of scratches in the surface, several in one diagonal direction and then several in the opposite direction in a crosshatched pattern. Let this first layer dry overnight. The crosshatched scratches create a key to help hold the top layer in place.
6. Mix some more render and apply it to the hole and smooth it flush with the wall surface. Once this layer has started to cure, it can be smoothed over some more with a wet sponge and evened out to match the surrounding wall.
7. If the surrounding wall has a textured finish, you'll need to match the existing finish texture.
8. Allow the patch to dry for several weeks before applying a coat of touch-up paint.

Bagging a wall

No, we are not talking about teasing your brickwork. Bagging is basically a thin coating of mortar applied to the face of the block wall to cover the surface and fill in any gaps and joints. The term 'bagging' refers to the tradition method of applying the mortar to the wall surface by rubbing it on with a rolled-up section of hessian bag, although these days a variety of application techniques can be used. Unlike a full cement render, a bagged finish is quite rustic, as the thin coating still reveals some of the characteristics of the brick or blocks below.

You can also use this technique inside your house—exposed brick walls were once very groovy but that signature look of the 70s is not so 'in' these days.

 ## WHAT YOU NEED

- mortar mix: 3 parts yellow brickie's sand,* 1 part washed sharp sand, 1 part off-white cement
- scrubbing brush
- water and bucket
- bonding additive (e.g. Bondcrete)
- sturdy wheelbarrow
- banister brush/paint roller
- builder's plastic
- rubber gloves
- hessian/sponge/roller/brushes for application
- waterproofing compound (e.g. Silasec).

* By varying the type of sand or cement you use in a mortar mix you can alter the final colour of the mix, and for more dramatic variations you can add powdered oxide pigments. If you're not sure about getting the mix right, premixed bags can be purchased at any hardware store; you just add the water.

 ## WHAT TO DO

1. With a wire brush, clean the wall to remove any dirt, dust or loose materials. Scrub off mould or moss with an outdoor surface cleaner.

2. Chip off any lumps of old mortar with a chisel.
3. Fill any large gaps or holes with a small amount of mortar mix and allow to dry before getting on with the rest of the wall.
4. Wet down the surface before applying a bagging mix to it, as dry, porous brick or concrete blocks will draw the water from your mix and make it too dry and difficult to apply—you may end up with a flaky, brittle result. Mix the bonding additive with water in a bucket and apply with a banister brush or paint roller to help the mortar stick better to the surface.
5. Lay down some builder's plastic or a row of timber boards at the base of the wall to catch any falling mortar.
6. Make the mix up in a barrow—only mix as much as you can apply in about half an hour. Make sure to match your mix colour and consistency from one batch to the next—measure out the ingredients using a small bucket rather than just adding them by the shovelful. Add some more binding agent to the water that goes into the mix. If you've decided to add an oxide it should also be added to the water before mixing it in, as should your waterproofing compound. The mix needs to be made quite wet, a thick custard sort of consistency, but not so wet that it runs down the wall.
7. Heap the mixture onto your bag with a trowel and then rub it onto the wall surface in a circular motion. Wear gloves and always start at the top of the wall and work down. You can use a sponge, brush or even thick roller to apply the mix, but I quite like the traditional method— a hessian bag. You can also use the end of broom to paint it on and then smooth it out with the hessian. Make sure you keep the hessian damp while you work. You can even combine tools to create effects; if you follow up with a broom, for example, you can create a lightly grooved surface or you can use a damp sponge for an even, yet slightly sandy, surface.

8. A second coat may need to be applied, after the first has dried, to achieve a heavier texture or cover more of the original mortar lines.

9. Wait for at least two weeks for the wall to dry if you want to paint it. Once it's dry, give the wall a quick once-over with a firm brush to remove any loose surface sand and then apply a good-quality self priming exterior acrylic paint. The surface will be quite thirsty, so you may want to dilute the first coat down a bit so you don't use up too much paint.

Repairing a cracked concrete path

It's common to see cracks in concrete paths. If the cracks are simple and one side hasn't lifted or dropped, then filling cracks with a sand/cement mix should be sufficient.

 WHAT YOU NEED

- cold chisel
- metal trowel
- stiff bristle brush
- PVA additive
- cement
- sharp sand (i.e. clean white beach sand)
- large sponge

WHAT TO DO

1. Use a cold chisel to chop into the old concrete, making the crack wide enough to accept the filler.

2. The recess you create should have clean, sharp angles that undercut slightly; this means the base of the crack should be made wider than the top, like a dovetail profile, to help hold the patch in place.

3. Poke out all loose material with a trowel or a spike and use a stiff bristle brush to remove dust.

4. Repairs to cracks can be improved with a PVA additive like Bondcrete. Brush the Bondcrete directly into the crack and leave to dry. Prepare a mixture using one part cement to three parts washed sharp sand, then add some more Bondcrete.

5. Just before you start, brush water into the crack until the old cement is saturated so that the old concrete doesn't draw the moisture from your mix, making it brittle.

6. Using the point of the trowel, force the concrete as far into the crack as possible. Keep pressing it down and work in more until full, then level with the trowel and smooth over with a damp sponge.

7. Try to keep the concrete moist for a day or two with a light spray of water and/or covering with plastic. Concrete will set better if it 'cures' slowly.

NON-SLIP SURFACE
If you're entertaining outdoors on paving, decking or concrete you'll want to limit the chance of people slipping over, especially kids and older guests. A once-over with a moss and mildew remover will remove slippery surfaces. You'll find a range of them in the cleaning product area of hardware stores. They just spray on and a few minutes later wash off with water.

Cleaning canvas blinds and awnings

Do you have a pale-coloured canvas awning or exterior blind that's very grubby? They can be challenging to clean as the problem with washing your exterior canvas is that you may remove the colour and/or water-proofing treatment.

You can try cleaning with a soft scrubbing brush and a solution of very salty water—use about one cup of salt per litre of water and add a dash of clove oil to maintain the waterproofing and remove mildew. Follow the cleaning with a spray of 50/50 white vinegar and water mix.

If this doesn't work, visit a ship's chandler store—they sell special pH-neutral solutions to help clean canvas, as well as mould and mildew removers and spray-on water repellents. And remember:

- don't roll up your awnings while they're still wet
- don't let water sit in pools on the surface
- clean them regularly.

Removing stains from concrete and masonry

The main thing to remember when trying out products you're not sure about is to always test them on a small inconspicuous spot first before proceeding with the whole job.

Tannin stains

Timber such as merbau is a very popular choice for outdoor structures like screens, decks and pergolas these days because of its high durability rating, resistance to termites and good fire rating. However, it's very rich in tannins and this can cause stains on surrounding concrete or pavers, like the marks left by gum leaves when they fall on a path and then get rained on.

To remove these stains, use a tannin stain remover or oxalic acid flakes mixed with water (85 grams of flakes to 4.5 litres) and scrub it on with a scrubbing brush—MAKE SURE you wear protective gloves, clothing and goggles, as it will burn!

To prevent tannin staining, seal the timber with a tannin-sealing preparation (e.g. WOODguard) before finishing it with your decking oil, then coat the concrete surfaces with a concrete sealer. Oh, and try to sweep up leaves as soon as they fall. Easier said than done, I know!

Rust stains

Do you have metal angles or brackets on your house that have gone rusty? They may be causing rusty stains on your rendered walls. Also, driveways sometimes get rust stains from old radiators.

Firstly you'll need to treat the rust that's causing the stains. See 'Removing rust from outdoor metal' in Chapter 15, 'Your garden and yard'.

Once the rust has been treated you can tackle the stains with a rust remover product (Bondall Bore, Rust and Tannin Stain Remover and CLR—see below—are two examples). If this doesn't work, step up to a home-made acid mix such as the oxalic acid blend described earlier or a diluted mix of hydrochloric acid.

CLR
CLR (a brand name) stands for 'Calcium, Lime, Rust', and not only will it remove rust stains from concrete and tiles but it can be used in the bathroom to dissolve soap scum and calcium deposits from tubs, toilets and sinks, or in the kitchen to remove those deposits from glassware, tea and coffee pots, lime scales from coffee makers, humidifiers or even brown stains inside your kettle.

Oil stains

If you have oil stains on your driveway, try a bag of kitty litter and an old brick. Cover the stain with the litter and then grind it into a fine powder with the brick. Let it sit and soak up the oil for a day or two, then sweep it up. If the stain remains, try a commercial driveway cleaner or even some engine degreaser, but always try these chemicals on a discreet area of your concrete first in case they discolour it.

If you're not so keen on spraying chemicals around your property, then good old eucalyptus oil often works well too. Pour undiluted eucalyptus oil directly onto the stain and let it sit a while to dissolve the oily marks, before scrubbing the area clean with warm soapy water.

Most grease and tyre track marks can be removed with driveway cleaning products found in both hardware and motor accessory stores.

SEAL IT
If you have pavers, tiles or stencilling on your paths or driveway you should apply a fresh coat of sealer soon after cleaning to make them easier to clean in the future.

Fixing chalky concrete

Too much water or low temperatures can alter the chemical balance of wet concrete when it's poured, preventing it from curing correctly. The result is a chalky surface. This can happen on both exterior and interior cement.

Try using a water-based concrete floor sealer, which will dustproof and seal the surface. Another choice is to paint the surface with one of the excellent concrete driveway paints available on the market. While chalky concrete should not be directly topcoated, it certainly can be prepared for topcoating through the use of a concrete conditioner product like Bondall SBP. This is a water-based product designed to seal and bind porous, powdery surfaces and also to prime the surface prior to applying water-based decorative paint.

Make sure you test the product you choose on a small inconspicuous area first to ensure it's achieving the desired result before applying over the entire surface.

Fixing efflorescence on concrete

No, we're not talking about the pretty sparkly stuff found on tropical waters at night—that's phosphorescence. Efflorescence is the white crystalline or powdery stains that appear as fuzzy white deposits on the surface of masonry materials like concrete, brick and clay tiles. These are salt stains caused by water seeping through the masonry. The water dissolves salts inside the masonry while moving through it, and then evaporates, leaving the salt on the surface.

It can be relatively easy to remove compared to some other stains:

- The water-soluble salts can be removed by dry brushing or with soapy water and a stiff brush.
- Heavy accumulation or stubborn deposits of efflorescence salts can usually be removed with a solution of hydrochloric acid and water. The acid should be heavily diluted in water; check the label for correct dilution and safety procedures. Always wet the surface well before applying acid mix and then scrub off the marks before rinsing the area clean with water.

Rejuvenating tessellated tiles

Many Federation homes have tessellated tiles on their front verandas. These tiles are what are known as 'fully vitrified', which means they're a solid colour all the way through rather than just on the surface.

After a hundred years of built-up grime, the best way to clean them is with a special marble and tile cleaning agent. These alkaline-based cleaners won't eat into your cement-based grout. You mix the stuff with water and scrub it on with a plastic pot scouring pad, then leave it to sit and do its thing for 20 minutes before rinsing off. As always, cleaning a small test area first before proceeding to the whole floor is a very good idea.

Cleaning sandstone doorsteps

Often sandstone doorsteps get black and grimy with age. Scrubbing the stone is the go, but you'll need to make up a bleach solution and use it with a stiff synthetic-fibre scrubbing brush:

1. Lay down some plastic to protect surrounding gardens and structures, and put on some rubber gloves and safety goggles to protect yourself.
2. Wet the stone down with clean water and let it soak in.
3. Make up a solution of water and bleach mixed 3:1, apply the solution with a watering can to one area at a time, and allow about five minutes for it to react.
4. Get scrubbing.
5. Rinse well with more clean water and then allow to dry. If you're happy with the result you should apply a sandstone sealer.

You can also use this method on paths and sandstone garden edging, but make sure you protect the surrounding plants.

Refinishing a balcony railing

Do you have a powder-coated galvanised railing on your balcony or verandah? You know, the ones that look a bit like wrought iron but are only a decade old? You probably chose it as a low-care option over timber and rightly so, but even powder coating will eventually chip and peel off so you may want to revitalise it rather than replace it.

For a real quick fix (or just until you get around to the complete repaint) you could try your local car accessory shop. These shops sell car duco touch-up pens in a vast array of colours. These are just like a felt tip marker pen but are loaded up with paint rather than ink. If you can find a matching colour, the pen dispenser will make a touch-up job as easy as colouring in. But if the damaged areas are numerous or large, you're better off refinishing the whole thing. Here's how:

1. Start by washing the railing down with warm soapy water, then scour the entire powder-coated surface with a Scotchbrite pad or fine 240 grit wet and dry.

2. Prime any chips or areas where the galvanised coating is exposed with galvanised iron primer or similar.

3. Apply your top coat. The good news is that you can actually use a good-quality exterior acrylic paint straight onto the scoured powder coating. If, however, you want a more traditional high-gloss finish, you'll need to use enamel paint. Once again this can be painted straight onto your prepared surface.

FOR COAST DWELLERS
If you live close to the coast, to maximise the life of your exterior paint it's good practice to clean it regularly with some mild detergent to remove salts and other contaminants.

Chapter 15
YOUR GARDEN AND YARD

Obviously this is not a book about gardening, plants, soil or any of those other great topics which have been written about at length. In this chapter you'll find some tips on how to fix or improve the look of the structures that are in or around your garden. And because most of them are always out in the weather, they do need plenty of TLC.

Fixing your fence

The fence is probably the number one structure in most people's garden. A well-built fence should last many years, but they certainly can take a beating out there in the elements. Regular maintenance and quick repair of problems as soon as you notice them will not only keep your fences looking good but extend their life further. One rotten post can be the start of an entire fence collapse!

Re-nailing a timber fence

Check your timber fence regularly for loose pickets or palings—they'll often come loose if plain steel nails, which will rust, have been used. (You should always use galvanised or stainless steel nails.) Often nails will also let go as the timber dries and shrinks over time, or if excessive force is applied to the paling (e.g. me climbing over the fence to retrieve a ball).

Here's what to do:

1. Remove the old nail if possible.
2. Replace with a larger one—twisted decking nails work quite well. Sometimes the extra strength of a galvanised screw may be necessary, particularly if the timber around the nail has decayed and made the hole larger.

Replacing a paling or picket

If a paling or picket is very twisted or split, you'll have to replace it. Any timberyard will carry a range of standard sizes and shapes.

Palings are usually made from low-grade timbers and are cut thin, so they'll often split when nailed. Therefore, drill a small pilot hole for the nail first; this will hold the nail in place for you, leaving one hand free to position the paling and the other to swing the hammer.

Straightening fence posts

Never force a loose or leaning fence post into position. Instead follow this simple method:

1. Dig the soil from around the post out to make the repositioning easier.
2. Push the leaning post back into position and check that it's plumb (straight up and down) with a spirit level.
3. If desired, nail some temporary timber braces to either side of the post to help keep it in the right position. These should run diagonal to the ground and be secured with small timber stakes.
4. Once the post is braced in the right position, the base can be repacked. A bag of rapid-set concrete mix will make the job quick. Before using rapid-set, pour a bucket of water into the hole to wet the earth around; once this has soaked in, pour a second bucket of water into the hole quickly followed by the bag of dry rapid-set. The rapid-set requires no mixing; it will draw the moisture it requires from the water in the hole and will dry to structural strength in one hour.
5. Once dry, remove the braces.

Treating rot in timber fences

Rot is the number one enemy of outdoor timber structures. For how to find, treat and prevent wood rot have a look at 'Removing rot from outdoor timber areas' in Chapter 14, 'The outside bits—your home's exterior'.

If you're too late to prevent or treat a rotted spot on your fence, sections of timber can often be repaired or replaced (see 'Replacing a paling or picket' above). If it's a rail end that needs repair, then galvanised steel brackets or plates can be used for support; prop the rail into position and then screw the bracket into position.

Post repairs can be a little more difficult, but if the rot doesn't extend more than 100 mm or so above ground level it can be done:
1. Remove several palings from either side of the post and then support the fence with a few bricks.

Many hands make light work, especially when straightening a fence post

2. Cut the bottom of the offending post away with a handsaw and dig out the old footing. Place a treated pine or hardwood replacement section of post into the hole and position it under the original post.
3. Place timber splints down either side of the post to span the join. Fix these in place with large galvanised bolts or sections of threaded rod with a nut at each end; place two bolts though the original post and two through the new section.
4. Reform the footing with concrete.
5. Once dry, replace the palings.

Lifting a sagging gate

Do you have a gate that drags on the ground when it's opened so that you have to lift it to make the latch meet when you close it?

Firstly, do a quick inspection. A bit of a poke with a screwdriver will tell if the timber is still sound (no rot or splits). If that's OK, make sure to check the posts that support the gate are straight with a spirit level.

Next check that the hinges are strong and straight and that the screws are well bedded into the timber in both the post and the gate frame. If they're loose, the quickest fix is to replace them with larger screws or put matchstick and PVA glue packing in the holes.

If all is well there and the gate is still dragging, you may need to add a tensioning cable. All good gates have a diagonal brace that runs from the top outer corner (latch side) to the bottom corner on the hinge side to add strength and support. Sometimes, though, even a hefty cross-brace won't stop a gate sagging over time, particularly if the kids like to use it as swing, so a little extra help may be needed in the form of a tensioning cable. This runs diagonally down the back of the gate in the opposite direction to the brace (if there is one)—that is, from the top of the hinge side to the bottom of the latch side. By fitting a turnbuckle (a threaded device for adjusting tension) in the cable, line tension can be added to pull the bottom corner of the gate that's dragging on the ground back up so that the gate swings freely. The turnbuckle can be loosened or tightened to keep the gate in the right shape and position for the latch to work smoothly.

 WHAT YOU NEED

- length of 3 mm galvanised cable—at least half a metre more than the diagonal measurement of your gate

- 5 mm galvanised turnbuckle—eye to eye style.
- 2 large eye screws
- 4 x 3 mm galvanised cable grips
- cordless drill
- small drill bits
- pliers
- small shifting spanner.

 WHAT TO DO

1. Working with the gate secured in the latch, drill a small pilot hole at the top corner of the hinge side.
2. Twist your eye screw into this. Be sure to make a small pilot hole and use a large eye screw and drive it in as deep as possible; you don't want the screw flying loose as you tighten the cable.
3. Repeat this on the bottom of the latch side. You could use eye bolts instead for extra strength if your gate's up to it.
4. Between these eye screws run the cable. Feed one end of the cable through the top eye first, fit the cable grip and secure it by tightening the small nuts on the clamp.
5. Find a good position for the turnbuckle—somewhere it can turn freely without rubbing on any of the timbers—then cut the cable to the appropriate length, allowing enough extra cable for the next clamp.
6. Fit the cable to one end of the turnbuckle. Open the turnbuckle to its maximum extension before fitting the second piece of cable. Feed the remaining end of the cable through the second eye screw and grab the end of it with some pliers to pull it taut before fitting the last grip.
7. Tighten the turnbuckle with a shifting spanner or by feeding a screwdriver through the centre and turning it. Tighten until you see the gate lift a bit in the latch, then test to see if it opens and closes freely.

8. Cut off any excess cable and bind the ends with some black electrical tape to stop the cable fraying.

Tensioning cable attached to straighten a gate

Fixing outdoor timber furniture

One of the most common questions I'm asked is what to use on outdoor furniture and timberwork in the garden. I've covered this extensively in

'Looking after your deck' in Chapter 14, 'The outside bits—your home's exterior', so if you're interested take a look at that.

As you may be serving food from your outdoor table you may wish to choose a natural non-toxic product on it, like Ecowood Oil tinted with a teakwood enhancer (available from major hardwood stores), or you can blend your own by combining pure tung oil with natural orange oil.

Fixing your rotary clothesline

Usually the other main construction in any Aussie backyard is the clothesline. It provides great service, so you need to look after it.

The good old Hills Hoist

If you still have one of the old bulky original Hills Hoists and are not interested in upgrading to a new one, you may still be interested in overhauling the one you've got:

- Frayed or broken wires can be replaced with new plastic-coated wire found in any hardware store. There's no great trick to replacing the wire as it doesn't need to be extremely taut; just start in the middle, one run at a time, always returning to the same arm. Pull each line tight with a pair of pliers and tie it off with a galvanised gable clamp.
- The old gearbox mechanism may have stopped working—try bringing it back to life by cleaning it out and re-oiling. If you do get it operating again, keep the oil up to it and make sure the drainage hole is kept clear. According to the Hills original instructions, one teaspoon of oil should be applied through the hole in the elevating shaft and a few drops through the hole in the gear case.

- If you need to replace any part, all the original parts can still be obtained from Hills. You can even download an owner's manual with a full set of diagrams from their website.

Modern clotheslines

Not a lot goes wrong with modern folding and retractable clotheslines (other than spider webs), unless they're used inappropriately. Unlike the Hills Hoist workhorses, modern lines will not handle having a couple of doors from an HG Holden suspended from them for a respray. If the moving parts on your foldaway clothesline become stiff or squeaky, a little squirt of WD-40 will have it swinging freely again. (It will also kill the spiders.)

> **USEFUL FACT**
> The ideal height for a clothesline is approximately 50 mm above the head of the person who uses it the most.

Waterproofing retaining walls and planter boxes

Do you have a cement or masonry block retaining wall and planter boxes in your garden? It's a good idea to waterproof them by painting on the back of the wall or the inside of the box. Good old-fashioned bitumen is the go—you can pick up a can of Ormanoid Bitumen Paint and a couple of cheap disposable brushes from the hardware store.

Removing rust from outdoor metal

Do you have metal outdoor furniture or a wrought iron balustrade on a balcony? Well, chances are at some stage it'll start suffering from a bit of rust.

Stopping rust before it starts, or treating it as it appears, should be a regular part of any maintenance plan. Be it door hardware, railings, balustrades, fences, sheet metal or decorative iron lacework, architectural metal work is everywhere outside our homes—old or new. And unless it has been galvanised, architectural iron and mild steel has to be protected from the elements through protective coatings such as paint or it will corrode and eventually rust away—and the closer you are to the coast, the worse it is. The right paint products will do the trick but, as always, good preparation is the key.

 WHAT YOU NEED

- wire brush or some wire wheels for your drill or angle grinder
- sandpaper or emery cloth
- scraper
- some rust converter

- anti-corrosion primer
- paint and brush
- safety gear, including eye and ear protection and an appropriate dust mask.

Remember: if you're working on an old house the old paints you remove may contain lead.

 ## WHAT TO DO

1. Remove all loose or flaking paint and rust material with the scraper and a wire brush. I like the wire wheels that fit on your power drill as they work quickly and come in a range of shapes and sizes to help your get into awkward spots. You may find that sanding is also helpful in removing any loose rust—you don't have to remove all the rust, just the loose material. Be absolutely sure to wear your safety glasses when operating a wire brush on a power tool, as small pieces of wire tend to break off and may end up in your eye!

2. Apply the rust converter to any remaining rust that may be pitted into the metal surface or in tight areas that you can't sand. Rust converter contains tannic acid; the tannin reacts with the iron oxide (rust), converting it into iron tannate, a stable blue/black protective substance. (Do not apply rust converter to any areas of bare shiny metal without rust.) Rust converter will be touch-dry in about 20 minutes but it's best to wait at least three hours before moving onto the next step.

3. Clean and degrease the surface. Wash with a strong detergent followed by a thorough rinsing. The light 'flash rust' that appears after washing can be removed with a cloth dampened with paint thinner.

4. Priming is next. Water-based paints are now produced which have fantastic rust-inhibiting properties, and they have some advantages over the old solvent-based products. Besides being low odour and

easy to clean up, an added advantage to water-based paints is their ability to meld in with any trapped moisture which may not be visible to the naked eye. These coatings will force the moisture up to the surface and replace it with rustproofing chemicals that seal the surface off. You may see rusty-looking spots in your dried primer but don't worry, most can be wiped off with a cloth—it's just rusty moisture that has been forced to the surface.

5. For topcoating I'd recommend at least two coats of a good-quality exterior paint. You can use a water-based paint, which will be easier to apply and to clean up, but if you live anywhere near saltwater, or if your metalwork is prone to a bit of wear and tear, try a single-pack epoxy finish. Once dry, these paints are usually highly glossy and very resistant to scratching and abrasion.

Looking after your BBQ

For many families, the barbie is the most important thing in the backyard. These days they can do just about anything but sing and tap dance, and they cost about as much as a small car, so it's a good idea to look after them.

Cleaning the inside

The secret to cleaning a BBQ is . . . (drum roll please!) . . . do it EVERY time you use the barbie, but don't OVERDO it, as a natural coat of food oils on the cast iron parts protects them from corrosion. Having said this, at least once a year you should do a big clean:

- Warm barbeques are easier to clean than cold ones, so fire it up for a little while first then turn it off and disconnect the gas.
- Dismantle the entire BBQ to wash all the parts separately. Remove

the hood, plates, grills, tray of rocks and drip tray; pull the knobs off the gas taps; then release and lift out the burners.

- Spread the grills out on some newspaper and scrape with a 'griller killer' (a specially shaped scraper designed to fit around the grill bars). Or you can use a grill stone; these manufactured stone blocks are soft enough to grind to the shape of the grill, removing grease and burnt food as you go.

- If the grills aren't too dirty, clean off any grease with warm water and soap mixed with white vinegar; don't overdo it as leaving some greasy residue will protect from rust. Once dry, spray on a little more cooking oil and spread it with a paper towel. If the grills are particularly dirty, oven cleaner can be used, but it's very caustic and you'll need to remove all residues. Ceramic cooking grids should be cleaned with soapy water and a brass wire BBQ brush. (Note that all the cleaning tools needed for your big clean are available at BBQ shops.)

Cleaning the outer casing

If your BBQ has a stainless steel outer casing and trolley like mine, then all it will need is cleaning rather than de-rusting (see below). Don't use harsh cleaners and abrasives on the metal as they will scratch it; the soapy water and vinegar mix is all that is needed. After cleaning the outer casing of your stainless BBQ, you can buff it with a commercial stainless steel cleaning oil, or even a little baby oil. The oil will remove watermarks and fingerprints, and will also make it easier to clean next time.

De-rusting and re-oiling

If your grills and burners are made of cast iron, they may have rusted up. You'll need to scrape off any flaking rust and then give the surface a good going-over with a wire brush, then give them a light spray of that cooking oil before they rust up again.

If the outer casing is developing rust spots, rub them back with steel wool and treat with rust converter before retouching with heat-resistant paint.

Timber BBQ trolleys can be kept in good order by re-oiling them once a year. Give them a light sanding, then use outdoor furniture oil. Or you can pick up a can of specially formulated BBQ trolley oil; this will not only soak through grease stains on the top of your trolley but help protect against new ones.

Renewing the rocks

Renew volcanic heating rocks each year, as they become clogged with grease and oil. Empty the old sand from the drip tray, clean the tray and give it a spray of vegetable oil before lining it with aluminium foil. Place new washed sand or unscented kitty litter on top of the foil.

Keeping it working (and safe)

Gas taps can become stiff, causing plastic controls to break. Remove the plastic knobs and spray the mechanisms with WD-40 to free them. The WD-40 is not a permanent lubricant, however, so apply a drop of sewing machine oil to each tap and then cover them with petroleum jelly to keep the oil in.

If one or more of your burners doesn't seem to generate a flame like the others, then it may be because a gas jet has become clogged. If you lift the burner out of the BBQ you'll see the small brass jets; these are like a small covered nuts with tiny holes through them. They're removed with a small spanner. If you can't clear the blockage, buy new ones from a BBQ shop for a couple of dollars each.

Reconnect the gas and check all the connections for leaks by coating them with a mix of 50/50 dishwashing liquid and water—if gas is leaking, you'll detect bubbles forming in the soap. Try tightening the connections or replacing the seals. You should also consider fitting a gas fuse at the bottle, which will not only indicate the amount of gas left in the bottle but shut down the gas supply if a major leak occurs.

BBQ EMBARRASSMENT

How many times have you invited people around for a barbie only to find you've run out of gas? It's usually by guesswork that I keep track of my gas tank, and this has led to some embarrassing, mad dashes to the servo! There's a smart mathematical method for working out how much gas is left—weigh your gas bottle on the bathroom scales and compare the weight of the bottle with the 'tare weight' marked on the side of the shroud on the bottle. The difference in the weights will give you an idea on how full it is.

Chapter 16
USEFUL INFORMATION

Throughout this book I've referred to a number of specialty products, companies and sources of information. Here are the website and phone details of some sources of these kinds of products. It's far from an exhaustive list—I'm based in NSW so there's a strong leaning there—so I suggest you also try your local *Yellow Pages*.

These details were checked at time of writing, but, as you know, things change quickly in the modern digital age and businesses come and go, so apologies if by the time you read this the contact details are no longer current. We'll add updated information as it comes to hand on our website **www.otr.com.au/fixit**, and you can contact us via this website as well.

Safety while you work

The Lead Group

Has a free info and referral service about lead. The website has some useful fact sheets.

www.lead.org.au

1800 626 086

NSW Government

The NSW Government has a website on DIY safety.

www.diysafe.nsw.gov.au

Accident Research Centre

Monash University's Accident Research Centre has downloadable DIY safety brochures.

www.monash.edu.au/muarc/reports/Other/diyfacts.html

Blackwoods

Bulk industrial and safety product suppliers.

www.blackwoods.com.au

(02) 9203 0111

Protector Alsafe

Safety gear.

www.protectoralsafe.com.au

Energy saving

Water Efficiency Labelling and Standards (WELS) Scheme

The website explains the WELS scheme and details some products.

www.waterrating.gov.au

1800 803 772

Your Home

A website created by the Australian Greenhouse Office with masses of info on how to make your home more energy efficient.
www.greenhouse.gov.au/yourhome

Websites full of water saving tips include:
(Your local water supplier's website will have information relevant to your area.)

Savewater!

www.savewater.com.au

Sydney Water

www.sydneywater.com.au

Melbourne Water

www.melbournewater.com.au

ActewAGL

www.actewagl.com.au

Timber and furniture restoration

For your restoration needs, including French polishing supplies, cabinet-making and a great range of door hardware try:

Mother of Pearl & Sons Trading

Supplier of high-quality imported shellacs and shellac brushes, cabinet-maker's hardware and fine finishing products.
www.motherofpearl.com
(02) 8332 6999

Goods & Chattels
Ditto!
www.goodsandchattels.com
(07) 3391 5764

For woodworking tools as well as a huge range of consumables try:

The Wood Works Book & Tool Co
Also has lots of good books!
www.thewoodworks.com.au
(02) 9979 7797

Carba-Tec
Huge supplier of tools and consumables. Streaming video on the website. Each state has its own website and phone number, access via the national one.
www.carbatec.com.au
1800 683 583

Timber finishes
Here are some specialist manufacturers/distributors of timber finishing products (waxes, polishes and oils):

U-Beaut Enterprises
Marketing website for the U-Beaut range of products; also hosts Woodworking Australia's Woodwork Forums.
www.ubeaut.com.au
(03) 5221 8775

Organoil

Australian company manufacturing timber finishes, including Ecowood Oil.

www.organoil.com.au

1800 060 654

Gilly Stephenson

Another Australia company producing waxes, stains and polishes.

www.gillystephenson.com

(08) 9295 1973

Howard Products Australia

www.howardproducts.com.au

1800 672 646

Liberon

www.liberon.com.au

(02) 6280 9720

Acecroft

For Scratch Fix pens and repair kits, and metal and jewellery cleaners and polishes.

www.acecroft.com.au

1800 815 636

Timbecon

Masses of tools and specialist timberwork products.

www.timbecon.com.au

1300 880 996

Trade Time
Make my favourite tool bags, pouches and leather belts.
www.tradetime.com.au
(08) 8552 3347

General timber info
Timber and Working with Wood Show
These are expos that occur around the country; the website details what's on where.
www.workingwithwood.com.au

Timber Preservers Association of Australia
Information about treated timbers.
www.tpaa.com.au
(03) 9596 8155

Timber Development Association
Great source of info on timber.
www.timber.net.au
1300 734 822 (Timber Advisory Service)

Specialist timber suppliers include:

Anagote Timbers
Newtown, Sydney
(02) 9558 8444

Lazarides Timber
www.lazaridestimberagencies.com
(07) 3267 3899

Trend Timbers
www.trendtimbers.com.au
(02) 4577 5277

Britton Timbers
Tassie company but they have offices in Melbourne, Brisbane and Sydney.
www.brittontimbers.com.au
(03) 6452 2522

Australian Furniture Timbers
www.afttimbers.com
(03) 9646 1081

Building protection
For products that protect your buildings against damp, rot and other problems (like graffiti) try:

Tech-Dry
Damp prevention products and anti-graffiti.
www.techdry.com.au
(03) 9699 8202 (head office)

Preschem
Makes No Rot sticks, among many other useful DIY goodies.
www.preschem.com
(03) 9532 0679

Timbermate
Specialist wood filler and wood rot treatments supplier, including Earl's Wood Hardener.
www.timbermate.com.au
1800 354 811

AGS (Anti-Graffiti Systems)
Graffiwipe product and Graffiti Attack range.
www.antigraffiti.com.au
(02) 9586 4555

Doors and windows
Australian Window Association
Represents over 350 timber, aluminium and PVC manufacturers throughout Australia. Some useful Q&As on the website.
www.awa.org.au
(02) 9498 2768

Window Energy Rating Scheme (WERS)
This system rates the efficiency of various windows and will guide you in selecting the best product for the climate you live in.
www.wers.net
(02) 9498 2768

Cyclone Industries
Window screen meshes.
www.cyclone.com.au
(03) 8791 9300

In addition to companies like Mother of Pearl and Sons mentioned above, the following companies sell all kinds of door and window furniture:

H.M. Cowdroy
Also have track systems, door seals, etc.
www.cowdroy.com.au
1300 269 376

Häfele
This company sells a huge range of kitchen fittings, tools and architectural hardware.
www.hafele.com.au
1800 806 307

Hettich
Ditto!
www.hettich.com.au
1800 687 789

Lockwood
Offers various catalogues of lock styles you can look at and lists suppliers in your area. Has installation instructions and videos.
www.lockweb.com.au

Kitchens and wet areas
Laminex and Formica
Useful technical info and ideas on what you can do with laminate.
www.laminex.com.au
www.formica.com.au
132 136

Caesarstone

Individual state phone numbers available on the website.
www.caesarstone.com.au

Corian

www.casf.com.au
1800 267 426

Spirit Marble and Tile Care

Sells tile and marble cleaner/sealer; the website has very useful info on treating different types of stone (with their products of course!).
www.spiritsealers.com
(02) 9734 6937

Paint and other finishes

All of the big, well-known paint companies offer very useful technical assistance lines.

DULUX (and British Paints)

www.dulux.com.au
132 525

Wattyl

www.wattyl.com.au
132 101

Taubmans

www.taubmans.com.au
131 686

Haymes

www.haymespaint.com.au
1800 033 431

Cabot's

Manufactures a broad range of timber finishes for both internal and external uses. The website contains loads of useful info on finishes and how to choose and apply the appropriate product.
www.cabots.com.au
1800 011 006

Feast Watson

The description for Cabots above applies also to Feast Watson.
www.feastwatson.com.au
1800 252 502

The Natural Paint Place

Natural non-toxic paints, oils, polishes and associated products.
www.thenaturalpaintplace.com.au
(02) 9519 0433

Porter's Original Paints

Specialist traditional paints for interior and exterior.
www.porterspaints.com.au
1800 656 664

White Knight Paints

Tub and tile paints, grout pens and all kinds of specialty paints and exterior products.
www.whiteknightpaints.com.au
131 686

Resene

Great colour selection tool on their website.

www.resene.com.au

1800 738 383

For waterproofing/coating paints and cleaners for masonry and metal try:

Durobond Paints

Specialist coatings, including Super-Prime and Concoat, for waterproofing and protection.

www.durobond.com.au

(02) 9905 0811

Flood

All sorts of primers, bonders, sealers—one well-known product is Penetrol.

www.floodaustralia.net

1800 226 113

Galmet

Metal protection products.

www.galmet.com.au

(02) 9757 8800

Zinsser

Makes all sorts of waterproofing products, anti-mould paints, primers/sealers and shellac.

www.zinsser.com.au

1300 784 476

Crommelin

Makes a wide range of sealers and waterproofers.
www.crommelin.com.au
1800 655 711

Concrete Technologies

Patterned concrete products and sealers.
www.concretetech.com.au
1300 737 787

Bondall

Products include their Bore, Rust Stain Remover, Silasec and PondTite.
www.bondall.com
1800 810 123

Davco

Waterproofing, adhesives and grout; Ormonoid is one of their products.
Lots of good information on tiling on the website.
www.davco.com.au
1800 653 347

Senseal

Epoxy sealers and adhesives. One product is Multi-Primer.
www.senseal.com.au
(03) 9533 2444

ProtectAll Security Products

For StopClimb paint.
http://protectall.bigpondhosting.com
(07) 3800 0505

I-Strip
Makes a large-scale paint stripping product.
www.i-strip.com.au
1800 224 953

Peelaway
Another paint stripping solution.
www.peelaway.com.au
(02) 9746 6733

Gutters
These companies all make different kind of gutter guards:

Leafbusters
www.leafbusters.com.au
1300 488 837

Gumleaf Gutter Protection
www.gumleafgutterguard.com
1300 486 532

Gutter Shield
www.guttershield.com.au
1300 365 377

General/miscellaneous
Archicentre
Archicentre is the Royal Australian Institute of Architects Home Advisory Service.
www.greenweb.com.au/archicentre
1300 134 513

Kidsafe

Lots of information about making your home safe for children. This organisation has offices in each state with their own website and phone details—see the national site.

www.kidsafe.com.au

(02) 9845 0890

Gyprock

Useful info on the uses of this product—some good DIY projects.

www.gyprock.com.au

1300 306 556

Soundblock

Distributors of Barrierboard and other acoustic insulation products.

www.soundblock.com.au

(02) 9327 7410

Whitworths

Lots of useful cleaning and paint products suitable for marine/wet area use.

www.whitworths.com.au

(02) 9907 3344

Hills Hoist

www.hillshoist.com.au

1300 300 564

Off The Rails Productions
Ruwenzori Retreat

Scott McGregor and Wendy Gray.

www.otr.com.au

www.ruwenzori.com.au

INDEX

abrasives 39
acoustic matting 912
acrylic baths, rejuvenating 202
acrylic gap filler 50
acrylic paint 223, 233–4
air conditioning 76
Allen keys 23
aluminium doors 148
aluminium windows 157, 162–3
angle grinder 29
arris 16
awl 15
awnings, cleaning 280–1

bagging a wall 275–8
balcony railing, refinishing a 285–6
bamboo furniture 190
baths
  acrylic, rejuvenating 202
  enamel, rejuvenating 201–2
bathroom taps 214
BBQ, looking after your 298–301
benchtops
  laminate 173, 174
  stone/granite/marble 175
  timber 174–5
bevels 16–17
birdbaths 296
Black Japan 226
boards 54–5
bolster 21
bolts 44–5
bookshelves 189
borers 124–5, 182
bricklayer's trowel 22

bricks
  getting paint off 237
  painting 235–7
brickwork, repairing cracks in 269–72
building protection 309

cane furniture 190
canvas blinds, cleaning 280–1
carpets
  fixing a small damaged spot (burn
    hole/impossible stains) 132
  fixing snags 130–2
  removing furniture indentations 132
cat's paw 15
caulking gun 15
ceiling rose, attaching a new 107–8
ceilings
  ceiling rose, attaching a new 107–8
  cornice, installing or repairing a new
    105–7
  insulation 69, 91
  painting 229
cement 51
cement paint 226
chairs, fixing 186–8
chamfer 16
chisels 14, 21
circular saw 29
clamps 14, 187
claw hammer 10
cleaners 52
clothesline, fixing your rotary 294–5
club hammer 22
cold chisel 21
concrete

fixing chalky 283
fixing efflorescence on 284
painting 235–7
removing stains on 281–3
path, repairing a cracked 278–80
construction abhesive 48
coping saws 21
co-polymer 50
cork floors 128
cornice, installing or repairing a new 105–7
cramps 14
cupboards, built-in
benchtops, laminate 173, 174
benchtops, stone/granite/marble 175
benchtops, timber 174–5
door handles, replacing 176–7
doors, fixing sagging corner 168
doors, updating 173–4
drawers, fixing 169–70
kitchen doors that no longer line up 167–8
laminate kitchen, looking after and updating your 171–4
shelf supports 170–1
wardrobe doors, fixing swinging 168–9
curtains 75

damp, dealing with 93–7
decks
cleaning 259–60
looking after your 256–64
replacing damaged boards 257–8
'silvered' 261–2
staining treated pine 262
timbers 256–7
distemper 226
door handles 140–1
replacing cupboard 176–7
doorframe, repairing 144–5
doors 310–11
aluminium 148
broken, repairing 144–5
corner cupboard, fixing sagging 168
cupboard, updating 173–4
cupboard door handles, replacing 176–7
dents, fixing 142–3

draught-proofing 71–2
furniture, restoring 137–42
kitchen cupboard, that no longer line up 167–8
rattling, fixing 133–4
sliding, fixing 145–8
sliding glass screen doors, fixing 200–1
that don't close properly 134–7
wardrobe, fixing creaky 188–9
wardrobe, fixing swinging 168–9
doorsteps, cleaning sandstone 285
double glazing for windows 74
drain cleaner 215
drainage, poor 95–6
drawers, fixing 169–70
draught-proofing your house 70–5
drill attachments 25, 28
drills
cordless 24–7
electric 27–8
dust (roof space) 63

electric
drills 27–8
sanders 29–30
tools 29–30
electrical
circuits, watts, amps and fuses 204
dimmers 208
fuse, fixing a blown 204–6
lightbulbs 206–10
safety 63–4, 205
safety switches 205
enamel baths, rejuvenating 201–2
enamel paint 223–4, 233, 239–41
energy efficient 68–80
air conditioning 76
draught-proofing your house 70–5
installing or updating your insulation 69
on standby 76–7
reducing energy used for hot water 77–8
refrigerators 75–6
saving water 78–80
energy saving 304
expanding foam fillers 51

fasteners 41–6
fences
  fixing 287–90
  metal, painting 238
  timber, painting 233–5
  treating rot 289–90
files 20
fillers 50–1
finish/topcoat (paint) 223
fire hazards 64
first aid 62
float 22
floorboards
  creaking, fixing 109–13
  damaged tongue and groove, fixing a 117–19
  fixing draughts 74–5
  gaps in, fixing 116–17
floors
  cork 128
  painting 235
  protecting your polished 119–22
  fixing scratches in timber 120–2
  pests in and under 122–6
  under-floor ventilation problems 126–7
  rot, wet/dry 125–6
  slate 127
flooring types 127–30
flyscreens, making and fixing 158–62
French polishing 245–8
furniture
  bamboo 190
  cane 190
  metal 190
  removing animal hair 180
  wardrobe doors, fixing creaky 188–9
furniture, timber
  borer 182
  chairs, fixing 186–8
  dents and scratches 178–81
  French polishing 245–8
  outdoor, fixing 293–4
  removing white heat rings 181–2
  restoring 182–6, 305
  veneer that's lifting 189–90
  waxing 245
furniture indentations in carpets 132

fuse, fixing a blown 204–6
fuses 204

G-clamp 23
garden and yard
  BBQ, looking after your 298–301
  clothesline, fixing your rotary 294–5
  fences, fixing 287–20
  gate, lifting a sagging 291–3
  metal, removing rust from outdoor 296–8
  planter boxes, waterproofing 295
  retaining walls, waterproofing 295
  timber furniture, fixing outdoor 293–4
gate, lifting a sagging 291–3
glass
  painting 238
  replacing putty around 153–4
  scratched, broken or cracked 154
  screen door, fixing a sliding 200–1
glues 46–9
graffiti, removing 281
grout
  acrylic 193
  cleaning and repairing 192–3
  removing from tiles 193
gutters 316
  cleaning and fixing 253–6

hacksaw 11
hammers 10, 22, 65
hawk 22
hinges, fixing door 134–6
hot water, reducing energy used for 77–8
hot water systems 216–17

instant bonding glue 48–9
insulation, installing or updating your 69, 91

jeweller's screwdriver 23
jigsaw 29

keyhole saw 11
kitchens 311–12
  benchtops, laminate 173, 174
  benchtops, stone/granite/marble 175

benchtops, timber 174–5
cupboard door handles, replacing 176–7
cupboard doors, fixing sagging corner
   168
cupboard doors, updating 173–4
doors that no longer line up 167–8
drawers, fixing 169–70
laminate 171–4
shelf supports 170–1

ladder safety 64–5
ladders 16
laminate benchtops 173, 174
laminate kitchens 171–4
laminates, painting 238–9
lead paint 65–7
lightbulbs 206–10
lime wash 226
linoleum 128
linseed oil 260
locks, fitting window 154–7
long-nosed pliers 19
loo, fixing a leaky 215–16
lubricants 40
lump hammer 22

magnets 15
mallets 20
markers 40–1
masonry, removing stains on 281–3
masonry walls
   damp 272–3
   fixing chips on corners of 85–6
   repairing holes in 86–7
measures 10
metal
   painting 237–8
   removing rust from outdoor 296–8
metal effect paints 226
mildew on walls 198–9
milk paint 225
mirrors, hanging 103–5
mitre box 20–1
mullion/muntin, repairing 143–4
multigrips 13

nails 41–3

oil finishes 57
oil stains 58, 282–3
oil-based urethanes 56, 250–1
on standby (appliances) 76–7
outside your home
   bagging a wall 275–8
   balcony railing, refinishing a 285–6
   BBQ, looking after your 298–301
   brickwork, repairing cracks in 269–72
   canvas blinds and awnings, cleaning
      280–1
   clothesline, fixing your rotary 294–5
   concrete path, repairing a cracked
      278–80
   concrete, fixing chalky 283
   concrete, fixing efflorescence on 284
   concrete, removing stains on 281–3
   deck, looking after your 256–64
   fences, fixing 287–90
   gate, Lifting a sagging 291–3
   graffiti, removing 281
   gutters, cleaning and fixing 253–6
   masonry, removing stains on 281–3
   metal, removing rust from outdoor
      296–8
   painting 228, 233–7, 251–2
   render, patching damaged 274–5
   sandstone doorsteps, cleaning 285
   stairs, fixing outdoor timber 264–7
   tessellated tiles, rejuvenating 284–5
   timber areas, removing rot 267–9
   timber furniture, fixing outdoor 293–4
   waterproofing 272–4
   waterproofing retaining walls and
      planter boxes 295
   see also garden and yard

paint 312–16
   acrylic 223, 233–4
   additives 225
   anti-climb 280
   anti-slip 236
   bricks 235–7
   brush reviver 222
   concrete 235–7
   disposing 242–3
   enamel 223–4, 233, 239–41

finishes 224–5
floors 235
lead 65–7, 243
matching 87
MDF/chipboard 235
rollers 219–22
scraper 15
speciality 225–6
storing 242–3
types of 222–6
see also timber finishes
paint tin holder 230
paintbrushes 218–19, 220–2, 241
painting
acrylic over enamel 233
the basics 226–39
ceilings 229
getting a good straight edge 241–2
glass 238
laminates 238–9
metal 237–8
outside of your house 228, 233–7, 251–2
plasterboard 231
reusing old turps 243
surface preparation 226–8
tiles 238–9
timber 231–3
timber fences 233–5
and the weather 228
where to start 228
paths, repairing a cracked concrete 278–80
pests in and under floors 122–6
pictures, hanging 97–101
pinch bar 23
pipe wrench 23
pipes
frozen 213
repairing leaky PVC 212–13
water hammer 213
plane 22
planter boxes, waterproofing 295
plasterboard
cutting 85
painting 231
repairing 81–5
pliers 13, 19

plugging chisel 21
plumbing
drain cleaner 215
frozen pipes 213
hot water system 216–17
loo, fixing a leaky 215–16
PVC pipes, repairing leaky 212–13
shower recess, leaky 214
taps, changing, bathroom/laundry 214
taps, dripping 211–12
trap, clearing a blocked 215
water hammer 213
plunger 15–16
pointing trowel 22
polyurethane 50
ponds 296
pozidriv screwdriver 12
power tools 24–31
primer (paint) 222
primer-sealer (paint) 223
pry bar 15
PVA (polyvinyl acetate) 46–7
PVC pipes, repairing leaky 212–13
pull saw 21
punch set 16
putty, replacing around glass 153–4
putty knife 15

quick-fitting clamp 14

rasps 20
refrigerators 75–6
render, patching damaged 274–5
rendered walls, fixing cracks in 87–9
retaining walls, waterproofing
reversable ratchet socket spanner 19
rollers, paint 219–22
ropes 53
rot
removing from timber areas 267–9
in timber fences 289–90
wet/dry 125–6
rotary clothesline, fixing your 294–5
router, high speed 30
rubber bands 53
rules 10
rust stains 282

safety
  electrical 63–4, 205
  equipment 9–10
  fire 64
  first aid 62
  invisible dangers 62–3
  ladder 64–5
  lead paint 65–7
  while you work 10, 59–67, 303
sanders, electric 29–30
sandpaper 37–8
sandstone doorsteps, cleaning 285
sash windows, maintaining 149–53
saws 10–11, 20–1, 29
screwdrivers 12–13, 19, 23
screws 43–4
sealants 50
sealer (paint) 222
shadow board 17–18
sharpening tools 32–6
shelf supports 170–1
shellac 56–7
shelves, installing on your walls 101–3
shifting spanner 13–14
shower head, mineral build-up in 216
shower recesses
  leaky 214
  sliding glass screen door, fixing a 200–1
side cutters 19
silasec 274
silicone 50
  replacing grubby 199–200
slate floors 127
sliding bevel 10
sliding doors 145–8
sliding glass screen door, fixing a 200–1
solvents 40
soundproofing your house 91–3
spanners 13–14, 19
spiral ratchet screwdriver 19
spirit level 14
spring clamp 14
staining timber surfaces 243–5
stairs
  fixing creaky timber 113–16
  fixing outdoor timber 264–6
Stanley knife 12

staple gun 22
steel rule 10
storing and disposing of paint 242–3
strap clamp 187
straps 53
strings 53
stud finder 24

tack hammer 10
tannin stains 281–2
tape measure 10
tapes 53
taps
  changing, bathroom/laundry 214
  dripping 211–12
tenon saws 20
termites 123–4
tessellated tiles, rejuvenating 284–5
tiles
  attaching a towel rail 197
  cracked/damaged 193–5
  cutting 195–7
  painting 238–9
  removing grout from 193
tiling
  grout, cleaning and repairing 192–3
  over tiles 198
  preparing a painted surface for 197–8
  wet areas 191–8
timber 54–5
  areas, removing rot from outdoor 267–9
  benchtops 174–5
  deck 256–7
  dents and depressions 179–80
  fences, painting 233–5
  finishes 306–7
  general information 307–9
  French polishing 246–8
  kitchens 174–5
  painting 231–2
  restoring 305
  staining 243–5
  stairs, fixing creaky 113–16
  stairs, fixing outdoor 264–7
  surfaces, treating in wet areas 202
  veneer that's lifting, fixing 189
timber finishes 56–8

clear finishes 56–8
  oil stains 58
timber furniture
  borer 182
  chairs, fixing 186–8
  dents and scratches, fixing 178–81
  outdoor, fixing 293–4
  removing white heat rings 181–2
  restoring 182–6
timber-lined walls, fixing 89
tin snips 20
tools
  advanced toolkit 19–24
  care of 32
  basic toolkit 9–16
  electric 27–30
  hiring 31
  power 24–31
  shadow board 17–18
  sharpening 32–6
toxic chemicals 62–3
trap, clearing a blocked 215
tung oil 57, 58, 248–50
two-part epoxy 47

undercoats (paint) 223
urethane, applying oil-based 56, 250–1
utility knife 12

ventilation problems, under-floor 126–7
vinyl flooring 128–30

wall anchors 45–6
wallpaper, removing 89–90
walls
  bagging 275–8
  dealing with damp 93–7
  hanging pictures 97–101
  installing shelves 101–3
  lining 92–3
  masonry, damp 272–3
  masonry, fixing chips on corners of
    85–6
  masonry, repairing holes in 86–7

  mildew on 198–9
  mirrors, hanging 103–5
  plasterboard, repairing 81–5
  removing wallpaper 89–91
  rendered, fixing cracks in 87–9
  retaining, waterproofing 295
  soundproofing 91–3
  timber-lined, fixing 89
wardrobe doors
  creaky, fixing 188–9
  sliding 148
  swinging, fixing 168–9
water
  reducing energy used for hot 77–8
  saving 78–80
  see also hot water systems
Water Efficiency Labelling and
  Standards (WELS) 80
water hammer 213
water-based urethane (clear sealer) 56
waterproofing outside areas 272–4
waterproofing retaining walls and
  planter boxes 295
wax putty 51
waxing timber surfaces 245
wet areas 311–12
  baths, rejuvenating enamel 201–2
  bath, rejuvenating acrylic 202
  mildew on walls 198–9
  silicone, replacing grubby 199–200
  sliding glass screen door, fixing 200–1
  tiling 191–8
  treating timber surfaces in 202
Whirly Bird 69–70
window scraper 23
windows 310–11
  aluminium, maintaining powder-
    coated 162–3
  aluminium, sliding 157
  dents, fixing 142–3
  double glazing 74
  draught-proofing 72–3
  flyscreens, making and fixing 158–62
  hinges, fitting 157–8

locks, fitting 154–7
  masking tape, removing old 164
  putty around glass, replacing 153–4
  sash, maintaining 149–53
  tint, removing bubbling 164–5
wire cutters 19
wires 53

wood chisels 14
wood putty 51
wood saw, hand 10–11
work safety *see* safety
workbench, portable 18
woodworking vice 23
wrench 23